The Well-Crafted Sentence

A WRITER'S GUIDE TO STYLE

The Well-Crafted Sentence

Second Edition

A WRITER'S GUIDE TO STYLE

Nora Bacon

University of Nebraska at Omaha

Bedford / St. Martin's
Boston ▪ New York

For Bedford / St. Martin's

Senior Executive Editor: Leasa Burton
Developmental Editor: Sophia Snyder
Senior Production Editor: Karen S. Baart
Senior Production Supervisor: Jennifer L. Peterson
Executive Marketing Manager: Molly Parke
Editorial Assistant: Daniel F. Schafer
Copyeditor: Steven Patterson
Indexer: Mary Louise White
Permissions Manager: Kalina K. Ingham
Senior Art Director: Anna Palchik
Text Design: Lisa Buckley
Cover Design: Billy Boardman
Composition: Achorn International, Inc.
Printing and Binding: RR Donnelley and Sons

President, Bedford/St. Martin's: Denise B. Wydra
Presidents, Macmillan Higher Education: Joan E. Feinberg and Tom Scotty
Editor in Chief: Karen S. Henry
Director of Marketing: Karen R. Soeltz
Production Director: Susan W. Brown
Associate Production Director: Elise S. Kaiser
Managing Editor: Elizabeth M. Schaaf

Library of Congress Control Number: 2012940087

For information, write: Bedford/St. Martin's, 75 Arlington Street, Boston, MA 02116
(617-399-4000)

ISBN 978-1-4576-0673-1

Acknowledgments

Preface for Instructors

THE WELL-CRAFTED SENTENCE is designed to help undergraduates develop facility in writing smooth, clear, fully developed sentences and to encourage attention to the rhetorical effects of style choices. It is not a grammar book: it does not focus on avoiding or correcting errors, and it makes no attempt to offer a thorough description of English syntax. Instead, it asks students to examine prose written by accomplished stylists, to note the relationship between syntactic structures and their rhetorical effect, and to practice using specific structures that all adult writers *can*, but only the best writers often *do*, take advantage of in their work. The book invites student writers to take sentences seriously, and it invites you to make room for sentences in your curriculum.

Rediscovering Style

For several generations, writing teachers have struggled to find the appropriate place for sentences in writing courses. We know, from a long and trustworthy tradition of empirical research, that "traditional grammar instruction" does not improve students' writing; students who are taught to parse sentences, identify errors, and memorize usage rules seldom operationalize that knowledge as they write. Worse, such instruction may alienate them from their linguistic intuitions and leave them disinclined to write. So writing teachers have wisely abandoned traditional grammar instruction. It sometimes appears that we have abandoned sentences altogether. Certainly teachers try to help students write stronger sentences, but we have tended to do so privately, in tutorials rather than classrooms, rarely discussing the work in professional conferences or journals.

Fortunately, recent years have seen a renewed interest in sentence pedagogy. I would date the renewal to the year 2000, when *College Composition and Communication* published Robert Connors's article "The Erasure of the Sentence." Connors laments the decline of three sentence pedagogies — Francis Christensen's generative rhetoric, imitation exercises, and sentence-combining — considering the reasons they fell into disuse and reviewing the research demonstrating their effectiveness. Three important books published during the first decade of the twenty-first century — *Refiguring Prose Style* by T. R. Johnson and Tom Pace, *Out of Style* by Paul Butler, and Butler's collection *Style in Rhetoric and Composition* — similarly trace a decline from robust attention to style in Greek and Roman rhetoric and in the studies of "syntactic maturity" that held center stage in the 1960s and '70s to the virtual absence of style in late twentieth-century scholarship.

In spite of the "rise and fall" arc of the history they sketch, Johnson, Pace, and Butler are optimistic. They note the emergence of young scholars who, prompted by the study of classical rhetoric and by sensitivity to students' needs, have begun investigating approaches to teaching style. Style pedagogy has also gotten a boost from scholars working at the intersection of composition and creative writing, especially Wendy Bishop, who encouraged teachers and students to approach sentences in an experimental, playful spirit. And the growth of our field, especially the development of major programs in writing studies, has cleared curricular space for sentence structure and style. My hope is that *The Well-Crafted Sentence* will help teachers take advantage of these developments in the profession by providing classroom-ready materials for teaching style.

Teaching Students to Experiment with Style

While writing *The Well-Crafted Sentence*, I have been guided by three pedagogical principles. The first is that writers can improve their style by studying the work of excellent stylists. A distinctive feature of *The Well-Crafted Sentence* is the use of model texts by accomplished writers — Louise Erdrich, Drew Gilpin Faust, Henry Louis Gates Jr., Barack Obama, Tim O'Brien, Theodore Olson, Oliver Sacks, David Sedaris, Amy Tan, and Lily Wong Fillmore. These are engaging texts, and many of the sentences are remarkably beautiful; the passages not only provide a store of authentic examples, but they enliven the chapters. In addition, they motivate student writers. I could simply assert that appositives, for example, are a useful addition to a writer's toolbox, but why should student writers believe me? Why should they care enough to spend their time practicing apposition? When they see what Louise Erdrich or Oliver Sacks can accomplish with appositives, and when they find that in exercises they can successfully imitate the prose of these writers, students are more likely to experiment with appositives in their own work.

Second, the textbook stresses the principle of rhetorical variation. The model texts have been selected to illustrate contemporary prose in a range of genres. If a discussion of sentences is to be truly rhetorical, it is not enough to examine sentences in context to see how they contribute to the overall effect of a paragraph or essay (though that's certainly a good start). Equally important is the imperative to examine sentences from multiple genres. Students need to see published writers making one sort of choice on one occasion and making *different* choices on different occasions. These observations sensitize students to the relationship between text and context and protect them against the impulse to seek simple, over-generalized rules for good writing. Although it is possible to understand the chapters and complete most of the exercises in *The Well-Crafted Sentence* without reading the model texts in full, I encourage you to assign them. They're good reading. And the more students know about a text, its writer, and the sociopolitical context in which the text was written, the better prepared they will be to appreciate (or to criticize) the writer's choices.

The third principle is a commonplace of composition pedagogy: people learn to write by writing. After the opening paragraphs in each chapter explain and illustrate a stylistic principle, the exercises give students the chance to push words around on the page. Students are asked to analyze passages from the model texts, to practice particular structures in imitation and sentence-development exercises, to create and compare two versions of a passage. You'll probably want to use the exercises in multiple ways. Some are easy to do on the spot, so a class can go over them aloud; others are designed as individual writing tasks; those that ask students to evaluate the effects of different rhetorical choices are well suited for small-group discussion. What matters most is that, in the end, students turn from the exercises to their own texts, using their skills in crafting sentences to revise their own essays and stories, pushing their writing ever closer to truth, clarity, and beauty.

New to the Second Edition

I am grateful to the many teachers who, after using the first edition of *The Well-Crafted Sentence* in their classes, agreed to offer feedback on the text. Largely in response to their suggestions, I have revised the text in several ways:

- **A new first chapter, "Approaches to Style,"** defines the term and argues for attention to style in all writing, whether its primary purpose is to induce understanding, conviction, passion, or pleasure. In particular, the chapter argues that academic essays, like other genres, create occasions to make stylistic choices.
- **Five new model texts** have been added. The model texts represent the work of living authors recognized for the excellence of their prose. In this edition, I've updated the selections, choosing some shorter pieces and a wider range of texts. These include not only essays, stories, and excerpts from memoirs but also a speech (Barack Obama's "A More Perfect Union") and two academic articles (those by historian Drew Gilpin Faust and linguist Lily Wong Fillmore).
- **Exercises have been added and grammatical concepts are more fully explained.** New and revised exercises, drawing from new model texts, offer increased focus on revising and editing sentences.
- **New attention to style in academic writing.** Throughout the book, instruction, exercises, and examples illustrate how stylistic choices can work in academic writing.

Acknowledgments

I am indebted to many people who have helped in the creation of this book. Its approach to sentence pedagogy has roots in the work of theorists and teachers including Francis Christensen, Patrick Hartwell, Joseph M. Williams, and especially William Robinson and Jo Keroes.

I received invaluable help from my colleague at the University of Nebraska at Omaha, Joan Latchaw, who shared her insights as she used the first edition in her course, The Rhetoric of the Sentence. I am thankful to the students who have taken that course over the years, especially for their feedback on exercises. When we ran out of semester before all the exercises had been written, four readers volunteered to test-drive exercises in the later chapters: sincere thanks to Casey Tribolet, Holly Newman Dzyban, Kyle Simonsen, and Kimberly Schwab.

At Bedford/St. Martin's, I have had the pleasure of working with an extraordinary team of editors. Joan Feinberg offered crucial support at an early stage; Leasa Burton was unfailingly helpful and encouraging; Daniel Schafer provided assistance with the headnotes; Kalina Ingham ably managed text permissions; and Karen Baart, Anna Palchik, Lisa Buckley, and Steven Patterson effected the transformation from a manuscript into a book. I am especially grateful to developmental editors Michelle McSweeney (for the first edition) and Sophia Snyder (for the second) for guiding me through the writing process with an extraordinary blend of critical rigor, tact, and patience. They have made The Well-Crafted Sentence a better book, and if I succeed in learning from their example, they will have made me a better writing teacher.

My thanks to the teachers who have reviewed The Well-Crafted Sentence throughout its development. The teachers whose feedback on the first edition informed my work on the second were G. Douglas Atkins, University of Kansas; Audrey Bilger, Claremont-McKenna College; James Borton, University of South Carolina, Sumter; Tom Busey, Indiana University; Isaac Cates, University of Vermont; Cheri Crenshaw, Dixie State College; Drucella Crutchfield, Southeastern University; Christine Peters Cucciarre, University of Delaware; Lightsey Darst, North Hennepin Community College; Jonathan Deane, Rutgers University, Camden; Tom Deans, University of Connecticut; Alisa DeBorde, Southeastern University; Diana Epelbaum, College of Staten Island; Christopher Ervin, Western Kentucky University; William Fitzgerald, Rutgers University, Camden; Melissa Goldthwaite, Saint Joseph's University; Rebecca Gordon, Oklahoma City University; Gary Hafer, Lycoming College; Jessica Hausmann, Georgian Court University; John Isles, City College of San Francisco; T. R. Johnson, Tulane University; Scott Kaukonen, Sam Houston State University; Nate Kreuter, Western Carolina University; Joan Latchaw, University of Nebraska at Omaha; Krysten Leonard, Radford University; Zachary Martin, College of Staten Island; Tom McGohey, Wake Forest University; Star Medzerian, Nova Southeastern University; Ann

Modzelewski, Edmonds Community College; Barry Nowlin, University of South Alabama; Megan O'Neill, Stetson University; Tom Pace, John Carroll University; Doreen Piano, University of New Orleans; Daniel Shea, Mount St. Mary College; Elizabeth Signorotti, Binghamton University; Allison Smith, Middle Tennessee State University; Carol Spaulding-Kruse, Drake University; Elizabeth Stansell, Clemson University; Daniel Wallace, Rutgers University, Camden; and Lothlórien Watkins, San Francisco State University.

I also remain grateful to those who responded to drafts of the first edition: Charlotte Brammer, Samford University; Marc. C. Conner, Washington & Lee University; Laurie Cubbison, Radford University; Joan Frederick, James Madison University; Susan M. Grant, University of Missouri–St. Louis; Paul Harris, Loyola Marymount University; Joseph C. Holobar, Penn State University; Katherine Kapitan, Buena Vista University; Jennifer Lee, University of Pittsburgh; Mary Hurley Moran, University of Georgia; David A. Nentwick, Syracuse University; Jill Onega, University of Alabama–Huntsville; Howard Sage, Hunter College; Alf Seegert, University of Utah; Julie Clark Simon, Southern Utah University; Jo Beth Van Arkel, Drury University; and Venise Wagner, San Francisco State University.

Closer to home, I would like to thank my colleagues Sam Walker and Anna Monardo for their contributions to the introduction and my husband, Dana Joiner, for unwavering support.

Nora Bacon

Digital and Print Resources

THE WELL-CRAFTED SENTENCE doesn't stop with this book. Here, you'll find both free and affordable premium digital resources to help students get even more out of the book and your course as well as package options that can save your students money. You'll also find convenient instructor resources. To learn more about or order any of the products below, contact your Bedford/St. Martin's sales representative, e-mail sales support (sales_support@bfwpub.com), or visit the Web site at **bedfordstmartins.com/wellcrafted**.

Digital Options for Students

bedfordstmartins.com/wellcrafted
Send students to free and open resources, choose flexible premium resources to supplement your print text, or upgrade to an expanding collection of innovative digital content.

Free and open resources for *The Well-Crafted Sentence* provide students with easy-to-access reference materials, visual tutorials, and support for working with sources.

- A new guide to the parts of speech
- Sample responses to exercises
- A searchable glossary of grammatical terms
- 5 free videos of real writers from VideoCentral
- 3 free tutorials from *ix: visualizing composition* by Cheryl Ball and Kristin Arola
- *Research and Documentation Online* by Diana Hacker
- *The Bedford Bibliographer*: a tool for collecting source information and making a bibliography in MLA, APA, and *Chicago* styles

Re:Writing Plus gathers all of Bedford/St. Martin's premium digital content for composition into one online collection. It includes hundreds of model documents, the first ever peer review game, and Video-Central. *Re:Writing Plus* can be purchased separately or packaged with the print book at a significant discount. An activation code is required. To order *Re:Writing Plus* packaged with the print book, use **ISBN 978-1-4576-4598-3.**

ix 2.0: visualizing composition helps students put into practice key rhetorical and visual concepts. To order *ix 2.0: visualizing composition* packaged with the print book, use **ISBN 978-1-4576-4596-9.**

i-claim 2.0: visualizing argument offers a new way to see argument — with 6 tutorials, an illustrated glossary, and over 70 multimedia arguments. To order *i-claim 2.0: visualizing argument* packaged with the print book, use **ISBN 978-1-4576-4867-0.**

E-Book Options

bedfordstmartins.com/wellcrafted/formats
Bedford/St. Martin's e-books let students do more and pay less. For about half the price of a print book, the e-book for *The Well-Crafted Sentence* offers the complete text of the print book combined with convenient digital tools such as highlighting, note-taking, and search.

Package and Save

Add more value to your course by packaging a handbook or reader with *The Well-Crafted Sentence* — and save 20%. To learn more about package options or any of the products below, visit the Web site at **bedfordstmartins.com/wellcrafted/catalog** or contact your Bedford/St. Martin's sales representative.

- *The Everyday Writer*, **Fifth Edition, by Andrea Lunsford,** is the first tabbed handbook to help students, who are writing more than ever — in classrooms, workplaces, and social spaces — build on the smart decisions they make as social writers and use their skills in their academic and professional work. To order *The Everyday Writer* packaged with *The Well-Crafted Sentence*, use **ISBN 978-1-4576-4870-0.**

- *EasyWriter*, **Fourth Edition, by Andrea Lunsford,** distills Andrea Lunsford's teaching and research into the essentials that today's writers need to make good choices in any rhetorical situation. To order *EasyWriter* packaged with *The Well-Crafted Sentence*, use **ISBN 978-1-4576-4863-2.**

- *Emerging,* **Second Edition, by Barclay Barrios,** offers readings to engage students with meaningful contemporary issues so that they can develop the skills they need to address the large questions that will shape their lives. To order *Emerging* packaged with *The Well-Crafted Sentence,* use **ISBN 978-1-4576-4869-4.**

- *Language Awareness: Readings for College Writers,* **Eleventh Edition, by Paul Eschholz, Alfred Rosa, and Victoria Clark,** collects contemporary and classic readings about language that not only make students more aware of its uses and more capable of analyzing its effects, but also help them to deploy language more effectively in their own writing. To order *Language Awareness* packaged with *The Well-Crafted Sentence,* use **ISBN 978-1-4576-4868-7.**

Instructor Resources

bedfordstmartins.com/wellcrafted/catalog
You have a lot to do in your course. Bedford/St. Martin's wants to make it easy for you to find the support you need—and to get it quickly.

Teaching Central offers the entire list of Bedford/St. Martin's print and online professional resources in one place. You'll find landmark reference works, sourcebooks on pedagogical issues, award-winning collections, and practical advice for the classroom—all free for instructors.

Bits collects creative ideas for teaching a range of composition topics in an easily searchable blog format. A community of teachers—leading scholars, authors, and editors—discuss revision, research, grammar and style, technology, peer review, and much more. Take, use, adapt, and pass the ideas around. Then, come back to the site to comment or share your own suggestions. Visit *Bits* at **bedfordstmartins.com/bits**.

Coursepacks for the most common course management systems—Blackboard, WebCT, Angel, and Desire2Learn—allow you to easily download digital materials from Bedford/St. Martin's for your course. To find the coursepacks available with *The Well-Crafted Sentence,* visit **bedfordstmartins.com/coursepacks**.

About the Author

NORA BACON is a professor of English and writing program administrator at the University of Nebraska at Omaha. She started her career at San Francisco State University in the late 1970s when its writing courses highlighted sentence structure, encouraging students to experiment with style by joining and developing their sentences.

Nora went on to teach at Stanford University, where she helped to launch a service-learning program called Community Service Writing. As she worked with students writing in multiple settings — English classes, classes in other disciplines, and community organizations — she was intrigued by the variation in the texts they created and by the learning strategies they used to make successful adaptations. Her research, begun at UC Berkeley in the 1990s, has examined service-learning pedagogy, the development of "writing agility," and the relationship between texts and the contexts in which they are written and read. Nora's current research focuses on the stylistic choices preferred in different disciplines, uniting her interest in variation and her abiding fascination with sentences.

Contents

ANTHOLOGY

Model Texts for Writers 157

The Well-Crafted Sentence

A WRITER'S GUIDE TO STYLE

Introduction

IF YOU'VE GROWN UP speaking English, or if you've been speaking it regularly for several years, then it's likely that you create hundreds of well-formed sentences every day. You open your mouth and words spill out: it doesn't require much effort for you to create sentences or for your listeners to understand them. Maybe the sentences aren't *perfect* — you might make a false start, or interrupt yourself, or mispronounce a word — but they're clear enough, they're easy, and chances are that nobody criticizes your style.

There are, I'm told, people who enjoy a similar fluency when they write. It's said that Shakespeare never blotted a line. But for most of us, writing is far more difficult than speaking: we take on more complicated intellectual tasks (longer stretches of language, more challenging concepts, ideas with more complex relationships), and, aware of the permanence of written texts, we aspire to higher standards of accuracy and eloquence. When we write, we don't have the opportunity to watch our listeners and make repairs if they seem puzzled or resistant; instead, we have to anticipate the reactions of readers who may be complete strangers.

Writing, then, rarely involves the spontaneous production of language; instead, we write and rewrite, revise and edit, arranging and rearranging words. Because writing rests on the page, we have the opportunity to return to it, to tinker with it, to play with it and work on it, before we send it on to a reader. That's why it makes sense to speak of writing as a craft: we writers begin with the raw material of language and shape it until it expresses something of ourselves — our experiences, observations, and feelings, our ideas and convictions. This book is designed to help you become more skillful at the craft of writing and editing sentences.

Like other skills, skill in crafting sentences develops through observation, practice, and feedback. *The Well-Crafted Sentence* is designed to give you opportunities to *observe* by reading with a writer's eye, attending to the choices that other writers have made, and to *practice* by imitating excellent sentences and creating sentences of your own. For *feedback*, you'll have to rely on people you trust. Ideally, you will read this book while enrolled in a writing class where the teacher and your classmates can provide helpfully critical responses to your work.

Chapter 1 summarizes ways of thinking about style, suggesting that an effective style is the result of choices — choosing words, choosing where to place them — with an eye to achieving a particular rhetorical effect. Chapter 2 is also foundational; it provides a bare-bones refresher of grammatical terms and concepts that most people learn in the eighth grade and forget in the ninth. You will make use of these terms and concepts when you read subsequent chapters and any time you wish to carry on a reasonably precise conversation about sentences (with, say, an instructor, classmate, coworker, or editor). Note that all grammatical terms and concepts in the book are highlighted in boldface when they appear for the first time, and they are included, with definitions, in the glossary at the back of the book.

The following chapters introduce strategies for writing well-focused, well-balanced, and well-developed sentences. Chapter 3 examines the heart of any sentence, the subject and verb, stressing the importance of choosing subjects that will get a sentence off to a strong start. In Chapter 4, I describe the construction of pairs and lists, highlighting the need for parallel, or matching, structures. Chapter 5 shows how sentences can be expanded and enriched with the use of modifiers.

Chapters 6 through 9 continue the discussion of modification, focusing on specific structures that published writers use frequently but that undergraduate writers tend to overlook. The structures are illustrated in passages drawn from "model texts," essays and stories by distinguished contemporary writers. Along with the sample passages, you'll find commentary drawing your attention to the choices the writer has made and the effects of those choices.

The commentary is followed by exercises in which you will identify the structure of interest and then practice using it. The exercises are intended not only to clarify a concept but, more important, to get you to practice using the structure so that it begins to feel perfectly natural to you. Borrowing a time-honored instructional technique that the ancient Romans called *imitatio*, I've written several exercises that ask you to rework a passage from one of the model texts. These exercises call for imitation and variation. If you retain the ideas of the model passage, you'll vary its structure; if you retain the structure, you'll create new content.

It's important that you work through the exercises with care. Some exercises (especially those early in the book or early in a chapter) have specific correct answers, but most are open-ended, with a virtually unlimited range of possible responses. Please don't think of the exercises as tests: they're rehearsals, not performances. When you've finished an exercise, you can check your work by comparing your responses to those on the *Student Site for The Well-Crafted Sentence*, **www.bedfordstmartins.com/wellcrafted**.

As you're studying each syntactic structure, make it a point to practice it when you write and revise your own prose. Use a draft of your current essay or story to reinforce what you're learning about sentences, inserting the new structure into three or four sentences to see how it works. Show your writing to others to learn how your experiments with sentence structure affect them as they read.

Who are these distinguished contemporary writers whose sentences you will analyze and imitate? They are ten authors whose work is published in highly respected books, journals, and magazines. Louise Erdrich is a short-story writer and novelist, David Sedaris a humorist. Tim O'Brien writes fiction inspired by events in his own life, blurring the line between memory and imagination. Amy Tan is best known for her novels, though the selection you'll be working with is a personal reflection written as a speech and later included in a collection of "musings." Theodore Olson is a lawyer, and Barack Obama was, at the time he wrote the speech printed here, a presidential candidate. The other model texts are by scholars. While the pieces by historian Drew Gilpin Faust and linguist Lily Wong Fillmore are written for academic journals, neurologist Oliver Sacks addresses a general audience. The selection by literary theorist and historian Henry Louis Gates Jr. is a chapter from his memoir; the events recalled in this text foreshadow his lifelong academic interest in the African American experience. The model texts have been selected not just for their excellence but for their variety. They show how ten skillful writers tune their prose to particular occasions.

You can see that I admire these texts. Still, I hope you won't approach them with undue reverence. You may love a sample sentence and approve of the writer's choices, or you may not. In either case, it is worthwhile to articulate what the sentence does to you and to imagine how a different arrangement of words might change the impact. Please read with an experimental eye, thinking of how any given sentence might have developed in the hands of another writer—like you.

When your writing class has ended, it is unlikely that you will ever again approach a writing task saying "In this piece, I'm going to use at least five verbal phrases." Most of the time, as we write, our attention is fixed on what we want to say. We think about the *meaning* that we're pushing into existence, and the words arrange themselves accordingly. But then we pause to look back—to reread, to reflect, to revise—and that's when we see that no, it's not quite right: this sentence doesn't quite capture what I meant to say, or that one doesn't deserve so much space; this sentence contradicts itself, or that one is hopelessly tangled; this sentence could be misinterpreted and that one doesn't sound like me.

At those points in the writing process, it is useful to be able to draw upon a rich store of linguistic resources. The principal goal of this book is to expand the repertoire of syntactic structures available to you when you write and revise. As you work through the following chapters, you will examine structures that most undergraduate writers readily understand but seldom use. With practice, you will make them your own.

CHAPTER 1

Approaches to Style

WELL-CRAFTED SENTENCES ARE essential to an effective style. Everybody agrees to that; I can make the claim without fear of contradiction. But what is an effective style? What, for that matter, is style? If you're about to spend several weeks working with "a writer's guide to style," what kind of work have you undertaken? The term *style* has a long history and many meanings, some of them inconsistent with others. So I'd like to begin by considering three widespread ideas about style. Style can be understood as the quality of writing that makes it uniquely and recognizably the creation of one writer; as the ornamentation that transforms pedestrian prose into something beautiful or memorable; and as the effort to make language clear and concise. All three conceptions of style have merit; there are useful insights embedded in each, and each sheds light on specific qualities and skills that writers need to develop.

Style as Identity

Few twenty-first-century readers have ever heard of George-Louis Leclerc de Buffon, but many are familiar with his assertion about style. "Style," he said, "is the man himself."

Style, this quotation suggests, is identity; style is the unique voice that distinguishes one writer from all others. This idea has become a commonplace in conversations about style. When we speak of Jane Austen's style, for example, we mean the quality that makes her writing unmistakably hers, distinct from the work of any other writer. Austen may not sound exactly the same in her letters as she does in her novels, and she may not sound the same in *Persuasion* as she does in *Northanger Abbey*, but she always sounds like Jane Austen. If you read much of her work, you quickly learn to recognize her voice. Something similar could be said of Charles Dickens, Ernest Hemingway, Virginia Woolf, David Foster Wallace, Joan Didion . . . Insert Your Favorite Author Here. Style, in this view, is a quality intrinsic to the writer, and we recognize a well-loved writer by his or her style just as we recognize friends and family by the sound of their voices.

Many writers I've worked with over the years have aspired to develop their own unique writing styles. This is a commendable aspiration. But paradoxically, the best way to achieve it is not to focus on it too deliberately: it's a mistake to try to develop a distinctive style by inserting oneself into every text, or by writing spontaneously as one speaks, or by trying to sound different from everyone else. A writer who is trying hard to sound charming or sophisticated or erudite usually sounds, in the end, like somebody trying hard. Instead, a distinctive style is likely to develop in the writer who focuses on the subject, on what he or she has to say. "Good writing," Virginia Woolf wrote, "has for backbone some fierce attachment to an idea." The writer who is fully engaged with an idea will quite naturally use language revealing his or her mind at work; the prose style will reflect the individuality of the mind.

It is probably most useful to think of your individual style not as a single voice but as a range of voices. All of us are capable of being thoughtful, serious, bawdy, silly, humorous, sarcastic, sweet, tart, bold, deliberative, confessional — not all at the same time, but all quite authentically. Developing an individual style might begin with testing many ideas and many voices to discover which ones ring true. Here, then, is another paradox: an excellent strategy for improving your own style is to imitate the style of other writers. You are what you read, not just because reading informs your store of knowledge and values but because it extends the range of words and stylistic choices that feel authentic to you.

Style as Embellishment

A second view of style is the one we have in mind when we contrast *style* with *substance*. It's possible to say the same thing in more than one way. If you adjust the wording of a sentence without altering its essential meaning, what you're doing is playing with style.

The most famous example of this kind of play comes from Desiderius Erasmus, the sixteenth-century author of *Copia: Foundations of the Abundant Style*. Erasmus was convinced that of all the possible stylistic virtues, variety was the most important; he encouraged writers to have plenty to say and many ways to say it. "The speech of man," he explained,

> is a magnificent and impressive thing when it surges along like a golden river, with thoughts and words pouring out in rich abundance. . . . Richness of expression involves synonyms . . . metaphor, variation in word form, equivalence, and other similar methods of diversifying diction.

At one point, Erasmus illustrates richness of expression by writing 195 variations on the sentence, "Your letter pleased me greatly" — everything from "Your letter was the source of singular gladness" to "Your communication poured vials of joy on my head." The list of 195 sentences may strike a modern reader as excessive, but you have to give Erasmus credit for this: he remembers that speaking and listening — for our purposes, we can shift that to writing and reading — can be a source of pleasure (not to mention joy, gladness, happiness, delight, satisfaction, and a refreshment of spirits).

While writers naturally like to take and give pleasure, the conception of style as embellishment has an unfortunate consequence: it can make work on style seem trivial and even vaguely dishonorable. You've figured out what you want to say. You've said it. Now, why would you keep on messing around with the words? Richly ornamented language is criticized by advocates of the plain style, who prefer stripped-down prose that gets straight to the point.

The Plain Style

Over the centuries, many philosophers have argued that the purpose of speaking and writing is to seek or to communicate truth. So, they say, the goal of speaking or writing should be to find the words that convey information or express an idea in the most straightforward possible way—simply, clearly, so that the language captures the truth without distractions or distortions. In this view, work on wording or sentence structure ought to be undertaken in the interest of clarity, period; efforts at variety, beauty, or wit are a waste of time and, more to the point, likely to get in the way of clear communication. Writers who strive for eloquence are viewed with some suspicion because they may be trying to manipulate readers, short-circuiting readers' critical thinking by charming them or appealing to their emotions.

Objections to stylistic embellishment have never been more strongly articulated than in the work of Thomas Sprat, who was so troubled by "the luxuries and redundancy of speech"—indulgences appealing to the passions rather than to reason—that he believed "eloquence ought to be banished out of all civil societies as a thing fatal to peace and good manners." In 1667, Sprat published a history of the Royal Society, the association of "natural philosophers" (we would call them scientists) who came together in seventeenth-century London to share their discoveries. Members of the Royal Society, he said, rejected stylistic flourishes of all kinds:

> They have . . . been most rigorous in putting in execution . . . a constant Resolution, to reject all the amplifications, digressions, and swellings of style: to return back to the primitive purity, and shortness, when men deliver'd so many *things*, almost in an equal number of *words*. They have exacted from all their members, a close, naked, natural way of speaking; positive expressions; clear senses; a native easiness: bringing all things as near the Mathematical plainness, as they can: and preferring the language of Artizans, Countrymen, and Merchants, before that, of Wits, or Scholars.

Sprat has no time for Erasmus's golden river of words flowing in rich abundance; on the contrary, he prefers the everyday to the ornate, the direct to the allusive, the short to the "copious." Sprat's insistence on the plain style anticipates the view that dominated style books, writing classes, and even government position papers about style throughout the twentieth century.

Perhaps you have read or heard of *The Elements of Style*. It's a charming little book first published in 1918 by Cornell professor William Strunk and, after Strunk's death, republished with revisions and additions by the essayist E. B. White, who had been a student in Strunk's

English class. For many generations of writers, teachers, and editors, *The Elements of Style* has been the final authority on what makes prose effective. In the final chapter, "An Approach to Style," White strongly cautions against writing that calls attention to itself. His reminders include these: *Place yourself in the background; write in a way that comes naturally; do not overwrite; do not overstate; avoid fancy words; avoid foreign languages; use figures of speech sparingly; prefer the standard to the offbeat.* The chapter — and, in fact, the book as a whole — is a manual for achieving the plain style.

There's a lot of wisdom to be found in *The Elements of Style*. Strunk and White stress the importance of clarity and conciseness, and in my judgment, these are essential to good writing on almost all occasions. An especially memorable injunction is "Rule 13: Omit needless words." Strunk explains that "a sentence should contain no unnecessary words, a paragraph no unnecessary sentences, for the same reason that a drawing should have no unnecessary lines and a machine no unnecessary parts. This requires not that the writer make all his sentences short . . . but that every word tell." This is solid, commonsense advice: no reader wants to spend time slogging through superfluous words, and every example that Strunk offers (reducing "the question as to whether" to "whether"; "there is no doubt but that" to "no doubt"; "the fact that I had arrived" to "my arrival") clearly represents an improvement.

I was brought up on Strunk and White. I take real pleasure in lean, clear prose, and I have no patience with wordiness or pretension. While writing *The Well-Crafted Sentence*, I have been continually reminded of my debt to Strunk and White and other, more recent advocates of the plain style. And yet. When you read Strunk and White's rules and reminders, don't you find yourself asking, "Is that all there is?" Surely clarity and conciseness are desirable, surely writing that sounds natural is better than writing that sounds contrived . . . but when Strunk and White boil good style down to principles like those, aren't they missing something?

For a glimpse of what's missing, we might look to E. B. White himself, in this paragraph from his introductory chapter. After an affectionate recollection of Strunk's lesson on "Rule 13: Omit needless words," White makes a confession:

> The Professor devotes a special paragraph to the vile expression "the fact that," a phrase that causes him to quiver with revulsion. The expression, he says, should be "revised out of every sentence in which

it occurs." But a shadow of gloom seems to hang over the page, and you feel that he knows how hopeless his cause is. I suppose I have written "the fact that" a thousand times in the heat of composition, revised it out maybe five hundred times in the cool aftermath. To be batting only .500 this late in the season, to fail half the time to connect with this fat pitch, saddens me, for it seems a betrayal of the man who showed me how to swing at it and made the swinging seem worthwhile.

White's prose here is, as always, perfectly lucid, and he gets his money's worth for every word. But what makes this passage fun to read is that White permits himself to fool around. Professor Strunk didn't really quiver with revulsion, and no shadow of gloom really hangs over the page; White is exaggerating. Composition isn't really hot and revision isn't really cool, and we don't measure the frequency of "the fact that" with a batting average; White is using metaphors. My point is not that White is using figures of speech or that, in doing so, he violates one of his own rules. My point is that he is having some fun. I suspect that *The Elements of Style* owes its place as America's best-loved style book not only to the wisdom of Strunk and White's advice, not only to the vigor and clarity of their prose, but also to the sense of whimsy that White brought to the enterprise.

What I would argue for, then, is a *both/and* view of style. A writer who masters the stylistic principles of the plain style, earnestly seeking clarity and conciseness, is off to a fine start. But the best writers also seek pleasure, perhaps for themselves as they write and certainly for us as we read. This doesn't mean trying hard to be clever or to plant a lot of metaphors or hyperbole or alliterative phrases in a text; instead, it means relaxing, being open to figures of speech when they suggest themselves, and taking an experimental, even playful attitude toward language. A sentence that ends up sounding inappropriate or over-wrought can always be deleted in the next draft. But you can't decide against "vials of joy on my head" until you've given yourself permission to write it.

Style in Context: Making Rhetorically Smart Choices

The conception of style as a reflection of the writer's distinctive person-ality reminds us how important it is to write with integrity—which can mean a commitment to becoming knowledgeable and thoughtful about the topic at hand, or to telling the truth, to writing from the heart, to writing in a voice that strikes one's own ear as authentic. The conception of style as embellishment, at least as Erasmus presents it, reminds us of the value of being generative, producing many ideas, many words, many ways to say something, and it highlights the possibility of pleasure in written language. Discussions of the plain style call attention to the value of keeping prose clear, concise, and uncluttered.

What still has to be stirred into the mix is the variation in readers. It's safe to make some generalizations about readers — they like a writer who respects their intelligence, they dislike tangled syntax, they appreciate humor — but this road won't take us very far. Readers aren't all the same, and what a reader will like or understand depends on the situation. You may have noticed this in yourself as a reader: you'll tolerate more ambiguity in a poem or story than in a booklet at the doctor's office; you'll spend more time figuring out difficult sentences in a chemistry textbook than you would in a magazine article; a comment that seems funny in a personal e-mail might strike you as tasteless in a published editorial. Every time you pick up a text, you have expectations for what that sort of text will do and how it will sound. Although your expectations may not be rigid or well defined, there they are, and they shape your response to a text.

For writers, then, choices about crafting sentences can be made only in reference to the particulars of a rhetorical context (who is saying what to whom, when, where, and why). I can't stress this point enough: if anyone asks what makes a good sentence, the only honest answer is "It depends." Whether a word is right or wrong, whether an idea should be emphasized or subordinated, whether a sentence should be short or long, simple or complex — it all depends on the purpose of the text, the intended audience, and the sentences before and after. Writing involves a continual series of judgment calls, some so minor and easy that they feel automatic, others so important and difficult that a single paragraph can take hours to write.

Let's take the case of a writer who knows his or her subject and who has an adequate vocabulary to talk about it. To achieve an effective style, this writer needs (at least) three more things: enough mastery of sentence structure to imagine a range of options for expressing an idea, enough understanding of the rhetorical context to predict a sentence's impact on readers, and enough commitment to the idea itself to keep testing options until the sentence says just what it should. As an example of the kind of choices I have in mind, I'll show you two successful writers at work, creating and choosing among various ways to arrange their words.

In the spring of 1994, novelist Anna Monardo sat down to write a story exploring the mind-set of young people in the late 1960s and early 1970s. She began with this line:

> Natassia was born in Rome, while Mary and Ross were on a junior-year-abroad program.

As she worked on the story, she revised the opening:

> Natassia was conceived in Rome, while Mary and Ross were students in a junior-year-abroad program, when another couple, also students, dared them not to use birth control. "Do it with no birth control. We'll do it if you do it."

This is a significant revision. Monardo moves back nine months, from Natassia's birth to the more telling moment of her conception. As the sentence introduces Mary and Ross, it provides not only their names but a glimpse of their circumstances and their frame of mind at this turning point in their lives. And this opening is more pleasing to the ear. The prose has its own rhythm: if you read it aloud, you'll find that your voice rises and falls. Important information comes in short, dramatic clauses — "Natassia was conceived in Rome," "Do it with no birth control" — while less important information ("also students") is tucked into the middle of the sentence.

The story eventually grew into a novel, *Falling in Love with Natassia*. As the story took shape, Monardo realized that her opening sentence needed to direct readers' attention to Mary, to establish her as the main character. When the novel was published in 2006, the opening sentence appeared as follows:

> Mary and Ross were in Rome on a junior-year-abroad program when they had their baby, Natassia, who was conceived on a dare: "Do it with no birth control," another couple challenged. "We'll do it if you do it."

To signal the importance of the parents, Monardo made "Mary and Ross" the subject of the sentence. By contrast, the phrase "also students" has disappeared so that the other couple, who never reappear in the novel, have little presence as individuals. And Monardo reinforced the idea of a dare, adding the verb "challenged" and setting off the dare with a colon — strong punctuation to say "*here it comes.*"

Monardo's choices were guided by her goals as a writer of fiction. A novel is a work of art, so Monardo crafted her opening sentences with an eye to the beauty of the language. And a novel tells a story driven by the actions and interactions of a set of characters, so Monardo very intentionally led readers toward a particular understanding of Mary and Ross.

Other writers, creating different kinds of texts in different circumstances, may respond to a different set of goals. For example, consider the choices made by historian Sam Walker as he composed *Presidents and Civil Liberties, From Woodrow Wilson to George W. Bush: A Story of Poor Custodians.* For two years, Walker traveled around the country conducting research in presidential libraries, concerned first of all with writing an accurate, well-detailed account of the presidents' decisions affecting civil liberties. As he crafted the book, he also attended to style, imagining how readers might respond to his sentences.

Like Monardo, Walker understands the importance of opening lines. In an early draft of *Presidents and Civil Liberties,* when he was first getting his ideas on paper, Walker began the chapter about Lyndon Johnson as follows:

> Assuming the presidency in an atmosphere of national crisis following the assassination of President Kennedy on November 22, 1963, Lyndon Johnson wasted no time proving his commitment to civil rights. Passage of Kennedy's civil rights bill was still uncertain, and civil rights leaders distrusted him as a southerner who they believed had weakened the 1957 Civil Rights bill.

This is, in my view, a strong opening, especially with its reminder of the "atmosphere of national crisis" that followed Kennedy's assassination. But it's indirect. Although the passage begins a chapter about Lyndon Johnson, it starts by stepping back to the assassination of President Kennedy, and the second sentence presents Johnson only through the eyes of others, the civil rights leaders who distrusted him. While these background ideas are clearly relevant, Walker wanted to paint a more compelling picture of Johnson himself — and he wanted drama. In later drafts, he placed Johnson on center stage and turned up the spotlight.

The published chapter opens with these sentences:

> The president paused, and very slowly and deliberately told the nation,
> "And . . . we . . . shall . . . overcome." On national television the night
> of March 15, 1965, President Lyndon Johnson spoke to Congress
> and the nation about the urgent need for a federal voting rights law.
> Leaving no doubt about the depth of his commitment, he embraced
> the slogan of the civil rights movement.

In this version, Johnson is present from the first words — "the president paused" — and every sentence has a word or phrase referring to Johnson as its subject ("The president," "President Lyndon Johnson," and "he"). We hear Johnson's voice, complete with punctuation to cue the pacing, as he assures the nation that "we shall overcome" — words whose emotional power is grounded in the civil rights movement, borrowed by Johnson, and evoked again by Walker.

Explaining his revisions to the passage, Walker points to the effects he intended to have on readers: he hoped to direct their attention to the chapter's topic, to awaken readers' interest so they would keep turning the pages, and to help them understand civil rights issues in terms of decision-makers' human motivations and actions.

Style in Academic Writing

In creative writing, style plays an important role. Literary texts are read for pleasure; we expect the sentences to be beautiful or at least striking. And literary texts often have, as their underlying subjects, abiding truths about human life and human relationships; they often tell stories whose essential truth has been expressed many, many times before. In James Baldwin's words, "While the tale of how we suffer, and how we are delighted, and how we may triumph is never new, it always must be heard. There isn't any other tale to tell." Novels, short stories, and literary essays rarely provide us with new information; they hold our attention because they teach familiar truths with an immediacy that resembles the immediacy of learning through experience (but without the same risk of pain). What pulls us in, what holds us in the world of the story, is the beauty and power of the language; that is what makes the experience vivid. So nobody questions why creative writers should take care in crafting their sentences.

But what about all the other writing people generate, the writing that does not aspire to the status of art but that does the work of the world in newspapers, magazines, journals, letters, reports, memos? If literary writing is creative, is other writing uncreative? I'm especially interested in the style of academic writing, which I both write and teach. There's no escaping the fact that academic writing has a bad reputation: it's thought to be dry, dusty, dull . . . or wordy and pretentious . . . or objective and therefore impersonal and therefore dry, dusty, and dull.

The worst of it is that so many people believe academic writing is *supposed to be* flat. My impulse is to blame Thomas Sprat for having argued so forcefully that the work of science requires "Mathematical plainness." But if Sprat hadn't said it, somebody else would have. Most writing done in universities has, as its purpose, the discovery and communication of knowledge: when scholars write for an audience of other scholars, they usually do so to report the findings of their research, and when they write for other audiences — students or the public — they inform them of the current state of knowledge in their fields. One consequence of this purpose is that academic writers tend to care, above all, about accuracy and clarity; those are the principal goals that govern their choices. Another consequence is that, because they know that readers take up their work in order to learn new information, they don't rely on the novelty or beauty of their language to draw readers in. So in academic writing, artfulness in choosing words or crafting sentences is rarely essential to getting the job done.

The mistake is to conclude that artfulness actually interferes with getting the job done. Thomas Sprat believed that: he thought language could appeal *either* to "the passions" *or* to reason, and eloquent language was on the wrong path. He believed that if readers were pleased by a metaphor, or surprised by a clever word choice, or carried along by the rhythm of a particularly lovely sentence, they would be distracted from the scientific content of the work — as if people couldn't think and smile at the same time. By contrast, everything in my experience as a reader, writer, and teacher leads me to believe that we are more likely to comprehend new information and are more receptive to new ideas if the style of their presentation is not only clear and orderly but also pleasurable.

I think it's time that we raised our expectations for style in academic writing. To the goals of clarity, conciseness, and accuracy, we can add grace, rhythm, wit, and power. We can push back at dichotomies like appealing to the passions vs. appealing to reason, or creative vs. academic, or clarity vs. eloquence. And we can dispute the misconception that academic writers don't or shouldn't care about the sound of their language. Academic writing is writing: if the writer is making choices about how to arrange words in sentences, the prose has style.

Let us turn, then, to the matter of fitting words into sentences, beginning with a review of the possibilities afforded by English grammar.

The Sentence's Working Parts

AS A WRITING TEACHER, I occasionally find myself in conversation with people — students, neighbors, strangers at parties — who reveal peculiar beliefs about grammar. "I'm not a good writer," they tell me. "I don't know anything about grammar." Depending on when and where they went to school, they may once have been able to diagram a sentence or define *predicate nominative*, but if they can't do it today, they despair of ever improving their writing. They believe that a thorough understanding of grammar is essential for writers.

By contrast, there are people who dismiss grammar altogether. Observing that every five-year-old can generate sentences without having learned a single grammatical term, they conclude that studying sentence structure is a waste of time. People develop language skills effortlessly just by being part of a human community; this intuitive knowledge, they believe, is all they need.

I'd like to suggest an alternative view of the relationship between writing and grammar. I'd prefer not to ask "Do writers need to know grammar?" and then answer "yes" or "no." Instead, we might ask "How much grammar do writers need to know?" and then answer "It depends."

Perhaps the most useful way to think about grammatical knowledge is to consider the many fields of human activity in which technical knowledge lies on a continuum, with different levels of activity corresponding to different levels of expertise. Take cooking as an example. If you fix your meals by zapping frozen dinners in the microwave, you don't need to know much about cookery. But if you want to improve as a cook, you'll need some technical knowledge: in order to follow recipes and talk to other cooks, you have to learn the difference between *broil* and *braise*. You will acquire the words for *chives* and *chervil* about the time you learn to identify them by taste, and that's when you'll know which one to put in the soup. Professional chefs typically have a very discriminating palate; a wide vocabulary of terms for ingredients, tools, and techniques; and even some understanding of the chemistry underlying food preparation. A cook's analytical knowledge informs his or her hands-on practice in the kitchen.

You can probably think of many other activities — playing basketball, drawing portraits, playing the piano — that people can participate in with varying levels of technical knowledge. Beginners can jump right in, and with practice, they will improve. As their proficiency develops, they acquire a vocabulary for talking about the activity, and they learn to observe other athletes, artists, or musicians with an appreciation of their technique.

How much grammar do you need to know? For everyday speech, your intuitive knowledge is adequate. For everyday writing at school and work, you need to know enough terminology to comprehend a handbook and to understand editing suggestions from your classmates, teachers, coworkers, or boss. To gain still more control over written language, you'll want to read the work of other writers with a discriminating eye; this requires the ability to look at sentences analytically, seeing what the parts are and how they fit together.

In this chapter, our mission is to break the English sentence into pieces and take a look at each piece, reviewing the terminology used to describe sentences.[1] When a grammatical term appears for the first time, it is printed in boldface and is followed by a definition, which appears again in the glossary (p. 275). If you need a refresher on the parts of speech — noun, verb, adjective, adverb, preposition, conjunction, pronoun, determiner — consult the glossary for a brief definition or **www.bedfordstmartins.com/wellcrafted** for a more thorough explanation.

Since every sentence has at least one clause, we'll begin with the clause. Later in the chapter, we'll consider some of the options writers use to expand on clauses or join them together.

Clause Structure

In "Loss of Family Languages," Lily Wong Fillmore tells the story of the Chens, a family that moved from China's Canton province to northern California. Like most good writers, Wong Fillmore varies her sentences: some are short, some long; some are simple, some complex; some are declarative, making statements, while others are interrogative or imperative. But for our present purpose — clarifying the structure of clauses — I'm going to chop her sentences into units of a single clause:

> The Chen family arrived in the United States in 1989. They settled in a suburban town in the San Francisco Bay Area. Father, Mother, and Uncle had jobs in a restaurant. They worked in the restaurant's kitchen. The kitchen workers were all Chinese. As a result, their lack of English was not a handicap. Mother and Father usually left the house early and returned close to midnight. Grandmother watched the children. For the children, school was difficult initially. But they did not complain much.

A **clause** is a group of words containing a **subject** and a **predicate**. Most English speakers find that if they're asked to divide a clause into two parts, they intuitively split it between the subject and predicate. In a basic, uncomplicated clause, the subject names the actor or topic and the predicate says what the subject is or does.

SUBJECT	PREDICATE
The Chen family	arrived in the United States in 1989
They	settled in a suburban town in the San Francisco Bay Area
Father, Mother, and Uncle	had jobs in a restaurant
They	worked in the restaurant's kitchen
The kitchen workers	were all Chinese

The clause's subject is a **noun phrase**, a noun or a group of words headed by a noun. If you examine the clauses above, you'll notice that two of them have "they" as the subject. "They" is a **pronoun**, a word English speakers substitute for a noun phrase so that we don't have to keep repeating "the Chen family" or "Father, Mother, and Uncle." A pronoun counts as a noun phrase; it can perform all the same grammatical functions as other noun phrases.

The predicate is a **verb phrase**, a verb or a group of words headed by a verb. In most of the sample sentences, the verb itself is a single word — "arrived," "settled," "had" — but notice that in the paragraph's final sentence, the verb includes an auxiliary, "did," as well as the main verb "complain." When an **auxiliary** precedes a verb, its function is to establish the time, duration, or certainty of the action, as in *had complained, were complaining, would complain, must complain.*

EXERCISE 2A

Divide each of the following clauses into its subject and predicate.

Examples

Kai-fong and Chu-mei / attended a school with many minority group children.

Many / had limited English.

1. The school had no bilingual or ESL classes.
2. The teacher spoke English only.
3. She gave the non-English speakers special attention.
4. Chu-mei soon befriended some classmates.
5. She learned some English from them and from the teacher.
6. She was neat, agreeable, and sociable.
7. She became comfortable in the social world of the school.
8. Kai-fong had quite a different experience in school.
9. He was not outgoing.
10. Some of the boys in his class teased him mercilessly.

In any clause, the verb will be one of three types: transitive, intransitive, or linking. If the verb takes an object, it's a **transitive verb**:

SUBJECT (NOUN PHRASE)	TRANSITIVE VERB	OBJECT (ANOTHER NOUN PHRASE)
Mother and Father	left	the house
Chu-mei	befriended	some classmates
Kai-fong	had	a different experience
Some of the boys	teased	him

In all of the sentences, the subject names the actor, the verb names the action, and the **object** is a noun phrase naming the person or thing that receives the action. What did Mother and Father leave? The house. Whom did Chu-mei befriend? Some classmates. What did Kai-fong have? A different experience.

If the verb has no object, it's an **intransitive verb**:

SUBJECT (NOUN PHRASE)	INTRANSITIVE VERB	
The Chen family	arrived	(in the United States in 1989)
They	settled	(in a suburban town in the SF Bay Area)
Mother and Father	returned	(close to midnight)
The children	did (not) complain	(much)

What did the Chen family arrive? The question doesn't even make sense; you don't arrive *something*, you just *arrive*. *Arrive* is always an intransitive verb. Other verbs can be transitive or intransitive, depending on how they're used; for example, you can imagine that people could settle something (a bet) or return something (a broken toaster). But in the sentences above, the family isn't settling *something*, they're simply settling; they aren't returning *something*, they're simply returning. So the verbs are intransitive.

Perhaps you're wondering why "in the United States" isn't an object. Notice the meaning: the phrase does not say *what* the Chen family arrived. Also, an object has to be a noun phrase, so expressions like "in the United States" or "close to midnight" could never function as objects.

A third type of verb is called a **linking verb** because it links the subject to a word or phrase that appears after the verb, called the **complement**. By far the most common linking verb is "to be" in all its forms — *am, is, are, was, were, will be, could be,* and so on.

SUBJECT (NOUN PHRASE)	LINKING VERB	COMPLEMENT (NOUN OR ADJECTIVE PHRASE)
The kitchen workers	were	all Chinese
Their lack of English	was (not)	a handicap
School	was	difficult initially

SUBJECT (NOUN PHRASE)	LINKING VERB	COMPLEMENT (NOUN OR ADJECTIVE PHRASE)
She	was	neat, agreeable, and sociable
She	became	comfortable in the social world of the school

In "Their lack of English was not a handicap," the complement is a noun phrase that is identified with the subject; in the other sentences, the complement is an adjective phrase that describes the subject. The tight relationship between the subject and the complements explains why the verb is called "linking."

To review, the three types of verbs are transitive, intransitive, and linking. A transitive verb takes an object:

> At the end of the day, the kitchen workers *cleaned* the stove.

An intransitive verb does not have an object:

> At the end of the day, the kitchen workers *showered*.

A linking verb ties a complement to the subject:

> At the end of the day, the kitchen workers *felt* exhausted.

One last point about subjects and predicates. The subject of a clause is, as I've said, a noun phrase — sometimes a single word (a noun or pronoun) and sometimes a cluster of words headed by a noun. The predicate is a verb or a cluster of words headed by a verb. When we divide a clause into its subject and predicate, it's a simple matter of splitting the clause into parts:

> The boys in Kai-fong's class / teased him about his appearance.

Often, it's useful to identify the **headword** in each part of the clause — the key noun in the noun phrase, the verb itself in the predicate.

> The <u>boys</u> in Kai-fong's class / <u>teased</u> him about his appearance.

In this sentence, the headwords "boys teased" constitute the **subject-verb pair**. The subject-verb pair is the beating heart of an English clause; readers intuitively focus their attention on these words, expecting them to name the clause's key actor and action. For a more detailed discussion of the stylistic importance of the subject-verb pair, see Chapter 3.

EXERCISE 2B

The following clauses are split into subject and predicate. The subject is a noun phrase: underline the headword once. The predicate is a verb phrase: underline the verb twice. When you identify verbs, include auxiliaries like *have, should,* or *will.*

Examples

Rodriguez's autobiography — describes the role of language in his family's relationships.

A teacher — had advised his parents to stop speaking Spanish to their children.

Rodriguez and his siblings — moved from Spanish to English.

1. The children — spoke to their parents less frequently.
2. Their mother — grew restless and anxious about the silence in the house.
3. She — would ask Rodriguez questions about his day at school.
4. She — smiled at small talk.
5. Her intrusions — often stopped her children's talking.
6. Their father — retired into quiet.
7. His English — improved somewhat over time.
8. His children and his wife — helplessly giggled at his garbled English pronunciation of the Catholic Grace before Meals.
9. His wife — said the prayer, even on formal occasions.
10. Her voice — became the public voice of the family.

EXERCISE 2C

Examine the verbs you've underlined in Exercise 2B. Identify each of them as a transitive, intransitive, or linking verb. For transitive verbs, identify the object.

Examples

Rodriguez's autobiography describes the role of language in his family's relationships.
transitive (object is "the role of language")

Exercise 2C continued

A teacher <u>had</u> <u>advised</u> his parents to stop speaking Spanish to their children.
transitive (object is "his parents")

Rodriguez and his siblings <u>moved</u> from Spanish to English.
intransitive

Transformations within the Clause

While all verbs can be described as transitive, intransitive, or linking, the sentence patterns are not always so easy to recognize. Speakers and writers often use sentences in which the core elements have been rearranged. Beginning with the sentence "Parents teach their children by word and example," we could generate variations such as these:

NEGATION	Parents don't teach their children by word and example.
QUESTION	Do parents teach their children by word and example?
PASSIVE VOICE	Children are taught by word and example.

These transformations change the meaning of the sentence in significant ways. The structural changes are significant, too; for example, the subject of the passive-voice sentence is no longer "parents" but rather "children." Nevertheless, beyond observing that these transformations are possible, we will take little notice of them because every English-speaking adult creates sentences like these with no trouble.

Extending the Clause

As a general rule, an English sentence will have at least one **independent clause**, one clause that can stand alone to constitute a complete sentence. Each of the sample sentences we've examined so far is composed of a single independent clause. You can identify them as clauses because they have a subject and predicate; you can identify them as independent because, when you read them aloud, they sound complete.

Return for a moment to the paragraph on page 19 in which I revised Lily Wong Fillmore's sentences to isolate the clauses. Except for two introductory phrases ("as a result" and "for the children"), the paragraph is a string of independent clauses. In published writing, you'll rarely see a whole paragraph made up of such sentences. Because the sentences are so short, averaging just 8.1 words, the prose starts and stops, starts and stops, moving along in short spurts that sound choppy and childlike.

In its published form, Wong Fillmore's paragraph contains 118 words in six sentences. The average sentence has about 20 words, which is far more typical of published writing:

> The Chens settled in a suburban town in the San Francisco Bay area where Father, Mother, and Uncle had jobs waiting for them in a restaurant owned by a relative. They went to work in the restaurant's kitchen, and because the kitchen workers were all Chinese, their lack of English was not a handicap. They worked long hours each day, leaving home early in the morning and returning close to midnight. Grandmother stayed at home with the children, and everything was fine at first. She got the children ready for school and was at home to care for them when they were out of school. School was difficult for the children initially, but they did not complain much. . . .

Each sentence in this paragraph contains at least one independent clause — but it doesn't stop there.

The next sections describe three ways that independent clauses can be extended. First, one independent clause can be joined to another. Second, a clause can be extended by means of words or phrases used as modifiers. Third, dependent clauses — structures that contain a subject and predicate but can't stand alone — can be added to the independent clause.

Joining Independent Clauses

When two independent clauses are closely related in meaning, it makes sense to join them with a **coordinating conjunction** such as *and* or *but*. Each of the sentences below contains two independent clauses:

> Grandmother stayed home with the children, and everything was fine at first.

> School was difficult for the children initially, but they did not complain much.

> One day, there was a rock-throwing incident at school, and Kai-fong was caught with rocks in his hands.

English has seven coordinating conjunctions: *and, or, nor, but, for, yet, so.* When two independent clauses are joined with a coordinating conjunction, they have roughly equal emphasis. A more detailed discussion of coordination appears in Chapter 4.

Writers frequently join independent clauses without the conjunction, relying instead on punctuation — specifically, the semicolon, colon, or dash. Take a moment to examine the punctuation in these passages:

> The other children could tell their side of the story; Kai-fong could not.
>
> The home language is nothing; it has no value at all.
>
> The ideological stance is this: to be American, one must speak English.
>
> There is tension in this home: the adults do not understand the children, and the children do not understand the adults.

I can imagine using a coordinating conjunction to join the independent clauses in the first sentence. To my ear, it sounds fine to say "The other children could tell their side of the story, *but* Kai-fong could not" because *but* captures the contrast between the other children's situation and Kai-fong's. But for the most part, these sentences pair clauses whose relationship is not accurately signaled by *and, but,* or any of the other coordinating conjunctions.

Instead, Wong Fillmore uses semicolons and colons. The semicolon appears when the sentences are of about equal importance, and it's especially apt when, as in the first sentence, the clauses are symmetrical (the other children could; Kai-Fong could not) or, as in the second sentence, when the clause after the semicolon restates what came before.

When one clause sets the stage for another, a colon works well. In the third sentence above, "The ideological stance is this" sets the stage quite explicitly; with those words and the colon, Wong Fillmore commits herself to spelling out the ideological stance. In the fourth sentence, the opening clause and the colon similarly commit her to describing the tension in the home.

In these sentences, then, Wong Fillmore illustrates how semicolons and colons typically function between independent clauses, with the semicolon establishing parity between the clauses and the colon suggesting that the opening clause be interpreted as a drum roll leading up to something more specific or more dramatic. The choice between a semicolon and colon is not a matter of correctness — another writer might have chosen differently — but it is worth attending to because it has a subtle effect on how a reader processes a sentence, what he or she expects of the ensuing clause.

"Loss of Family Languages" was published in *Theory Into Practice*, a journal for educators and educational researchers. In this context, Wong Fillmore chooses punctuation marks that maintain a relatively formal tone. In a less formal piece — a magazine article, short story, blog, or letter — the independent clauses might be joined by dashes. Having struggled with a dash addiction for many years, I have to advise you that dashes can be habit-forming. But they can be used effectively between independent clauses when you want to lengthen the pause or to create an air of spontaneity or surprise. Emily Dickinson does it — you can, too.

EXERCISE 2D

The passage below comes from "A More Perfect Union," one of the most influential speeches delivered during Barack Obama's 2008 campaign for the presidency. In these sentences, he explains some of the causes and consequences of black and white anger.

Use the passage to experiment with ways to join or separate independent clauses. Your choices are:

- period
- coordinating conjunction — *and, or, nor, but, for, yet, so* — preceded by a comma
- colon
- semicolon
- dash

Insert one of these in each of the underlined spaces between clauses. When you've finished, compare your choices to Obama's (p. 206, paras. 32–33). The point of the comparison is not to determine whether your choices or Obama's are better but rather to notice how the conjunction and/or punctuation affect the passage's style.

That anger is not always productive _____ indeed, all too often it distracts attention from solving real problems _____ it keeps us from squarely facing our own complicity in our condition and prevents the African American community from forging the alliances it needs to bring about real change _____ the anger is real _____ it is

---

Exercise 2D continued

powerful _____ to simply wish it away—to condemn it without understanding its roots—only serves to widen the chasm of misunderstanding that exists between the races.

In fact, a similar anger exists within segments of the white community _____ most working- and middle-class white Americans don't feel that they have been particularly privileged by their race _____ their experience is the immigrant experience _____ as far as they're concerned, no one handed them anything _____ they built it from scratch _____ they've worked hard all their lives, many times only to see their jobs shipped overseas or their pensions dumped after a lifetime of labor _____ they are anxious about their futures _____ they feel their dreams slipping away _____ in an era of stagnant wages and global competition, opportunity comes to be seen as a zero-sum game, in which your dreams come at my expense.

EDITING NOTE: Notice that a comma alone is not among the options for linking independent clauses. Published writers do sometimes use a comma in this way, but the choice is infrequent and appears only when both sentences are short. Pasting two independent clauses together with a comma is usually viewed as an error—a "comma splice"—and it's one worth watching for as you edit because it is highly stigmatized.

Modifiers

A **modifier** is a word, phrase, or clause that elaborates upon some other element in the sentence, describing it, limiting it, or providing extra information. For example, in "The younger children quickly learn to speak English," "younger" modifies "children" and "quickly" modifies "learn."

When a modifier is longer and more complex, it becomes more interesting from a stylistic point of view: writers can make choices about where to place a modifier, and we manipulate emphasis by deciding whether an idea should be presented in a modifier or allowed to occupy a sentence of its own. Chapters 5 through 8 discuss various kinds of clauses and phrases used as modifiers.

The most common modifier is the prepositional phrase. You won't find a chapter on prepositional phrases because you don't need one: virtually all English speakers use prepositional phrases effortlessly from an early age. However, we should take a moment to observe their structure.

Chu-mei is the only child in the family who can still

communicate with the adults in Cantonese.

A **prepositional phrase** is made up of a preposition and a noun phrase. The noun phrase is called the object of the preposition. For example, "in" is a preposition with "the family" as its object, and "with" is a preposition with "the adults" as its object.

Prepositional phrases can modify many kinds of words and phrases — nouns, verbs, adjectives, adverbs. "In the family" modifies the noun "child." "With the adults" and "in Cantonese" modify the verb "communicate," telling how Chu-mei communicates.

Dependent Clauses

Examine these clauses:

Grandmother cut Kai-fong's hair	After grandmother cut Kai-fong's hair
Mother and Father scolded him	When Mother and Father scolded him
Some of his friends retained their primary languages	Although some of his friends retained their primary languages

Your ear will immediately tell you that the clauses on the right are not complete sentences. They sound unfinished, as if they are waiting to be attached to something else. While the clauses on the left are independent, those on the right are dependent. A **dependent clause** (also called a **subordinate clause**) is a group of words that contains a subject-verb pair but that cannot stand alone as a complete sentence.

EDITING NOTE: If you write a phrase or a dependent clause and leave it standing alone, you've created a fragment. Fragments are common in advertising, and some fiction writers like to use them as well. In formal writing such as academic essays, fragments are usually regarded as errors, so don't leave a dependent clause standing alone in a formal paper unless you have a truly compelling reason to do so — unless it sounds so *right* that your reader will respond with "ahh" rather than "oops." Fragments are discussed in more detail in Chapter 9.

Dependent clauses come in three varieties: adverb clauses, adjective clauses, and noun clauses.

Adverb Clauses

Adverb clauses are introduced by **subordinating conjunctions** like the "after" in "after Grandmother cut Kai-fong's hair" and "when" in "when Mother and Father scolded him." English has dozens of these subordinating conjunctions (sometimes called **subordinators**). Here's a partial list:

as	if	provided that	just as
because	as if	in order that	inasmuch as
since	as though	now that	while
unless	in case	so that	whereas
though	before	as soon as	where
although	after	as long as	whenever
even though	until	when	wherever

An **adverb clause** can be recognized by the presence of a subject-verb pair (this makes it a clause) and by the subordinating conjunction at the beginning. Adverb clauses do the characteristic work of an adverb, telling when, where, why, or how some action takes place.

Subordination with adverb clauses permits a writer to manipulate emphasis. For example, compare these sentences:

Even though I want a piece of cherry pie, I'm committed to my diet.
Even though I'm committed to my diet, I want a piece of cherry pie.

You can tell that the writer of the first sentence will stick to that diet, while the writer of the second is already reaching for a fork. The sentences read differently because in both cases we see the independent clause — "I'm committed to my diet" in the first, "I want a piece of cherry pie" in the second — as having more weight. Information tucked into the adverb clause is de-emphasized.

Adverb clauses can be appended before or after an independent clause, or they can be embedded in the middle:

While virtually all children who attend American schools learn English, most of them are at risk of losing their primary languages as they do so.

As they learn English, they use it more and more until English becomes their dominant language.

My friend Alexandra, when she's dieting, eats dessert alone in the kitchen after the rest of the family has gone to bed.

Adjective Clauses

Adjective clauses are discussed at length in Chapter 6. For now, it is enough to say that an **adjective clause** (also called a **relative clause**) is a dependent clause used to modify a noun. Most adjective clauses are introduced by these words:

who	which	when
whom	that	where
whose		

Two hundred and twenty-one years ago, in a hall that still stands across the street, a group of men gathered and . . . launched America's improbable experiment in democracy.

Farmers and scholars, statesmen and patriots who had traveled across an ocean to escape tyranny and persecution finally made real their declaration of independence at a Philadelphia convention that lasted through the spring of 1787.

This was one of the tasks we set forth at the beginning of this presidential campaign—to continue the long march of those who came before us, a march for a more just, more equal, more free, more caring, and more prosperous America.

These sentences illustrate the usual placement of adjective clauses, immediately following the noun phrase they modify.

Noun Clauses

Noun clauses are dependent clauses that perform the function of nouns. Unlike adverb and adjective clauses, noun clauses are not modifiers. Instead, they perform an essential grammatical function within

another clause, serving as a subject or an object. Noun clauses often —
but not always — begin with *that* or *what*.

> The school cannot provide children <u>what is most fundamental to success in life</u>.

> When parents send their children to school for formal education, they understand <u>that their job of socializing their children is far from done</u>.

> Rodriguez is trying to figure out <u>who he is</u>, <u>where he belongs</u>, and <u>what his culture means</u>.

In these sentences, the noun clauses are objects. What is the school unable to provide? "What is most fundamental to success in life." What do parents understand? "That their job of socializing their children is far from done."

Noun clauses can also serve as subjects, as in these sentences:

> <u>What Rodriguez's writings reveal to this reader</u> is a deeply conflicted and lonely man.

> <u>What is at stake in becoming assimilated into the society</u> is not only children's educational development but their psychological and emotional well-being.

A quick review:

- Every clause has a noun phrase as subject and a verb phrase as predicate. Independent clauses can stand alone as complete sentences.

  > The Chen family serves as an example of the immigrant experience.

- Adverb clauses begin with subordinators like those listed on page 30. An adverb clause performs the usual function of adverbs, telling where, when, why, or how something happened. It can be placed before, after, or in the middle of the clause it modifies.

  > Because their language learning illustrates an increasingly common pattern, the Chen family serves as an example of the immigrant experience.

- Adjective clauses usually (not always) begin with a relative pronoun: *who, whom, whose, which, that, where, when*. An adjective clause modifies a noun, and it follows the noun it modifies.

  > The Chen family, whose children become English-dominant within a few years, serves as an example of the immigrant experience.

- Noun clauses usually (but not always) begin with *that* or *what*. A noun clause is not a modifier; instead, it functions as other nouns do, serving as a subject or object.

What the Chen family illustrates is an increasingly common pattern of language learning in immigrant families.

EXERCISE 2E

The passages below are copied or adapted from "Loss of Family Languages" by Lily Wong Fillmore (p. 259) and "A More Perfect Union" by Barack Obama (p. 199).

The sentences have been broken up into clauses. In each clause, identify the subject-verb pair: in the noun phrase that serves as the subject, underline just the headword (the key noun) once, and underline the verb (including any auxiliaries) twice. Then, identify each clause as independent or dependent. Finally, identify each dependent clause more specifically as an adverb clause, an adjective clause, or a noun clause.

Examples

Kai-fong had a small group of friends who played with him on the playground. Several boys were Vietnamese, one was Filipino, the others were Thai. Their English had many dialect features that they had picked up from the African American children in the school, although they had little interaction with them.

Kai-fong <u>had</u> a small group of friends
independent clause

who <u>played</u> with him on the playground.
dependent (adjective) clause

Several <u>boys</u> <u>were</u> Vietnamese,
independent clause

<u>one</u> <u>was</u> Filipino,
independent clause

the <u>others</u> <u>were</u> Thai.
independent clause

Their <u>English</u> <u>had</u> many dialect features
independent clause

Exercise 2E continued

that they had picked up from the African American children in the school,
dependent (adjective) clause

although they had little interaction with them.
dependent (adverb) clause

Over time, Grandmother became withdrawn too. She had chronic headaches, which often immobilized her. The headaches made it hard for her to care for the younger children. Each day, while her sisters were young, Chu-mei hurried home from school to play with them and teach them things that she was learning in school.

1. Over time, Grandmother became withdrawn too.
2. She had chronic headaches,
3. which often immobilized her.
4. The headaches made it hard for her to care for the younger children.
5. Each day, while her sisters were young,
6. Chu-mei hurried home from school to play with them and teach them things
7. that she was learning in school.

The dilemma facing immigrant children is less a problem of learning English than of primary language loss. While virtually all children who attend American schools learn English, most of them are at risk of losing their primary languages as they do so.

8. The dilemma facing immigrant children is less a problem of learning English than of primary language loss.
9. While virtually all children . . . learn English,
10. who attend American schools
11. most of them are at risk of losing their primary languages
12. as they do so.

I chose to run for president at this moment in history because I believe deeply that we cannot solve the challenges of our time unless we solve them together.

13. I chose to run for president at this moment in history
14. because I believe deeply
15. that we cannot solve the challenges of our time
16. unless we solve them together.

Exercise 2E continued

Americans are anxious about their futures, and they feel their dreams slipping away; in an era of stagnant wages and global competition, opportunity is seen as a zero-sum game, in which your dreams come at my expense.

17. Americans are anxious about their futures,

18. and they feel their dreams slipping away;

19. in an era of stagnant wages and global competition, opportunity is seen as a zero-sum game,

20. in which your dreams come at my expense.

CHAPTER 2 NOTE

[1]Analyzing sentences would be simpler if everybody used the same terminology. In fact, however, analysts with different objectives use different sets of terms. The most thorough and precise terminology is used by linguists, who sometimes explain their project as an effort to spell out the thousands of rules that a native speaker knows intuitively. Why do you say *the big blue truck* rather than *the blue big truck?* You have the intuitive knowledge to place *big* before *blue* when you speak or write, but you probably can't articulate the rule you're following. A linguist can. To do the work of linguistic science, linguists have developed an extensive technical vocabulary.

Writers and editors need to talk about sentences in clear and consistent ways, but we don't need to account for every conceivable grammatical expression. We rely on a simpler vocabulary with broader categories. For writers and editors, the most important reference book is a good handbook or trustworthy grammar Web site—the sort of resource you consult with questions about grammatical correctness (Is this a fragment? Is that a dangling modifier?), about usage (*affect* or *effect? less* or *fewer?*), and about mechanics (colon or semicolon? italics or underlining?). With any luck, the terms you'll encounter throughout this book will match those in your handbook.

Well-Focused Sentences

The Subject-Verb Pair

WHEN LINGUISTS DESCRIBE languages, they categorize them according to the typical order of a sentence's key components. English is said to be an SVO language. The core of an English clause is made up of a Subject, Verb, and Object, most often in that order: *Cats eat mice; Matthew caught the ball; Elizabeth assumed the throne; Calculus teachers assign problem sets; I love you.*

We pick up the SVO pattern at an early age. When babies are learning to speak, they begin with one-word utterances — "ball," "Mama," "peekaboo," "hot" — but soon graduate to two-word and three-word strings. By the age of two, toddlers demonstrate an understanding of the SVO order: with remarkable consistency, they say "baby eat," "eat cereal," or "baby eat cereal," never mixing up the word order (never, for example, saying "cereal baby eat"). In English-speaking communities, we hear and produce hundreds of SVO sentences every day.

For writers, the SVO order has particular significance because it represents the norm. Without really thinking about it, readers develop an expectation that, as they approach a new sentence, they'll encounter first the subject, then the verb, and then an object. Of course, many English sentences are more complex than *Cats eat mice*, many are cast in other patterns (with, for example, an intransitive or linking verb — see pp. 21–22), and some use alternative word order. Still, the SVO norm has a great deal of power in shaping readers' expectations and in determining how easily they process sentences.

In this chapter, I want to make a case for choosing subjects carefully, taking full advantage of the subject position. Because readers intuitively expect the first noun phrase in a clause to be the subject, they pay attention to that noun phrase. A wise writer will direct the reader's attention to the key player, using the subject position to name the person or thing that the clause is really *about*. A sentence is well focused when the most important actor and action appear as the subject and verb.

Populated Prose

We'll begin with some examples of well-focused sentences from Tim O'Brien's book *The Things They Carried*. In a chapter titled "On the Rainy River" (reprinted on p. 211), the narrator describes a turning point in his life. In 1968, just out of college, he had to decide whether to comply with the military draft, virtually ensuring a tour in Vietnam, or flee to Canada. He spent a few days at a fishing lodge near the Canadian border, where his moral crisis was witnessed by the lodge's owner, Elroy Berdahl.

Note the subject of each clause:

> For ten or fifteen minutes Elroy held a course upstream, the river choppy and silver-gray, then he turned straight north and put the engine on full throttle. I felt the bow lift beneath me. I remember the wind in my ears, the sound of the old outboard Evinrude. For a time I didn't pay attention to anything, just feeling the cold spray against my face, but then it occurred to me that at some point we must've passed into Canadian waters, across that dotted line between two different worlds, and I remember a sudden tightness in my chest as I looked up and watched the far shore come at me. This wasn't a daydream. It was tangible and real. As we came in toward land, Elroy cut the engine, letting the boat fishtail lightly about twenty yards off shore. The old man didn't look at me or speak. Bending down, he opened up his tackle box and busied himself with a bobber and a piece of wire leader, humming to himself, his eyes down.

This paragraph is about two men. If you do a quick count, you'll find that twelve of the fifteen clauses have **human subjects**, nouns or pronouns referring to people. The narrator ("I") appears as the subject of five clauses, Elroy Berdahl is the subject of five more, and "we," refer-ring to the pair of them, is the subject of two. By consistently placing the narrator and Elroy Berdahl in the subject position, O'Brien ensures that even as we're visualizing a fishing boat or a shoreline, the human beings have a presence. The consistent focus unifies the paragraph as a whole.

The same consistent focus appears in this passage where, in a strik-ing move, O'Brien has the narrator address the reader directly:

> Twenty yards. I could've done it. I could've jumped and started
> swimming for my life. Inside me, in my chest, I felt a terrible squeez-
> ing pressure. Even now, as I write this, I can still feel that tightness.
> And I want you to feel it—the wind coming off the river, the waves, the
> silence, the wooded frontier. You're at the bow of a boat on the Rainy
> River. You're twenty-one years old, you're scared, and there's a hard
> squeezing pressure in your chest.

Again, the subjects capture the essential relationship, the interaction between the narrator and the reader: until the final clause, every subject is "I" or "you."

What would happen if the prose weren't so tightly focused? In the passage below, I've tried to retain as much of O'Brien's meaning as pos-sible without using so many human subjects.

> Twenty yards. It was do-able. It would have been possible to jump and
> start swimming for my life. Inside me, in my chest, there was a terrible
> squeezing pressure. Even now, as these words are being written, there
> is still that feeling of tightness. And it is important to me to share
> this feeling with you—the wind coming off the river, the waves, the
> silence, the wooded frontier. Imagine yourself at the bow of a boat
> on the Rainy River, twenty-one years old, scared, and there's a hard
> squeezing pressure in your chest.

To my ear, the altered passage is less effective — less cohesive, less vivid, with a slower pace. Words like *it* and *there* are just about meaning-free; as subjects, they have little power to focus a reader's attention or to steer a sentence in a clear direction. It's easy to understand O'Brien's prefer-ence for human subjects.

EXERCISE 3A

In the passages below, I've altered sentences from "On the Rainy River" by removing words referring to people from the subject position. Repopulate these passages to improve their focus. Ask who the passage is really about— who is doing something in the sentences—and whenever possible, use a noun or pronoun referring to that person as the subject.

Example
In the mornings it was sometimes our routine to go on long hikes into the woods, and at night there were usually Scrabble games or record-playing or reading in front of his big stone fireplace.

Restored to Original
In the mornings we sometimes went out on long hikes into the woods, and at night we played Scrabble or listened to records or sat reading in front of his big stone fireplace.

1. Even after two decades it is possible for me to close my eyes and return to that porch at the Tip Top Lodge. There is an image in my mind of the old guy staring at me. Elroy Berdahl: eighty-one years old, skinny and shrunken and mostly bald. His outfit was a flannel shirt and brown work pants. In one hand, if memory serves, was a green apple, a small paring knife in the other.

2. His fishing continued. His line was worked with the tips of his fingers, patiently, his eyes squinting out at his red and white bobber on the Rainy River. His eyes were flat and impassive. There was no speech. There was simply his presence, like the river and the late-summer sun.

Sentences with human subjects stand a good chance of having strong verbs. Compare, for example, the two versions of the example sentence in Exercise 3A:

In the mornings it was sometimes our routine to go on long hikes into the woods, and at night there were usually Scrabble games or record-playing or reading in front of his big stone fireplace.

In the mornings we sometimes went out on long hikes into the woods, and at night we played Scrabble or listened to records or sat reading in front of his big stone fireplace.

In the first sentence, the verbs are forms of *be*, the most colorless verb in our language. In the second sentence, the verbs are varied, and they name actions. This is a typical pattern in English prose: the writer who selects a human subject has a wide range of verbs to choose from, and his or her sentences have life and energy.

You can see the contrast again in the passages in which the narrator contemplates a swim to the Canadian shore. (The first passage is altered; the second is O'Brien's.)

> Twenty yards. It was do-able. It would have been possible to jump and start swimming for my life. Inside me, in my chest, there was a terrible squeezing pressure. Even now, as these words are being written, there is still that feeling of tightness. And it is important to me to share this feeling with you — the wind coming off the river, the waves, the silence, the wooded frontier.

> Twenty yards. I could've done it. I could've jumped and started swimming for my life. Inside me, in my chest, I felt a terrible squeezing pressure. Even now, as I write this, I can still feel that tightness. And I want you to feel it — the wind coming off the river, the waves, the silence, the wooded frontier.

In the first version, five of the six verbs are forms of *be* (and the sixth, "are being written," is in the passive voice, a topic discussed below). A subject like *it* or *there* can't be paired with very interesting verbs — *there* isn't capable of doing much. By contrast, people can do many things, so human subjects license a wide variety of verbs.

EXERCISE 3B

Observe the stylistic effects of choosing human subjects.

1. Return to Exercise 3A, underlining the subject-verb pairs in each passage before and after your revisions. When you shifted to human subjects, did your verbs shift as well? Do the revised passages rely less heavily on forms of *be?*

2. It often happens that the choice of a human subject makes a sentence more concise. Examine the passages in Exercise 3A, counting the words before and after revision. When you revised, were you able to capture the meaning in fewer words?

3. A paragraph containing well-focused sentences often gains cohesion from the repeated appearance of a key person in the subject position. Examine the passages from Exercise 3A as Tim O'Brien wrote them (see "On the Rainy River," p. 218, para. 19, and pp. 225–26, para. 75). How many different words has O'Brien used in the subject position?

It's simple enough to populate the prose if you're telling a story about a person or group of people sharing an experience, but what happens when you're operating in the realm of ideas?

The paragraph below comes from "'We Should Grow Too Fond of It': Why We Love the Civil War," historian Drew Gilpin Faust's article about the growth of Civil War scholarship in the final years of the twentieth century. The paragraph illustrates a common pattern in academic writing: the main point—which is an idea, requiring abstract language—is spelled out at the beginning, and the writer continues by illustrating the point with specific examples.

Social historians have been attracted to the war by some of the same elements that engage military scholars. The Civil War offers an authenticity and intensity of experience that can rivet both researcher and reader; the war serves as a moment of truth, a moment when individuals — be they soldiers or civilians — have to define their deeply held priorities and act on them. War is a crucible that produces unsurpassed revelations about the essence of historical actors and their worlds. James McPherson has described his work with the papers of more than a thousand soldiers: "From such writings I have come to know these men better than I know most of my living acquaintances, for in their personal letters written in a time of crisis that might end their lives at any moment they revealed more of themselves than we do in our normal everyday lives." War can exact from individuals just what historians hope to find: expressions of their truest selves. We follow as historians in the footsteps of many of our century's — and our civilization's — greatest writers. As Ernest Hemingway once explained to F. Scott Fitzgerald, who enlisted too late for any significant World War I experience, "The reason you are so sore you missed the war is because war is the best subject of all. It groups the maximum of material and speeds up the action and brings out all sorts of stuff that normally you have to wait a lifetime to get." No wonder we love to study war.

In the opening sentences, Faust articulates her point, explaining that war is attractive to study because it is a "moment of truth," heightening human experience. In these sentences, six of the eight clauses begin with abstract subjects (three instances of "war" and three uses of "that" in reference to "elements," "intensity of experience," and "crucible"). Then the paragraph shifts gears. As Faust develops her point with specifics, we meet a rich cast of characters including James McPherson, the soldiers whose letters he read, Ernest Hemingway, F. Scott Fitzgerald, and "we" referring to historians.

While this movement from abstract ideas to personalized examples is conventional in many genres of writing, it is particularly effective in Faust's text because it reflects the purpose of the article. She is interested not only in the causes of historians' fascination with war but in its consequences. The work of historians, she suggests, makes war seem comprehensible, even acceptable. In the article's final paragraph, the key subject is "we" — historians — as Faust considers historians' responsibility for giving shape to records and memories of war:

> War is, by its very definition, a story. War imposes an orderly narrative on what without its definition of purpose and structure would simply be violence. We as writers create that story; we remember that story; we provide the narrative that by its very existence defines war's purpose and meaning. We love war because of these stories. But we should ask ourselves how in the construction of war's stories we may be helping to construct war itself. "War is a force that gives us meaning." But what do we and our writings give to war?

In the first two sentences, the subject is "war": war itself takes action, war itself imposes meaning on violence. But then the subject is "we": historians tell the story, historians make the meaning. In the final pair of sentences, Faust highlights the shift in agency. The pair is nicely balanced — war gives something to us, we give something to war — with the subject of each clause naming the relevant agent.

The first point for writers, then, is that prose is clearer and more engaging if it is populated. A second, equally important point is that an accomplished writer can take advantage of the subject position in a clause — of the extra attention the subject position commands, of the reader's expectation that a subject will name the key actor — to keep the reader on board as the train of thought moves forward.

EXERCISE 3C

Choose one of the following as an opening sentence and write a short paragraph that develops the statement with specific examples. The opening sentence has an abstract subject. Use human subjects in most or all of the subsequent clauses.

1. The legacy of the Vietnam War still haunts America.
2. The local economy has experienced some sharp reversals.

Exercise 3C continued

3. Communication is the key to employer-employee relationships.
4. Religious differences can cause friction in family life.

When the topic under discussion does not include any humans, the best subjects are concrete nouns — nouns naming something tangible, something a reader can visualize. Compare these sentences:

In the last thirty years, there has been a decline in the quality of produce in freshness and flavor.

In the last thirty years, a decline in the quality of produce in freshness and flavor has occurred.

In the last thirty years, produce has declined in freshness and flavor.

Of the three sentences, the third is the leanest and strongest. Vegetables will never have much dramatic power, but a concrete subject is a step in the right direction, focusing the reader's attention on what the sentence is about.

Active Voice and Passive Voice

The distinction between **active voice** and **passive voice** is useful to know, especially if your writing handbook is one of the many that advises writers to prefer the active to the passive voice. I'd like to take a minute to explain these terms, and then I'll echo the conventional advice, with the caveat that the preference for the active voice is stronger on some occasions than others.

In an active-voice construction, the subject names the actor, performing the action described by the verb. In a passive-voice construction, the subject does not name the actor; instead, it names the person or thing that receives the action of the verb, the person or thing being acted upon. Compare the sentences below:

Active Voice	Passive Voice
Faust and O'Brien take very different approaches to understanding the narrative construction of war.	Very different approaches to understanding the narrative construction of war are taken by Faust and O'Brien.

Active Voice	Passive Voice
Historians have shared the country's intoxication with the Civil War.	The country's intoxication with the Civil War has been shared by historians.
Faust describes an explosion of Civil War scholarship.	An explosion of Civil War scholarship is described by Faust.
Our seminar will examine Faust's claims.	Faust's claims will be examined by our seminar.

Because each of the sentences on the left has a transitive verb — which is to say, the verb has an object — these sentences can be transformed into the passive voice. The transformation moves the object into the subject position, and the verb is adjusted accordingly.

To forestall any confusion, let me point out immediately that voice is unrelated to tense. Whether a sentence is active or passive depends on whether the subject performs or receives the action, not on whether the action takes place in the past, present, or future. *Our seminar examines, our seminar examined, our seminar will examine* are all active; *the claims are examined, the claims were examined, the claims will be examined* are all passive.

How do the passive-voice sentences on pages 43–44 strike you? To my ear, the first three sound a bit stilted. While the active-voice "Faust and O'Brien take very different approaches" sounds easy and natural, the passive-voice "Very different approaches are taken by Faust and O'Brien" sounds forced. Probably because ours is an SVO language, because the subject-verb-object order of the active voice is so very common, readers may pause or stumble over a passive-voice sentence. So, given a choice, most good writers on most occasions will place the actor in the subject position, generating an active-voice sentence.

Under some circumstances, however, the passive voice is more effective.

First, the passive voice is used when the actor is unimportant or unknown. Consider these sentences, for example:

During the 1990s, dozens of books about the Civil War were published every year.

During the 1990s, trade and academic presses published dozens of books about the Civil War every year.

The actor in both sentences is "presses": it is presses that publish books. The active-voice construction "presses published" makes perfect sense. But perhaps your reader isn't likely to know much or care much about trade or academic presses; perhaps he or she is more interested in all those books. In that case, it makes equally good sense to move the books themselves into the subject position. Similarly, when the actor is unknown, speakers and writers often choose the passive voice, so that we might say "My car was vandalized" or "The copy machine was left on all night."

The passive voice may also be a good choice if you want to use the subject position to name a thing or idea carried over from an earlier sentence. In the list of passive-voice sentences on pages 43–44, the last one is the least jarring.

> Faust's claims will be examined by our seminar.

Because the previous sentences discuss Drew Gilpin Faust's assertions about Civil War scholarship, "Faust's claims" keeps the focus on the current topic, so it makes a fine subject.

Finally, the passive voice can emphasize the absence of agency and power in a person or thing that is acted upon. A dramatic example appears in the early pages of "On the Rainy River" when O'Brien describes the narrator's work in a meat-packing plant, removing blood clots from dead pigs. The pigs are, emphatically and graphically, acted upon:

> After slaughter, the hogs were decapitated, split down the length of the belly, pried open, eviscerated, and strung up by the hind hocks on a high conveyer belt.

Who performs those actions? People, machines. But they don't appear in the subject position — or even, for that matter, in the sentence. At this point in the paragraph, O'Brien uses the passive voice to keep our focus on the hogs, on the receiving end of the violence (an image that gains resonance as the narrator worries over his draft notice, "thinking about the war and the pig factory and how my life seemed to be collapsing toward slaughter").

In short, while writers usually prefer the active voice because of what we know about readers' expectations and their response as they process language, it is important to remember that the passive voice is available, too, as a stylistic option.

EXERCISE 3D

Recast each active-voice clause below into the passive voice by placing the object—the thing or person being acted upon—in the subject position.

Example
In 1990, Ken Burns produced a documentary called *The Civil War*.

Passive-Voice Version
In 1990, a documentary called *The Civil War* was produced by Ken Burns.

1. More than fourteen million people viewed the *The Civil War*.
2. Sam Waterston reads Abraham Lincoln's letters and speeches.
3. Morgan Freeman voices the words of Frederick Douglass.
4. The documentary awakened interest in Civil War scholarship.
5. Historians recognize the importance of Burns's work.

Now, recast each passive-voice clause below into the active voice by placing the actor in the subject position.

Example
More recently, a documentary about Prohibition was created by Ken Burns.

Active-Voice Version
More recently, Ken Burns created a documentary about Prohibition.

6. The consumption of alcohol was criminalized by the Eighteenth Amendment.
7. The amendment was supported by millions of women.
8. In 1933, Prohibition was repealed by Congress.
9. Prohibition is often cited by policy makers as an example of legislative excess.
10. Laws against marijuana use are questioned by many state legislators.

EXERCISE 3E

Rewrite the boldface clauses below to restore O'Brien's active-voice sentences. When you've rewritten each clause, underline the subject once and the verb twice to confirm that the subject performs the action.

Exercise 3E continued

Example
I was never confronted about it by the old man.

Restored to Active Voice
The old <u>man</u> never <u>confronted</u> me about it.

1. Most graduate school deferments had been ended by the government.
2. Fight songs were played by a marching band.
3. Cartwheels were done along the banks of the Rainy River by a squad of cheerleaders.
4. It seemed to me that when a nation goes to war it must have reasonable confidence in the justice and imperative of its cause. **Your mistakes can't be fixed.**
5. If you support a war, if you think it's worth the price, that's fine, but **your own precious fluids have to be put on the line.**

Variation in Sentence Focus

A general rule—even a fine, time-tested, oft-cited general rule like "prefer human or concrete subjects and active verbs"—is just a starting point. In the end, writing doesn't work by rules: it's a matter of judgment. And a writer's judgment will depend on his or her individual style and on what seems appropriate for the occasion—for the audience, purpose, and genre (memoir, editorial, novel, report, speech).

To see how sentence focus varies, let's consider the model texts. Stories and memoirs describe people's experiences as they interact with one another, so you'd expect these texts to have a high frequency of human subjects and active verbs. By contrast, academic writing typically reports the findings of research, with the findings themselves—which may or may not have to do with human behavior—taking center stage. So you'd expect academic writing to have more abstract or non-human words as subjects and more verbs that can be paired with non-human subjects (*be*, passive-voice verbs). And sure enough, when I analyzed the model texts, these expectations were confirmed.

	% of clauses with human subject	% of clauses with "I" as subject	% of clauses with passive-voice verbs
Stories Erdrich, "Shamengwa" O'Brien, "On the Rainy River" Sedaris, "Genetic Engineering"	67	33	6
Memoirs Gates, "Sin Boldly" Tan, "Mother Tongue"	63	24	7

Articles on Academic Topics
Faust, "We Should Grow Too
  Fond of It"
Sacks, "Papa Blows His
  Nose in G"
Wong Fillmore, "Loss of
  Family Languages"
	55	1	13

Arguments about Public Issues Obama, "A More Perfect Union" Olson, "The Conservative Case for Gay Marriage"	52	9	8

The numbers demonstrate several points:

- Taken together, the model texts illustrate writers' preference for human subjects and active verbs.
- The preference for human subjects and active verbs is stronger in some genres than in others. (The patterns visible in this small sample have been observed in larger studies as well, with more marked differences across genres.[1])
- There is no law against using *I*! Teachers sometimes encourage young writers to avoid *I* to push them toward more worldly topics or more formal prose. But the choice to use *I* — like other choices writers make — depends on a number of factors including the writer's personal style, the topic, the audience, the purpose, and the genre.

EXERCISE 3F

Write two brief texts, just a few paragraphs each, about a past or present job.

First, write a narrative about yourself in relationship with a coworker, capturing a moment of interaction. Choose an incident that reveals the dynamics of the relationship; feel free to use dialogue.

Exercise 3F continued

Second, explain the purpose of your workplace, describing the product or service it provides and the processes that employees engage in to achieve the overriding purpose.

When you've finished writing, identify the subject-verb pair in each clause. Are all of your sentences well focused? That is, do the subjects keep the reader's attention focused where it ought to be? Is the frequency of *I* or other human subjects about the same in the two texts, or does it differ? Is the frequency of active verbs, passive verbs, and *be* about the same, or does it differ? Might the similarities and/or differences be explained by the topics, by your rhetorical purposes, by your personal stylistic preferences?

Sharpening the Focus

In my experience, the concept of focus is useful at two points in the writing process. First, there's that moment early in a sentence's life, when it's not even a sentence yet but a thought waiting to be articulated. "Who is doing something?" I ask. "What is he or she doing?" When I can name the actor and action, when I can piece them together as the subject and verb of a clause, the sentence is on its way.

More frequently, I think about the subject-verb pair late in the writing process, when I read through a draft and find myself snagged by a clumsy, wordy, or confusing sentence. "Who is doing something? What is he or she doing?" These simple questions can be remarkably powerful in guiding a writer toward leaner, clearer sentences.

This section presents a series of exercises organized around five editing tips, all designed to keep the actor and action in focus:

- Double-check sentences that begin with an abstract subject.
- Double-check sentences with *there* in the subject position.
- In general, keep subject phrases short.
- When a sentence seems badly focused, see whether its subject is buried in an introductory phrase.
- When a sentence seems badly focused, see whether its verb is masquerading as a noun.

The tips overlap; for example, when an abstract word occupies the subject position (a problem you'll work on in Exercise 3G), it may have landed there because the sentence's natural subject is buried in an introductory phrase (see Exercise 3J). Please use the tips not to label faulty sentences but to guide your editing.

Double-Check Sentences with Abstract Subjects

When a sentence begins with an abstract subject, see whether you can streamline it by finding a human or concrete noun somewhere in the sentence and relocating that noun to the subject position.

ABSTRACT SUBJECT

The <u>phenomenon</u> of "boomerang children," young adults who return to live with their parents after graduating from college, is an occurrence faced by many families today.

<u>Disagreement</u> about financial matters such as the expectation of paying rent for the young adult's "own" room may be a point of difference between parents and children.

The first sentence links the abstract subject "phenomenon" to the equally abstract complement "occurrence," so the heart of the sentence, "the phenomenon is an occurrence," says almost nothing. The second sentence similarly links two abstractions: "Disagreement may be a point of difference." To revise, find a human or concrete noun somewhere else in the sentence — find the actor — and move that noun to the front.

BETTER

"<u>Boomerang children</u>" are young adults who return to live with their parents after graduating from college; many families face this phenomenon today.

Many <u>families</u> face the phenomenon of "boomerang children," young adults who return to live with their parents after graduating from college.

<u>Parents and children</u> may disagree about financial matters such as rent for the young adult's "own" room.

<u>Parents</u> may expect payment for a room that the young adult considers his or her own.

Sentences beginning *the next way, the second reason,* or *another aspect* are especially likely to appear as paragraph starters in academic papers. Yes, you have to make a transition — but you can do better than that!

ABSTRACT SUBJECT

A second _way_ that families can address the ambiguities of their new situation is to establish ground rules.

Another _reason_ that the U.S. invasion of Iraq was a mistake is that it caused the stature of the United States as a world leader to plummet.

BETTER

Second, _families_ can address the ambiguities of their new situation by establishing ground rules.

Furthermore, when the _United States_ invaded Iraq, its stature as a world leader plummeted.

EXERCISE 3G

In the sentences below, underline the abstract noun that occupies the subject position. Then find the actor, the person who is _doing_ something. Revise the sentence to place the actor in the subject position, once again underlining your subject.

Example
Compared with a generation ago, _relationships_ between parents and children seem to be much better.

Suggested Revision
Parents and children get along better than they did a generation ago.

1. The incidence of moonlighting among schoolteachers is high.
2. The reason for Maybelle's desire to leave Minneapolis was her desire to avoid the harsh winter weather.
3. Similarities exist in the strategies Jackson and LeGuin use to portray the conflict between individual conscience and the influence of the social group.
4. The reason the characters in the stories are willing to victimize their neighbors is because they think their own comfort depends on somebody's sacrifice.
5. With the widespread use of PowerPoint and Prezi in business settings, the advantages and disadvantages of presentation software should be considered by speakers.

Double-Check Sentences with *There* in the Subject Position

In a sentence whose purpose is to assert that something exists, *there* may be just the right subject. Often, however, *there* just takes up space, delaying the appearance of a sentence's true subject. Since *there* is almost invariably followed by a form of *be*, it displaces not only the subject but the whole subject-verb pair.

THERE AS SUBJECT

There <u>are</u> some television news programs that tell only one side of the story.

BETTER

Some television news <u>programs</u> <u>tell</u> only one side of the story.

EXERCISE 3H

Revise the sentences below to eliminate *there* from the subject position. In the new sentence, underline the subject-verb pair.

Example
There are many young mothers who want to work.

Suggested Revision
Many young <u>mothers</u> <u>want</u> to work.

1. Consequently there are far too many children who are spending their days in underfunded daycare centers.
2. To comply with the new laws, there are too many extra expenses that a family daycare provider must contend with.
3. Outside, there was an ice cream truck ringing its bell, but the children were all indoors watching television.
4. In the story "The Ones Who Walk Away from Omelas," there is a single boy who is chosen to suffer in order for the rest of the town to prosper.
5. There are three points in the story where the author uses foreshadowing.

Keep Subject Phrases Short

Readers expect a subject-verb pair. If the subject is a lengthy phrase, the reader is held in suspense waiting for the verb, and the sentence feels awkward.

LONG SUBJECT PHRASE

<u>Many hours of labor, several meetings, including an emergency meeting of the whole committee, and several revisions of the contract</u> were the result of one hasty e-mail.

BETTER

One hasty <u>e-mail</u> resulted in many hours of labor, several meetings, including an emergency meeting of the whole committee, and several revisions of the contract.

As this example demonstrates, sometimes the best revision strategy is to see whether the sentence can be inverted.

EXERCISE 31

In the sentences below, underline the long subject phrase. Then find a noun or noun phrase elsewhere in the sentence that would make a more concise subject. Rewrite the sentence, underlining the new subject.

Example
"<u>Short-term temporary employment, or, in some cases, contract labor paid daily</u>" describes the only promise the company will make.

Suggested Revision
The <u>company</u> will promise only "short-term temporary employment or, in some cases, contract labor paid daily."

1. Commitment to ethical behavior, respect for the rules of confidentiality, courtesy to coworkers and customers, and fully professional behavior on all occasions should be demonstrated by every employee.
2. Disorderly conduct, horseplay in the work area, fighting, threatening behavior, and profane or insulting remarks are strictly prohibited by company policy.
3. An unprecedented number of layoffs; a reduction of earnings, profits, and stock values; and a steadily worsening competitive position vis-à-vis the other high-tech companies in the area were among the factors being responded to by the CEO's decision to resign.
4. Accounting irregularities in both the purchasing office and the president's operating accounts were discovered by the auditors.
5. Planning your whole trip, from searching for the lowest airfare to finding an affordable rental car to locating a convenient hotel and even making restaurant reservations, can be done using the Internet.

Uncover Subjects Buried in Introductory Phrases

The sentence below illustrates a trap into which many hapless subjects have fallen:

> To the people of Minnesota, <u>they</u> develop a tolerance for freezing temperatures.

The writer has something to say about the people of Minnesota; the people are the sentence's natural subject. But because the sentence begins with "to", the people of Minnesota appear as the object of a preposition, and the writer is forced to cast about for a substitute ("they") to use as a subject.

An editor's task is simply to move the key noun phrase to the front of the sentence:

> The <u>people</u> of Minnesota develop a tolerance for freezing temperatures.

EXERCISE 3J

In the sentences below, identify the key noun phrase and move it to the subject position. Underline the new subject.

Example
By having a large selection of organic vegetables, this appeals to the high-end buyer.

Suggested Revision
A large <u>selection</u> of organic vegetables appeals to the high-end buyer.

1. At the health food store, there are good bargains featured every weekend.
2. According to the store manager, he said he would be happy to stock more locally grown produce if he saw evidence of customer demand.
3. Because of the desk clerk at the hotel not knowing, it was unclear whether the rooms would be available both nights.
4. On San Francisco's beaches, it is beautiful but too cold for sunning or swimming.
5. After a visit to Chinatown, it made her nostalgic for her childhood in Shanghai.

Transform Nouns to Verbs

When a sentence seems badly focused, see whether its verb is masquerading as a noun.

> An emphasis is placed on the development of research skills in our graduate program.

"Emphasis" makes a poor subject for reasons we've considered: as an abstraction, it can't do anything, so it leads to a passive-voice verb. But an alert editor will note that *emphasis* has a sister verb, *emphasize*, which names exactly the action that the writer wants to highlight:

> Our graduate program emphasizes the development of research skills.

EXERCISE 3K

Each of the nouns in boldface below has a sister verb. Refocus the sentence, pairing a well-chosen subject with the verb form of the word. Underline the subject-verb pair.

Example
As graduate students work on their dissertation projects, the **development** of sophisticated research skills is achieved.

Suggested Revision
As graduate students work on their dissertation projects, they develop sophisticated research skills.

1. The candidate's **decision** to drop out of the race occurred when she fell to sixth place in the polls.
2. There is a **tendency** in the main character to damage relationships with everyone she meets.
3. Every Saturday morning, the **distribution** of fresh, organic produce happens when local truck farmers bring organic produce to the farmer's market.
4. The **establishment** of a more equitable tax policy won't happen on the city council until council members have to answer to voters in district elections.
5. The **success** of the project will be achieved only if the **contribution** of every team member is a 100% effort.

These tips should help you produce tighter, more clearly focused sentences. But editing, like other aspects of writing, depends above all on your good judgment. If, as you work on your own prose, you follow these tips only to find that a sentence sounds worse, or that it suffers a loss of clarity, substance, or precision, then set the tip aside for another day.

CHAPTER 3 NOTE

[1]If you're interested in learning about how language use varies across contexts, look for the *Longman Student Grammar of Spoken and Written English* by Douglas Biber, Susan Conrad, and Geoffrey Leech (Essex, England: Pearson Education Limited, 2002). The Longman grammar is a descriptive grammar; its purpose is not to offer advice but to describe what English speakers and writers actually do. Because its description is based on a large corpus — over 40 million words — the Longman grammar can make well-documented claims about patterns within and across contexts. Biber, Conrad, and Leech present the frequency of passive-voice clauses in four contexts: about 1% in speech, 4% in fiction, 15% in news reports, and 25% in academic prose (167–168).

CHAPTER 4

Well-Balanced Sentences

Coordination and Parallel Structure

IN COLORED PEOPLE: A MEMOIR, Henry Louis Gates Jr. describes his first year of college in a chapter titled "Sin Boldly" (reprinted on p. 190). The theme of bold sins is introduced in the chapter's first paragraph. Delivering his high school valedictory address, the young Gates rejected the "traditional prepared speech" he had practiced with his English teacher, instead writing a speech of his own about topics of the day:

> My speech was about Vietnam, abortion, and civil rights, about the sense of community our class shared, since so many of us had been together for twelve years, about the individual's rights and responsibilities in his or her community, and about the necessity to defy norms out of love.

Look carefully at that sentence. It's long—49 words—but its structure is quite simple. The main clause begins with the subject-verb pair "speech was" and then describes the content of the speech in four prepositional phrases:

> about Vietnam, abortion, and civil rights

> about the sense of community our class shared, since so many of us had been together for twelve years

about the individual's rights and responsibilities in his or her
community

about the necessity to defy norms out of love

The prepositional phrases are joined by a kind of glue you can buy for
a penny at any sentence-structure shop: the coordinating conjunction
and.

This chapter begins with some observations about Gates's work in
"Sin Boldly" and goes on to examine other texts in which coordinating
conjunctions join pairs or series, exploring the stylistic options that coordination makes available to writers.

Coordination

Let's take a moment to review the concept of coordination. English has
seven coordinating conjunctions — *and, or, nor, but, for, yet, so* — which
are used to join two or more independent clauses or smaller units
within a clause. Almost always, the units joined by the coordinator will
be similar in structure.

In the sentence about his valedictory speech, Gates has used coordinators not only to link a series of four prepositional phrases but also to
connect some smaller units.

> Vietnam, abortion, **and** civil rights,
> *The coordinator* and *joins three noun phrases.*

> the individual's rights **and** responsibilities
> *The coordinator* and *joins two nouns.*

> in his **or** her community
> *The coordinator* or *joins two determiners.*

As noted in Chapter 2, coordinators can also link independent clauses.

> Certainly Maura and I had been no strangers to controversy, **but** we
> usually took pains not to invite it.

> We were apparently the first interracial couple in Mineral County, **and**
> there was hell to pay.

> The Potomac Valley Hospital was called the meat factory because one
> of the doctors was reputed to be such a butcher, **so** we drove on past it
> and headed for my house.

EDITING NOTE: When a coordinator joins two independent clauses, it is usually preceded by a comma. When it joins smaller units within a sentence, no comma is necessary.

EXERCISE 4A

The sentences below are by Henry Louis Gates Jr. ("Sin Boldly," p. 190), Louise Erdrich ("Shamengwa," p. 159), and Barack Obama ("A More Perfect Union," p. 199). Circle every coordinating conjunction and underline the units being joined. Some sentences have more than one coordinator, so you may need more than one set of underlines, as in the second example.

Example

My one year at Potomac State College of West Virginia University, in Keyser, all of five miles away, was memorable for two reasons: because of my English classes with Duke Anthony Whitmore (and) my first real love affair, with Maura Gibson.

It was he who showed me, by his example, that ideas had a life of their own (and) that there were other professions as stimulating (and) as rewarding as being a doctor.

1. Once we were at college, Maura and I started having long talks on the phone, first about nothing at all and then about everything.
2. In his own redneck way, 'Bama Gibson was a perfectly nice man, but he was not exactly mayoral material.
3. My grandfather was colored, my father was Negro, and I am black.
4. Geraldine, a dedicated, headstrong woman who six years back had borne a baby, dumped its father, and earned a degree in education, sometimes drove Shamengwa to fiddling contests.
5. He had taken the old man's fiddle because he needed money, but he hadn't thought much about where he would sell it or who would buy it.
6. I took my bedroll, a scrap of jerky, and a loaf of bannock, and sat myself down on the crackling lichen of the southern rock.
7. There were rivers flowing in and flowing out, secret currents, six kinds of weather working on its surface and a hidden terrain beneath.
8. Each wave washed in from somewhere unseen and washed out again to somewhere unknown.
9. The document they produced was eventually signed but ultimately unfinished.

Exercise 4A continued

10. It was stained by this nation's original sin of slavery, a question that divided the colonies and brought the convention to a stalemate until the founders chose to allow the slave trade to continue for at least twenty more years, and to leave any final resolution to future generations.

EXERCISE 4B

Combine each group into a single sentence by creating a coordinate pair or series, joining the units with *and.* Underline the units being joined.

Example
I made my way to Mr. Whitmore's table. I introduced myself tentatively. I stated my case, telling him my cousin Greg had said that he was a great teacher.

Suggested Revision
I made my way to Mr. Whitmore's table, introduced myself tentatively, and stated my case, telling him my cousin Greg had said that he was a great teacher.

1. I wrote to Harvard. I wrote to Yale. I wrote to Princeton.
2. Horse Lowe put his big red face into Maura's window. He beat on the windshield with his fist. He told me to get the hell off his property.
3. Geraldine was not surprised to see the lock of the cupboard smashed. She was not surprised to see the violin gone.
4. As the days passed, Corwin lay low. He picked up his job at the deep fryer.
5. I remember my father playing chansons on his fiddle. He played reels. He played jigs.
6. He smiled. He shook his fine head. He spoke softly.
7. Reverend Wright is a man who served his country as a United States Marine. He is a man who has studied and lectured at some of the finest universities and seminaries in the country. He is a man who for over thirty years led a church that serves the community by doing God's work here on Earth.
8. He strengthens my faith. He officiated my wedding. He baptized my children.

Parallel Structure

As a general rule, units in a series should have **parallel structure**; that is, they should be the same kind of grammatical unit, and they should fit into the same "slot" in the sentence. As I've noted, the series in Gates's sentence about his valedictory speech comprises four prepositional phrases, and any one of the phrases fits naturally after the subject and verb:

My speech was	about Vietnam, abortion, and civil rights
My speech was	about the sense of community our class shared, since so many of us had been together for twelve years
My speech was	about the individual's rights and responsibilities in his or her community
My speech was	about the necessity to defy norms out of love

In this sentence, the second prepositional phrase is longer and more complex than the others. Nevertheless, because all four units are prepositional phrases that fit naturally into the slot after "My speech was," the series is parallel and the sentence is easy to read.

Sometimes the units in a well-crafted series match very closely:

My one year at Potomac State College of West Virginia University, in Keyser, all of five miles away, was memorable for two reasons: because of my English classes with Duke Anthony Whitmore and my first real love affair, with Maura Gibson.

Here, the noun phrases are about the same length, the nouns are signaled by the same determiner ("*my* English classes," "*my* first real love affair"), and each noun is modified by a prepositional phrase beginning with "with" and ending with a person's name.

If a writer fails to use parallel structure in a series, the sentence will be awkward and potentially confusing. It's a good idea to check the parallelism in a series by considering two questions. First, are the units grammatically similar? Second, do they fit into the same slot in the sentence?

Somehow, for reasons having to do with nudity and sensuality, blacks were not allowed to walk along most beachfronts or attend resorts.

Are the units grammatically similar?

walk along most beachfronts *verb phrase*

attend resorts *verb phrase*

Do the units fit into the same slot in the sentence?

blacks were not allowed to walk along most beachfronts

blacks were not allowed to attend resorts

The sentence above passes both tests, so the most exacting editor can be at peace.

In the sentence below, the series is not parallel:

I was used to being the only black person on the beach, in a restaurant, or who would be staying at a motel.

If you read the sentence aloud, your ear will quickly tell you that something is wrong. The sentence violates your expectations: having read two prepositional phrases ("on the beach," "in a restaurant"), you expect another one after the conjunction. Instead, you get an adjective clause ("who would be staying at a motel").

The simplest way to correct the parallel structure is to create a series of prepositional phrases:

I was used to being the only black person on the beach, in a restaurant, or at a motel.

(This is the sentence as Henry Louis Gates wrote it, with one small difference. He chose to insert the conjunction twice: "I was used to being the only black person on the beach, or in a restaurant, or at a motel.")

In the sentence below, the parallel structure is seriously flawed:

Gates's essay tells about his high school commencement speech, then describing his college experience, then integrating a nightclub, and finally what happened when he dated a white girl.

The four-part series fails both tests for parallel structure:

Are the units grammatically similar?

tells about his high school commencement speech *verb phrase*

describing his college experience *"-ing" verbal phrase*

integrating a nightclub   *"-ing" verbal phrase*

what happened when he   *noun clause modified by an*

dated a white girl   *adverb clause*

Do the units fit into the same slot in the sentence?

Gates's essay   tells about his high school
                             commencement speech

Gates's essay   describing his college experience

Gates's essay   integrating a night club

Gates's essay   what happened when he dated a
                             white girl.

The answer to both questions is a resounding "no."

There are several ways an editor might correct the parallelism in this sentence. One possibility would be to fill the slot after "Gates's essay" with matching phrases:

Gates's essay tells about his high school commencement speech, describes his college experience, boasts about integrating a night club, and explains what happened when he dated a white girl.

This sentence passes both tests: all four units are verb phrases, and they all fit, and even make reasonably good sense, in the slot after "Gates's essay." So the series is parallel; the sentence is correct. I don't like it much, though—it strikes me as wordy—so I'd be inclined to experiment with other options. I might, for example, decide to begin the series later in the sentence:

Gates's essay describes his high school commencement speech, his college experience, his adventure integrating a night club, and the consternation he caused by dating a white girl.

Gates's essay describes his experiences delivering a high school commencement speech, finding his academic interests in college, integrating a night club, and dating a white girl.

These sentences pass both tests for parallel structure. In the first, all four units are noun phrases, and they all fit after "Gates's essay describes." In the second, all four units are -*ing* verbal phrases that fit after "his experiences." I invite you to play with the sentence to find other ways to structure the series.

EXERCISE 4C

Each of these sentences contains a series in which the parallelism has gone awry. If you hear the problem immediately, revise the sentence. If you don't hear the problem right away, first identify the units in the series and test for parallel structure; then you'll be prepared to revise.

Example
He will probably be admitted to Officer Candidate School because he is young, strong, he can work hard, and has a good education.
The series is mixed, with two adjectives, then a clause, then a verb phrase.

Suggested Revisions
He will probably be admitted to Officer Candidate School because he is young, strong, hardworking, and well educated.
Four adjectives fit into the slot after "he is."

He will probably be admitted to Officer Candidate School because he is young and strong, he can work hard, and he has a good education.
Three clauses fit into the slot after "because."

1. He was always looking for money—scamming, betting, shooting pool, even now and then a job.
2. My mother out of grief became strict with my father, my older sister, and hard on me.
3. Ashley finished her story, went around the room, asked everyone why they were supporting the campaign, and she listened to their stories.
4. The old man was not there because of health care or the economy or education or the war or it could have been any other issue.
5. Granted, that one moment of recognition is not enough to give health care to the sick, or jobs to the jobless, or improve education.
6. The function of a university is to develop the analytical skills of students and a place where they should learn to express themselves.
7. During her first two years, Lucienne declared four majors: French, history, philosophy, and her favorite subject was still computer science.
8. He argued for financial aid for the children of immigrants in order to ensure the equal right to study the liberal arts, an equal chance at higher-paying jobs, and to learn the communication skills that prepare young adults for full participation in a democracy.

Correlative Conjunctions

If you've heard a child describe his or her day ("We went to the playground and Jeremy fell off the high bar and there was blood all over his face and the teacher called his grandma . . ."), you get a sense of how heavily we depend on *and* (and, to a lesser extent, *but*) in our everyday speech. Naturally, then, all of us, from elementary school children to published authors, use coordination frequently when we write.

By contrast, coordinators' first cousins, the correlative conjunctions, are quite rare in spoken English, and you seldom see them in the work of young writers. It is experienced writers who use correlatives, exploiting their ability to join syntactic units and to manipulate emphasis.

Correlative conjunctions come in pairs:

both/and	not/but
either/or	not only/but
neither/nor	not only/but also

In living sentences, they sound like this:

> She shook her head as if she were **both** annoyed with me **and** exasperated with her father.

> The speck seemed to **both** advance **and** retreat.

> It was a canoe. But **either** the paddler was asleep in the bottom **or** the canoe was drifting.

The correlatives *not/but*, *not only/but*, and *not only/but also* give greater weight to the second unit in the pair. The sentences below are from "A More Perfect Union," Barack Obama's 2008 speech exploring racial tension in America. In the speech, Obama frequently uses correlative conjunctions to set forth a word or phrase, then to substitute another word or phrase that signifies his intent more precisely or more forcefully.

> The Reverend Wright's comments were **not only** wrong **but** divisive, divisive at a time when we need unity.

> What's remarkable is **not** how many failed in the face of discrimination, **but** rather how many were able to make a way out of no way for those like me who would come after them.

> The legacy of discrimination — and current incidents of discrimination, while less overt than in the past — are real and must be addressed. **Not** just with words, **but** with deeds.

The correlative conjunctions background the material following *not* while emphasizing the material following *but*.

Like other coordinators, correlatives call for parallel structure. The editor's task is to be sure that the two parts of the correlative conjunction are followed by similar grammatical units that fit into the same slot in the sentence:

> She shook her head as if she were **both** annoyed with me **and** exasperated with her father.

Are the units grammatically similar?

| annoyed with me | *adjective phrase* |
| exasperated with her father | *adjective phrase* |

Do the units fit into the same slot in the sentence?

| She shook her head as if she were | annoyed with me |
| She shook her head as if she were | exasperated with her father |

The sentence passes both tests. Now examine a sentence with faulty parallelism:

> I pretended to sleep, **not** because I wanted to keep up the appearance of being sick **but** I could not bear to return to the way things had been.

Are the units grammatically similar?

| because I wanted to keep up the appearance of being sick | *dependent clause* |
| I could not bear to return to the way things had been | *independent clause* |

Do the units fit into the same slot in the sentence?

| I pretended to sleep | because I wanted to keep up the appearance of being sick |
| I pretended to sleep | I could not bear to return to the way things had been |

This sentence fails both tests, so it requires revision. In Louise Erdrich's actual sentence, the subordinator *because* is repeated at the beginning of the second clause so that both clauses joined by *not/but* are dependent:

I pretended to sleep, **not** because I wanted to keep up the appearance of being sick **but** because I could not bear to return to the way things had been.

I sometimes like to experiment with the placement of correlative conjunctions, placing them early in the sentence to create some repetition or late in the sentence for maximum efficiency:

The old woman knew enough **not** to trust her vision **but** to trust her touch.

The old woman knew enough to trust **not** her vision **but** her touch.

The purpose of dialogue is **not** to help participants reach agreement **but** to help them achieve mutual understanding.

The purpose of dialogue is to help participants achieve **not** agreement **but** mutual understanding.

EXERCISE 4D

Join the following sentences, using the correlative conjunctions indicated.

Example
both/and
When my father died he left the fiddle to my brother Edwin. He also left it to me.

Joined
When my father died he left the fiddle both to my brother Edwin and to me.

1. *both/and*
   Shamengwa loved the fiddle. Shamengwa's father loved the fiddle.
2. *both/and*
   His mother lost her capacity for joy. Ultimately, his father lost his capacity for joy.
3. *not/but*
   The narrator does not give Corwin a break because he believes he is innocent. He gives Corwin a break because he hopes he can be redeemed.
4. *either/or*
   He would learn to play the violin. Otherwise, he would do time.

Exercise 4D continued

5. *neither/nor*
Billy Peace did not play fair in the race for the violin. His brother Edwin did not play fair in the race.

6. *both/and*
Shamengwa can face the past without blinking. Billy Peace, who owned the violin before him, can face the past without blinking.

7. *not only/but also*
The violin brings great heartache. It brings great joy.

8. *not only/but also*
The violin brings great joy. It brings great heartache.

Stylistic Effects in Coordinate Series

Long Series

The number of units in a series has a strong influence on its rhetorical effect. In general, a series with three units is unmarked — that is, the length of the series doesn't call attention to itself — so it simply suggests completeness.

> I wrote to Harvard, Yale, and Princeton.

> I had not realized how much I loved to hear him play—sometimes out on his scrubby back lawn after dusk, sometimes at those little concerts, and other times just for groups of people who would gather round.

And there you have it. The young Henry Louis Gates applied to college; Shamengwa played his violin; the three-part lists tell you what you need to know.

A series with four units begins to feel long, and one with five or more conveys a sense of abundance, perhaps excess, perhaps exhaustion. This effect is even stronger when the writer omits the conjunction. In the sentence below, Gates describes his drives from West Virginia to Delaware to meet Maura Gibson, stringing one prepositional phrase after another to create a long series and using no conjunction. By the end of the sentence, it's surprising to learn that he has any energy left:

> I'd leave work on Friday at about four o'clock, then drive all the way to Delaware, through Washington and the Beltway, past Baltimore

and Annapolis, <u>over the Chesapeake Bridge</u>, <u>past Ocean City</u>, arriving
at Rehoboth before midnight, with as much energy as if I had just
awakened.

In the sentence below, Barack Obama uses a series of four examples to
illustrate the history of discrimination against black Americans:

Legalized discrimination—where <u>blacks were prevented, often through
violence, from owning property</u>, or <u>loans were not granted to African-
American business owners</u>, or <u>black homeowners could not access FHA
mortgages</u>, or <u>blacks were excluded from unions or the police force or
the fire department</u>—meant that black families could not amass any
meaningful wealth to bequeath to future generations.

Racial discrimination is a familiar theme in American history and political discourse; if Obama had included just one or two examples, his
listeners would have understood the point. But the passage has more
emotional impact because the long list calls to mind how *many* kinds of
injustice people faced, one after another, day after day.

You can see a similar effect in Obama's list of difficulties facing the
country. "A More Perfect Union" argues that Americans cannot afford
to spend time and attention on the issues that divide us:

. . . we need to come together to solve a set of monumental problems:
<u>two wars</u>, <u>a terrorist threat</u>, <u>a failing economy</u>, <u>a chronic health care
crisis</u>, and <u>potentially devastating climate change</u>. . . .

The five-part list not only explains the need for unity but also helps to
achieve the underlying rhetorical purpose of any campaign speech: to
show why voters should elect Obama rather than his Republican opponent. In 2008, as a Republican administration was coming to a close,
Obama's long series highlighted the proliferation of problems during
those years, thereby reinforcing his call for change.

EXERCISE 4E

Analyze the effect of length in coordinate series. Choose a passage from
any text you admire; for example, you might examine paragraph 33 in Wong
Fillmore's "Loss of Family Languages" (p. 269), paragraph 35 in Gates's
"Sin Boldly" (p. 196), a sentence or two from paragraph 65 in O'Brien's "On
the Rainy River" (p. 224), or the famous 315-word sentence in Martin Luther
King Jr.'s "Letter from Birmingham Jail."

Exercise 4E continued

1. Spend some time with the passage: read it aloud and type it.
2. Make the structure of the series visible, identifying the units being joined and any coordinating conjunctions, as you did in Exercise 4A.
3. For each series, count the number of units. I've claimed that a series of three feels complete, a series of four feels longish, and a series of five or more suggests abundance or excess. Do these generalizations apply to the passage you've selected?
4. For each series, consider the writer's choice of a conjunction. Are the units joined by *and*? another coordinator? no conjunction at all? What is the effect of adding, deleting, or changing the conjunction?
5. Describe the role of the passage you've selected in the text as a whole. Is this an important moment in the development of the story or argument? Why? How does the use of coordinate series serve the writer's rhetorical purpose?

The Echo Effect: Pairs

The sentence below features a four-part series, but the list feels longer:

> What would be needed were Americans in successive generations who were willing to do their part—through protests and struggle, on the streets and in the courts, through a civil war and civil disobedience, and always at great risk—to narrow that gap between the promise of our ideals and the reality of their time.

Here, Obama amplifies his illustration of doing one's part by inserting several pairs: "protests and struggle," "on the streets and in the courts," "a civil war and civil disobedience." As a result, the list of four phrases provides more than four examples. If you read the sentence aloud, you'll probably find that it establishes a rocking, back-and-forth rhythm, and you'll notice that "on the streets" is echoed by "in the courts," "civil war" by "civil disobedience." This simple coordination—joining two words or phrases with *and*—can enrich a sentence's meaning and affect its rhythm, usually creating a sense of balance.

"On the streets" and "in the courts" is an example of a matching pair; the two phrases are similar to each other in sound and sense. By contrast, the pair that closes the passage—"the promise of our ideals and the reality of their time"—uses similar grammatical units to communicate opposing ideas. A conceptual contrast can be especially striking if the contrasting ideas are expressed in matching phrases.

Observe the pairs in Obama's description of the church in Chicago where his family worshipped:

> Like other predominantly black churches across the country, Trinity embodies the black community in its entirety—the doctor and the welfare mom, the model student and the gangbanger. . . . The church contains in full the kindness and the cruelty, the fierce intelligence and the shocking ignorance, the struggles and successes, the love and, yes, the bitterness and biases that make up the black experience in America.

All of the underlined pairs offer contrasts as Obama conveys the broad scope of human difference contained within the black church and the black community: the high-status doctor is contrasted with the low-status welfare mom, the model student with the gangbanger. In the second sentence, Obama heightens the similarity of the pairs with alliteration — kindness/cruelty, intelligence/ignorance, struggles/successes — even as the ideas are more starkly opposed. (The last pair in the sentence breaks the mold both by setting forth "love" without an alliterative counterpart and by interjecting "yes" before the contrasting terms — but the echo effect reappears in "bitterness and biases.")

Coordinate pairs, then, are a surprisingly powerful and versatile structure. They induce a reader to hold two images or ideas in mind at the same time so that their similarities or differences stand out.

EXERCISE 4F

In "A More Perfect Union," Barack Obama tells the story that defined him as a candidate, the story of his own multiracial family, suggesting both a unique perspective on race relations and the source of his enduring hope for a less fractious, more unified country. His description of his background relies heavily on paired phrases.

> I am the son of a black man from Kenya and a white woman from Kansas. I was raised with the help of a white grandfather who survived a depression to serve in Patton's Army during World War II and a white grandmother who worked on a bomber assembly line at Fort Leavenworth while he was overseas. I've gone to some of the best schools in America and lived in one of the world's poorest nations. I am married to a black

---

Exercise 4F continued

American who carries within her the blood of slaves and slave owners — an inheritance we pass on to our two precious daughters. I have brothers, sisters, nieces, nephews, uncles, and cousins, of every race and every hue, scattered across three continents, and for as long as I live I will never forget that in no other country on Earth is my story even possible.

Underline the paired phrases (in every case, they are joined by *and*) and then examine the stylistic effect of each pair. Be prepared to discuss these questions:

1. How similar are the two units in structure and sound?
2. How similar are the two units in meaning? Are they matching, contrasting, or both?
3. In general, two units joined by a coordinator have roughly equal emphasis. Does the pair seem balanced? What happens if you change the order of the units — does the emphasis shift?
4. How does the use of paired phrases help Obama achieve the purpose of his speech?

The Echo Effect: Repetition

One reason that coordinate series are so widely used is that they make sentences more concise: it is more efficient to write "I remember my father playing chansons, reels, and jigs on his fiddle" than to name the songs in three separate sentences. However, conciseness isn't the only virtue writers seek, and we sometimes opt to repeat a few words in a coordinate series. Compare these sentences:

I wrote to Harvard, Yale, and Princeton.

I wrote to Harvard, to Yale, and to Princeton.

One way to think about the difference in this pair is that they indicate different ways of defining the slot into which coordinate units fit. For example, in the first sentence, the slot begins after *to*, and it is filled with three nouns:

I wrote to   Harvard

               Yale

               Princeton

In the second sentence, the slot begins after *wrote*, and it is filled with three prepositional phrases:

I wrote   to Harvard

               to Yale

               to Princeton

Both versions of the sentence are perfectly correct, and both are concise and easy to read. In this case, Henry Louis Gates chose the first version, using the preposition *to* just once.

When a series is longer or more complex, writers often choose to repeat a word or two so that the structure of the list is immediately apparent. We've seen this choice in Gates's sentence about his commencement speech:

My speech was *about* Vietnam, abortion, and civil rights, *about* the sense of community our class shared, since so many of us had been together for twelve years, *about* the individual's rights and responsibilities in his or her community, and *about* the necessity to defy norms out of love.

The preposition *about* functions like a bullet or a number, signaling the beginning of each unit. It helps the reader piece the sentence together.

Finally, consider two versions of a sentence by Louise Erdrich:

Each wave washed in from somewhere unseen and out again to somewhere unknown.

Each wave washed in from somewhere unseen and washed out again to somewhere unknown.

Both sentences are easy to follow; with or without the repetition of "washed," the paired phrases are effective. Erdrich wrote the second sentence, repeating the verb. It seems to me that the choice is easily explained on esthetic grounds. The repetition of "washed" makes the image more vivid, and it creates a rhythm in the sentence that captures the movement of the waves, washing in, washing out.

In short, a coordinate series creates the option of repeating words or phrases. Most writers strive for conciseness, so the default position may be to avoid repetition — but in the interest of clarity, emphasis, or beauty, repetition is sometimes a wise choice.

Repetition and Paragraph Cohesion

In "Shamengwa," Erdrich plays with repetition not just within sentences but from one sentence to the next. Shamengwa's story of finding his violin on the lake closes like this:

> "That is how my fiddle came to me," Shamengwa said, raising his head to look steadily at me. He smiled, shook his fine head, and spoke softly. "And that is why no other fiddle will I play."

And, as the story of the violin's previous owner comes to a close, we again hear a repeated structure echoing over the lake:

> The uncles have returned to their houses, pastures, children, wives. I am alone on the shore. As the night goes black, I sing for you. As the sun comes up, I call across the water. White gulls answer. As the time goes on, I begin to accept what I have done. I begin to know the truth of things.

If you have heard or read many of Barack Obama's speeches, you will notice that this kind of repetition—using the same words to begin several sentences—is a hallmark of his style. It is the feature of his writing most clearly linked to the tradition of African American religious oratory:

> In the end, then, what is called for is nothing more, and nothing less, than what all the world's great religions demand: that we do unto others as we would have them do unto us. Let us be our brother's keeper, Scripture tells us. Let us be our sister's keeper. Let us find that common stake we all have in one another, and let our politics reflect that spirit, as well.

The repetition not only makes the text easy to follow but impresses the point upon the listener's or reader's memory.

EXERCISE 4G

Try your hand at writing like Barack Obama. After studying passages from "A More Perfect Union," imitate their structure, paying particular attention to series and to repeated words or phrases.

Keep in mind that Obama wrote his speech during a presidential election, when important social issues were being discussed and the stakes were high. As you complete this exercise, you can choose a similarly momentous topic so that the style feels appropriate. If, instead, you opt for a topic of local or personal interest, the style may feel overblown, even comical. Feel free to experiment: write the sentences and see what happens.

1. Most working- and middle-class white Americans don't feel that they have been particularly privileged by their race. . . . So when they are told to bus their children to a school across town; when they hear that an African American is getting an advantage in landing a good job or a spot in a good college because of an injustice that they themselves never committed; when they're told that their fears about crime in urban neighborhoods are somehow prejudice, resentment builds over time.

Think of a social group or phenomenon that, rightly or wrongly, elicits widespread fear or resentment — immigrants, big business, outsourcing, highly educated people, taxation, landlords. Following the structure of the passage as closely as you can, write a sentence that asserts how people feel, then a sentence that sets forth three examples showing how the fear or resentment has been generated.

2. The profound mistake of Reverend Wright's sermons is not that he spoke about racism in our society. It's that he spoke as if our society was static; as if no progress has been made; as if this country — a country that has made it possible for one of his own members to run for the highest office in the land and build a coalition of white and black, Latino, Asian, rich and poor, young and old — is still irrevocably bound to a tragic past.

Think of an occasion when somebody — a member of your family, a roommate, a teacher, a boss — has misunderstood you, or something you said, or something you did. What was the root of that person's mistake? Following the structure of the passage as closely as you can, explain that the mistake was not _____. It was that the person spoke or acted as if _____; as if _____; as if _____.

3. For we have a choice in this country. We can accept a politics that breeds division and conflict and cynicism. . . . We can play Reverend Wright's sermons on every channel, every day, and talk about them from now until the election and make the only question in this campaign whether or not the American people think that I somehow believe or sympathize with his most offensive words. We can pounce on some gaffe by a Hillary supporter as evidence that she's playing the race card, or we can speculate on whether white men will all flock to John McCain in the general election, regardless of his policies.
   We can do that.

Exercise 4G continued

> But if we do, I can tell you that in the next election, we'll be talking about some other distraction. And then another one. And then another one. And nothing will change. This is one option. Or, at this moment, in this election, we can come together and say, "Not this time. . . ."

Begin by completing this sentence: "For we have a choice in this _____."
(This country? family? dormitory? workplace? neighborhood? university?)
Following the structure of the passage as closely as you can, spell out the ways we could make a foolish choice. Explain that "if we do," we can expect negative consequences, and then close by hinting that we could make a wiser choice.

Well-Developed Sentences

Modification

IN THE LAST CHAPTER, we considered several examples of coordination, examining sentences in which the parts are lined up one after another, like beads on a string. This chapter turns to a different kind of relationship, modification, whereby one part of a sentence extends, clarifies, or qualifies another part.

We'll begin with an illustration from "Papa Blows His Nose in G" (p. 236), an essay by the neurologist Oliver Sacks. The essay discusses the phenomenon of absolute pitch. People with absolute pitch, Sacks explains, can immediately recognize the pitch of any note, much as the rest of us recognize colors. He describes several musicians whose gift is evident from childhood:

> *The Oxford Companion to Music* was a sort of Arabian Nights for me as a boy, an inexhaustible source of musical stories, and it gives many charming examples of absolute pitch. Sir Frederick Ouseley, a former professor of music at Oxford, for example, "was all his life remarkable for his sense of absolute pitch. At five he was able to remark, 'Only think, Papa blows his nose in G.' He would say that it thundered in G or that the wind was whistling in D, or that the clock (with a two-note chime) struck in B minor, and when the assertion was tested it would invariably be found correct." For most of us, such an ability to

> recognize an exact pitch seems uncanny, almost like another sense, a
> sense we can never hope to possess, such as infrared or X-ray vision;
> but for those who are born with absolute pitch, it seems perfectly
> normal.

The underlined sentence beginning "He would say" is organized by co-ordination; it lists three examples of the young Ouseley's identification of pitches, linking them with the coordinating conjunction *or*. As one would expect, the three items in the list are similar grammatical units performing the same function in the sentence:

He would say that it thundered in G
noun clause, object of "would say"

that the wind was whistling in D
noun clause, object of "would say"

that the clock (with a two-note chime) struck in
B minor
noun clause, object of "would say"

By contrast, the sentence beginning "For most of us" is developed by modification. The independent clause is quite simple: "such an ability to recognize exact pitch seems uncanny." Everything else modifies the main clause, or modifies a part of it, or modifies a modifier:

For most of us,
modifies the independent clause

such an ability to recognize exact pitch seems uncanny,
independent clause

almost like another sense,
modifies the independent clause

a sense we can never hope to possess,
modifies "another sense"

such as infrared or X-ray vision.
modifies "a sense we can never hope to possess"

A **modifier** is a structure — a word, a phrase, or a dependent clause — that is added to a sentence at the beginning, where it paves the way for the independent clause, or at the end, where it elaborates on the clause. To examine the effects of modifiers, we'll analyze a few more sentences by Oliver Sacks as well as passages from David Sedaris's story "Genetic Engineering" (p. 246), Theodore Olson's essay "The Conservative Case for Gay Marriage" (p. 227), and Barack Obama's speech, "A More Perfect Union" (p. 199).

Early Modifiers and Paragraph Cohesion

Early modifier is a shorthand way of referring to initial modifiers, which open their sentences, and medial modifiers, which are embedded within the main clause.

In "Genetic Engineering," David Sedaris describes the relationship between an engineer and his children.[1] "The greatest mystery of science," he writes, "continues to be that a man could father six children who shared absolutely none of his interests." In the passages below, Sedaris uses early modifiers to establish the time and circumstances of the action:

> As children, we placed a great deal of faith in his ability but learned to steer clear while he was working. The experience of watching was ruined, time and time again, by an interminable explanation of how things were put together. Faced with an exciting question, science tended to provide the dullest possible answer. . . .

> Once, while rifling through the toolshed, I came across a poster advertising an IBM computer the size of a refrigerator. Sitting at the control board was my dad the engineer, years younger, examining a printout no larger than a grocery receipt. When I asked about it, he explained that he had worked with a team devising a memory chip capable of storing up to fifteen pages' worth of information.

Later in the story, the narrator explains that his father's tiresome explanations of scientific phenomena affected the children's enjoyment of their annual trip to the beach. ("We enjoyed swimming," he writes, "until the mystery of tides was explained in such a way that the ocean seemed nothing more than an enormous saltwater toilet, flushing itself on a sad and predictable basis.") The next sentences begin with early modifiers:

> By the time we reached our teens, we were exhausted. No longer interested in the water, we joined our mother on the beach blanket and dedicated ourselves to the higher art of tanning. Under her guidance,

we learned which lotions to start off with, and what worked best for
various weather conditions and times of day.

"By the time we reached our teens" indicates the time of the action.
The next modifiers make a link from old information to the content
of the coming sentence. "No longer interested in the water" recalls that
dispiriting image of the ocean as "an enormous saltwater toilet" and
prepares us to learn what the children did instead of playing in the
water. "Under her guidance" is also transitional, referring to the mother
mentioned in the previous sentence and setting up the specific lessons
that constituted her instruction in the "higher art of tanning." Sedaris's
early modifiers not only provide useful detail, but they help the reader
move smoothly from one sentence to the next, creating cohesion within
the paragraph.

In texts whose purpose is to explain a point or make an argument,
early modifiers perform similar functions, sometimes establishing time
or circumstance, sometimes marking logical relationships, sometimes
making the structure of the paragraph visible. Because Oliver Sacks
writes about scientific topics for an audience of non-experts, he takes
particular care to guide readers through the material, frequently using
early modifiers to indicate a sentence's role in a longer passage. We've
already seen one example:

> For most of us, such an ability to recognize an exact pitch seems
> uncanny, almost like another sense, a sense we can never hope to
> possess, such as infrared or X-ray vision; but for those who are born
> with absolute pitch, it seems perfectly normal.

The essential relationship between the two independent clauses is indicated by the coordinator *but*: the two sets of people being described
have contrasting experiences. But it's also important to identify the two
sets of people. To accomplish that, Sacks uses an early modifier before each independent clause. Later, as he summarizes the findings of
a study about musicians with absolute pitch, he uses similar modifiers
to signal the movement from one set of research subjects to another:

> "For students who had begun musical training between ages four
> and five," [researcher Diana Deutsch and her colleagues] wrote,
> "approximately 60% of the Chinese students met the criterion for
> absolute pitch, while only about 14% of the US nontone language
> speakers met the criterion." For those who had begun musical training
> at age six or seven, the numbers in both groups were correspondingly
> lower, about 55% and 6%. And for students who had begun musical

training later still, at age eight or nine, "roughly 42% of the Chinese students met the criterion while none of the US nontone language speakers did so."

This paragraph gives readers a lot to keep track of: musicians from two countries (whose salient difference is that they speak Chinese, a tonal language, or English, a nontonal language) with musical training beginning at different ages. The early modifiers, which strategically repeat key words, make the paragraph easy to follow.

| EDITING NOTE: Early modifiers are usually set off by commas.

EXERCISE 5A

Examine the following passage from Theodore Olson's article, "The Conservative Case for Gay Marriage" (reprinted on p. 227).

Sadly, our nation has taken a long time to live up to the promise of equality. In 1857, the Supreme Court held that an African American could not be a citizen. During the ensuing Civil War, Abraham Lincoln eloquently reminded the nation of its founding principle: "our fathers brought forth on this continent, a new nation, conceived in liberty and dedicated to the proposition that all men are created equal."

At the end of the Civil War, to make the elusive promise of equality a reality, the 14th Amendment to the Constitution added the command that "no State shall deprive any person of life, liberty, or property, without due process of law; nor deny to any person the equal protection of the laws."

1. Underline the three early modifiers that make the structure of the passage visible.
2. Write a paragraph that moves forward in three steps, perhaps describing three sets of people as Sacks does in the paragraph about musicians trained at various ages, perhaps progressing chronologically as Olson does. Use early modifiers to signal the movement from one step to the next.

The Crescendo Effect: The Pleasures of the Periodic Sentence

By placing some material — information that's already been established, or stage-setting background information — in early modifiers, writers can delay the independent clause, creating suspense as the sentence climbs toward a dramatic closing. The stylistic principle at play in such a sentence reminds me of the buildup to a sneeze. When the person sitting next to me on the bus says "ahh . . . ahh . . . ahh . . . ," I expect a "kerchoo." I wait for it, leaving my reading or daydreaming on hold until it comes. More elegantly, the effect might be compared to a crescendo, the gradual increase in volume that lends emotional power to musical phrases.

Writers have several ways of creating a crescendo. In a coordinate series, for example, writers often arrange the items in ascending order of importance. These examples come from Theodore Olson's article:

> So there are now three classes of Californians: heterosexual couples who can get married, divorced, and remarried, if they wish; same-sex couples who cannot get married but can live together in domestic partnerships; and same-sex couples who are now married but who, if they divorce, cannot remarry. This is an irrational system, it is discriminatory, and it cannot stand.

> I have no doubt that we are on the right side of this battle, the right side of the law, and the right side of history.

When the crescendo builds through a series of early modifiers leading up to the independent clause, the sentence is called a **periodic sentence**. Watch how Theodore Olson and Barack Obama build periodic sentences:

> If all citizens have a constitutional right to marry, if state laws that withdraw legal protections of gays and lesbians as a class are unconstitutional, and if private, intimate sexual conduct between persons of the same sex is protected by the Constitution, there is very little left on which opponents of same-sex marriage can rely.

> Two hundred and twenty-one years ago, in a hall that still stands across the street, a group of men gathered and, with these simple words, launched America's improbable experiment in democracy.

> When [white Americans] are told to bus their children to a school across town; when they hear that an African American is getting an advantage in landing a good job or a spot in a good college because of an injustice that they themselves never committed; when they're told that their fears about crime in urban neighborhoods are somehow prejudice, resentment builds over time.

For the sake of comparison, read the same sentences with the independent clauses moved to the beginning. The sentences retain their meaning and remain grammatically correct—but listen to what happens:

> There is very little left on which opponents of same-sex marriage can rely if all citizens have a constitutional right to marry, if state laws that withdraw legal protection of gays and lesbians as a class are unconstitutional, and if private, intimate sexual conduct between persons of the same sex is protected by the Constitution.

> A group of men gathered and launched America's improbable experiment in democracy with these words, two hundred and twenty-one years ago, in a hall that still stands across the street.

> Resentment builds over time when [white Americans] are told to bus their children to a school across town; when they hear that an African American is getting an advantage in landing a good job or a spot in a good college because of an injustice that they themselves never committed; when they're told that their fears about crime in urban neighborhoods are somehow prejudice.

In this version, all the drama of the periodic sentences has fizzled.

In short, writers can add punch to a sentence by placing the key point at the end. One way to accomplish that is to begin a sentence with early modifiers.

EXERCISE 5B

Each of the numbered sentences below is a single independent clause. Develop each sentence by adding at least two modifiers before the independent clause, setting up the independent clause so that it has a strong impact.

These sentences do not appear in the model texts, but they make statements about characters in "Genetic Engineering" (p. 246) and ideas in "The Conservative Case for Gay Marriage" (p. 227). If you haven't already done so, read those texts for information to use in developing the sentences.

Example
Gretchen deserves to win the annual Miss Emollient pageant.

Suggested Revisions
Again this year, to the dismay of her sisters and her brother, Gretchen deserves to win the annual Miss Emollient pageant.

Exercise 5B continued

Because she has faithfully followed her mother's advice, seeking just the right balance of oils and lotions, lying outside when the sun was high, and using aluminum foil to reflect the sun's rays to those hard-to-reach spots, Gretchen deserves to win the annual Miss Emollient pageant.

1. The engineer is isolated from his family.
2. The fishermen have sold their homes near the ocean.
3. Many people were surprised by Olson's position on gay marriage.
4. Same-sex marriages promote conservative values.
5. It is time to overturn legislation that limits the right to marry.

EXERCISE 5C

Play with the placement of modifiers. Rewrite the sentences you created in Exercise 5B, placing the modifiers after the independent clause. As you review the sentences or discuss them with classmates, consider these questions: In which cases does the shift make a significant difference in the sentence's meaning, emphasis, or rhythm? Can you think of circumstances when you would strongly prefer one version to the other?

Leaping and Lingering: The Pleasures of the Cumulative Sentence

Oliver Sacks's example of Frederick Ouseley, the professor who enjoyed absolute pitch all his life, is balanced by several examples of people who suffered discomfort from absolute pitch, either when they lost their ability or when it made them acutely aware of ill-tuned instruments:

> The Oxford Companion to Music again gives many examples, including one of an eminent pianist who, playing the Moonlight Sonata (a piece which "every schoolgirl plays"), got through it only "with the greatest difficulty" because the piano was tuned to a pitch he was not accustomed to, and he "experienced the distress of playing the piece in one key and hearing it in another."

This is a good example of a cumulative sentence, a term coined many years ago by the rhetorician Francis Christensen.

A **cumulative sentence** begins with the main clause, then extends the sentence with one or more **end modifiers**. Christensen offers a sentence of his own as both a definition and an example of the cumulative sentence:

> The main clause, which may or may not have a sentence modifier before it, advances the discussion; but the additions move backward, as in this clause, to modify the statement of the main clause or more often to explicate or exemplify it, so that the sentence has a flowing and ebbing movement, advancing to a new position and then pausing to consolidate it, leaping and lingering as the popular ballad does."[2]

Christensen claims that the cumulative sentence is the mainstay of contemporary style because it serves both the writer, pushing him or her toward specificity, and the reader, who can follow the play of the writer's mind as it tests, expands, qualifies, and otherwise modifies ideas.

Oliver Sacks is a master of the cumulative sentence. He illustrates quirks of the human mind by writing extended case studies or, as in "Papa Blows His Nose in G," by telling stories about his patients and correspondents. Readers find the stories engaging because the rich accumulation of details — typically appearing in modifiers — makes us care about the people and feel that we understand their experience. Additionally, Sacks frequently uses modifiers to explain scientific concepts, interjecting the definition of a technical word or restating an idea in more precise or more familiar language.

The sentences below describe the experience of a composer who had but then lost absolute pitch, and the work of scientists who study the phenomenon. I've spread the sentences out on the page to show how the modification is working, using an outlining method adapted from Francis Christensen[3]:

This sense of loss was clearly brought out by one of my patients, Frank V., a composer who suffered brain damage from the rupture of an aneurysm of the anterior communicating artery.

This sense of loss was clearly brought out by one of my patients,
independent clause

    Frank V.,
    modifies "one of my patients"

        a composer who suffered brain damage from the rupture of an aneurysm of the anterior communicating artery.
        modifies "Frank V."

Originally, he perceived pitches instantly, absolutely, as he perceived colors—no "mental process" was involved, no inference, no reference to other pitches or intervals or scales.

> Originally,
> *modifies the independent clause, establishing the time*

he perceived pitches instantly, absolutely,
independent clause

> as he perceived colors—
> *modifies "instantly, absolutely"*

no "mental process" was involved,
independent clause

> no inference,
> *modifies independent clause, specifying a mental process*

>> no reference to other pitches or intervals or scales.
>> *modifies "no inference," describing the kind of inference Frank V. found unnecessary*

The neural coordinates of absolute pitch have been illuminated by comparing the brains of musicians with and without absolute pitch using a refined form of structural brain imaging (MRI morphometry) and by functional imaging of the brain as subjects identify musical tones and intervals.

The neural coordinates of absolute pitch have been illuminated
independent clause

> by comparing the brains of musicians with and without absolute pitch
> *modifies the independent clause, explaining one way the neural coordinates have been illuminated*

>> using a refined form of structural brain imaging
>> *modifies the phrase above, explaining how the brains were compared*

>>> (MRI morphometry)
>>> *modifies the phrase above, identifying the form of imaging*

> and by functional imaging of the brain as subjects identify musical tones and intervals.
> *modifies the independent clause, explaining a second way the neural coordinates have been illuminated*

EXERCISE 5D

Outline these sentences by David Sedaris and Barack Obama. Place the independent clause at the left margin, and indent the other clauses or phrases to show how they relate to the main clause or to each other. Add notes to explain what each modifier is doing.

How many pieces should you break the sentence into? For the purposes of this exercise, let the punctuation be your guide: place each unit set off by commas or dashes on its own line.

Example

During the first week of September, it was my family's habit to rent a beach house on Ocean Isle, a thin strip of land off the coast of North Carolina.

Sample Outline

>During the first week of September,
>*modifies independent clause below, setting the time*

it was my family's habit to rent a beach house on Ocean Isle,
independent clause

>a thin strip of land off the coast of North Carolina.
>*modifies "Ocean Isle"*

1. As youngsters, we participated in all the usual seaside activities—which were fun, until my father got involved and systematically chipped away at our pleasure.
2. We enjoyed swimming, until the mystery of the tides was explained in such a way that the ocean seemed nothing more than an enormous salt-water toilet, flushing itself on a sad and predictable basis.
3. Of course, the answer to the slavery question was already embedded within our Constitution—a Constitution that had at its very core the ideal of equal citizenship under the law; a Constitution that promised its people liberty and justice and a union that could be and should be perfected over time.
4. The man I met more than twenty years ago is a man who helped introduce me to my Christian faith, a man who spoke to me about our obligations to love one another, to care for the sick and lift up the poor.
5. There is one story in particular that I'd like to leave you with today—a story I told when I had the great honor of speaking on Dr. King's birthday at his home church, Ebenezer Baptist, in Atlanta.

Take a moment to read this passage from "Papa Blows His Nose in G." It appears in three versions, first pared down to the independent clauses, then with details added in new sentences, and finally as Sacks actually crafted it, with the details added in modifiers. If you compare the versions, you can see the degree to which Sacks relies on modifiers to communicate the content and to smooth out the rhythm of his sentences.

Pared down to the independent clauses:

Absolute pitch may cause problems too. One such problem occurs with the inconstant tuning of musical instruments. Thus the seven-year-old Mozart said, "Your violin is half a quarter of a tone flatter than mine here." (So it is related in *The Oxford Companion to Music;* there are many tales about Mozart's ear.) The composer Michael Torke instantly remarked that my own ancient piano was a third of a tone flat.

Developed with details in additional independent clauses:

Absolute pitch may sound like a delicious extra sense. It allows one to instantly sing or notate any music at its correct pitch. But it may cause problems too. One such problem occurs with the inconstant tuning of musical instruments. Thus the seven-year-old Mozart compared his own little violin to that of his friend Schactner. He said, "Perhaps you have not altered the tuning of your violin since I last played it. Then it is half a quarter of a tone flatter than mine here." (So it is related in *The Oxford Companion to Music;* there are many tales about Mozart's ear. Some are no doubt apocryphal.) The composer Michael Torke encountered my own ancient piano. It still has its original nineteenth-century strings. It is not tuned up to the 440 cycles per second standard of modern pianos. He instantly remarked that it was a third of a tone flat.

Developed with details in modifiers (as written by Oliver Sacks):

While absolute pitch may sound like a delicious extra sense, allowing one to instantly sing or notate any music at its correct pitch, it may cause problems too. One such problem occurs with the inconstant tuning of musical instruments. Thus the seven-year-old Mozart, comparing his own little violin to that of his friend Schactner, said, "If you have not altered the tuning of your violin since I last played on it, it is half a quarter of a tone flatter than mine here." (So it is related in *The Oxford Companion to Music;* there are many tales about Mozart's ear, some no doubt apocryphal.) When the composer Michael Torke encountered my own ancient piano, which—still having its original nineteenth-century strings—is not tuned up to the 440 cycles per second standard of modern pianos, he instantly remarked that it was a third of a tone flat.

But in the end, the point is not to analyze another writer's sentences. The point is to generate material of your own—to know that, before and after an independent clause, there are spaces where you can elaborate, and when you've elaborated, there are spaces where you can elaborate some more. Christensen called his model *generative* in the hope that it would help writers see the possibilities for pushing sentences toward further levels of specificity, precision, and clarity.

EXERCISE 5E

Think about a place you've visited more than once, perhaps a family vacation spot or a relative's house. Spend a few minutes remembering: think about what the place looked like, the buildings, the landscape, the people you met there, what those people did at work and at play. Then, using David Sedaris's sentences as models, imitating their structure as closely as possible, create well-developed sentences about the place and/or the people.

Example

    During the first week of September,
it was my family's habit to rent a beach house on Ocean Isle,
    a thin strip of land off the coast of North Carolina.

Sample Response

    Every other year in the summertime,
In a modifier, establish the time.

it was my family's habit to bunk up in a condo in the Ozarks,
independent clause

    a resort area surrounding an S-shaped lake in Missouri.

1.   On one of those walks,
  I came across my father
    standing not far from a group of fishermen
      who were untangling knots in a net the size of a circus tent.

Exercise 5E continued

_____

       In a modifier, establish the time.

_____

independent clause

_____

_____

2.   The men drank from quart bottles of Mountain Dew
         as they paused from their work to regard my father,
            who stood at the water's edge,
            staring at the shoreline with a stick in hand.

_____

independent clause

_____

_____

_____

3.   My father answered their questions in detail
    and they listened intently —
         this group of men with nets,
           blowing their smoke into the wind.

_____

independent clause

_____

independent clause

_____

_____

Exercise 5E continued

4.   Stooped and toothless,
    they hung upon his every word
       while I stood in the lazy surf,
          thinking of the upcoming pageant
          and wondering if the light reflecting off the water might tan
          the underside of my nose and chin.

_____

In a modifier, provide a detail about the subject of the main clause.

_____

independent clause

_____

_____

_____

The next three chapters continue the discussion of modification, each treating a particular kind of modifier. Chapter 6 focuses on adjective clauses, Chapter 7 on verbal phrases, and Chapter 8 on my personal favorites, appositives and absolutes.

CHAPTER 5 NOTES

[1] Sedaris writes in the first person, so it's very tempting to write as if the story were a true account of the Sedaris family. In struggling to distinguish between the writer and the narrator, I am inspired by this scene from "The Learning Curve"—another story in *Me Talk Pretty One Day*, one beloved by writing teachers. Sedaris the writer gives us "Mr. Sedaris," the narrator and main character in a story about a writing workshop:

... The way I saw it, if my students were willing to pretend I was a teacher, the least I could do was return the favor and pretend that they were writers. Even if someone had used his real name and recounted, say, a recent appointment with an oral surgeon, I would accept the story as pure fiction, saying, "So tell us, Dean, how did you come up with this person?"

The student might mumble, pointing to the bloodied cotton wad packed against his swollen gum, and I'd ask, "When did you decide that your character should seek treatment for his impacted molar?" This line of questioning allowed the authors to feel creative and protected anyone who held an unpopular political opinion.

"Let me get this straight," one student said. "You're telling me that if I say something out loud, it's me saying it, but if I write the exact same thing on paper, it's somebody else, right?"

"Yes," I said. "And we're calling that fiction."

The student pulled out his notebook, wrote something down, and handed me a sheet of paper that read, "That's the stupidest fucking thing I ever heard in my life." They were a smart bunch.

[2] Francis Christensen, *Notes Toward a New Rhetoric* (New York: Harper & Row, 1967), 6.

[3] The outlines used in this and subsequent chapters are adapted from Francis Christensen's work in "A Generative Rhetoric of the Sentence." The outlines are convenient because they make a sentence's structure visible, showing how each piece relates to the pieces before it. But don't try this at home — at least not unless you're pretty sure you're working with a cumulative sentence. While the technique is illuminating for the sentences Christensen loves best, those with an ebbing and flowing, "leaping and lingering" sequence of modifiers, it is difficult to adapt to sentences organized by any other plan.

CHAPTER 6

Adding Color
with Adjectivals

ONE OF THE MOST STRIKING differences between spoken and written language is the frequency of **adjectivals** — words, phrases, and clauses that modify nouns — in written texts. Listen to these sentences:

> In this essay, Amy Tan writes about her mother's "broken" English.

> In this engaging essay, Amy Tan, who is best known for her novel *The Joy Luck Club*, writes about her mother's "broken" English.

The first sentence sounds like something anyone might say, but the second one is clearly *written*. In everyday conversation, it would strike us as odd and pretentious.

In conversation, we generally interact with people we know, so they share our background knowledge, and we often talk about people and things that are easy to recall, perhaps even present in the room. In those circumstances, detailed description is unnecessary, so most of our nouns stand bare. In writing, when we can't be sure of what our readers know or what mental images they might be forming, we seek specificity by adding modifiers before or after noun phrases.

When asked to develop their sentences — to make them more specific, more vivid — many writers think immediately about adding adjectives. "My grandmother had a cat" grows into "My 85-year-old grandmother had a sleek, black cat," and "The Chevrolet sat in the parking lot" becomes "The dented, rusty, blue Chevrolet sat in the dark, windswept parking lot." This sort of addition comes easily to any adult writer. However, there's a limit to the number of adjectives you can pack in before a noun, and they don't do much for a sentence's rhythm. Modifiers that follow the noun represent an important extension of the writer's range of options.

This chapter examines adjective clauses and adjective phrases in two texts about immigrants' confrontation with English, Amy Tan's "Mother Tongue" (p. 252) and Lily Wong Fillmore's "Loss of Family Languages" (p. 259). Additional sample sentences are drawn from Oliver Sacks's essay, "Papa Blows His Nose in G" (p. 236).

The Structure of Adjective Clauses

An **adjective clause**, as you might imagine, is a clause — that is, a group of words containing a subject-verb pair — that functions adjectivally, supplying information about a noun. Adjective clauses, sometimes called relative clauses, are usually introduced by **relative pronouns** — *who, whom, whose, which, that* — and occasionally by *where* or *when.*

In the sentences below, the adjective clauses are underlined, and an arrow points to the noun being modified:

> The talk was going along well enough, until I remembered one major
>
> difference that made the whole talk sound wrong. My mother was in
> the room.

> I'll quote what my mother said during a recent conversation which I
> videotaped and then transcribed.

> My mother was talking about a political gangster in Shanghai who had
> the same last name as her family's, Du, and how the gangster in his
>
> early years wanted to be adopted by her family, which was rich by
> comparison.

> My mother told us about a wedding in Shanghai, where she grew up.

Writers frequently omit the relative pronoun, as in this sentence:

Just last week, I was walking down the street with my mother, and I

again found myself conscious of the English I was using.

You can recognize "I was using" as a clause by the presence of a subject-verb pair and as an adjective clause by its function, modifying the noun "English." While the clause could have begun with a relative pronoun — "the English that I was using" — the pronoun is not essential.

The best way to understand the structure of an adjective clause is to think of it as a sentence that has been embedded after a significant noun. So you could write two separate sentences: "*The Joy Luck Club* was written by Amy Tan. She lives in San Francisco." Or you could transform the second sentence into an adjective clause: "*The Joy Luck Club* was written by Amy Tan, who lives in San Francisco." The transformation is effected by changing the pronoun *she* to the relative pronoun *who.*

The following examples illustrate similar transformations:

Amy Tan has written several novels. They explore mother-daughter relationships.

Amy Tan has written several novels that explore mother-daughter relationships.

Amy Tan has written several novels. Critics praise them.

Amy Tan has written several novels that critics praise.

The hospital staff ignored Mrs. Tan. She was deeply worried about her CAT scan results.

The hospital staff ignored Mrs. Tan, who was deeply worried about her CAT scan results.

The hospital staff ignored Mrs. Tan. Her English was imperfect.

The hospital staff ignored Mrs. Tan, whose English was imperfect.

The hospital staff ignored Mrs. Tan. They found her difficult to understand.

The hospital staff ignored Mrs. Tan, whom they found difficult to understand.

EDITING NOTE: *Whose* can refer to people or things; it substitutes for *his, her, their,* or *its.*

EXERCISE 6A

The following passages, from Amy Tan's "Mother Tongue" (p. 252), contain a total of twelve adjective clauses. Underline each adjective clause and draw an arrow to the noun being modified. The first two have been done for you.

Fortunately, for reasons I won't get into here, I later decided I should

envision a reader for the stories I would write. And the reader I decided on was my mother, because these were stories about mothers. So with this reader in mind—and in fact she did read my early drafts—I began to write stories using all the Englishes I grew up with: the English I spoke to my mother, which for lack of a better term might be described as "simple"; the English she used with me, which for lack of a better term might be described as "broken"; my translation of her Chinese, which could certainly be described as "watered down." . . .

Why are there few Asian Americans enrolled in creative writing programs? Why do so many Chinese students go into engineering? Well, these are broad sociological questions I can't begin to answer. But I have noticed in surveys—in fact, just last week—that Asian American students, as a whole, do significantly better on math achievement tests than on English tests. And this makes me think that there are other Asian American students whose English spoken in the home might also be described as "broken" or "limited." And perhaps they also have teachers who are steering them away from writing and into math and science. . . .

EXERCISE 6B

The following sentences are based on the selection "Papa Blows His Nose in G" by Oliver Sacks (p. 236). In each set, transform the indented sentences into adjective clauses that modify the noun phrase in boldface. (If this exercise takes you more than five minutes to complete, you're over-thinking it. Just change the underlined word to *who, whom, whose, which, that, when,* or *where.*)

Example
Michael Torke noticed the pitch of **my ancient piano**.

I̲t̲ is not tuned up to the modern standard.

I̲t̲s̲ strings are more than a century old.

Exercise 6B continued

Sample Responses

Michael Torke noticed the pitch of my ancient piano, <u>which</u> is not tuned up to the modern standard.

Michael Torke noticed the pitch of my ancient piano, <u>whose</u> strings are more than a century old.

Sacks describes the neurologist **Steven Frucht**.

1. <u>He</u> is sometimes unable to hear intervals or harmonies because he is so conscious of the individual notes.
2. Sacks considers <u>him</u> a close friend.
3. <u>His</u> absolute pitch is both a blessing and a curse.

Sacks now lives in **New York City**.

4. <u>It</u> is an ideal home for a music lover.
5. Every week, you can hear live performances of jazz, rock, or classical music <u>there</u>.

Absolute pitch was found to be more common among **Chinese students**.

6. Diana Deutsch compared <u>them</u> to English-speaking American students.
7. <u>They</u> began studying music at an early age.
8. <u>Their</u> tonal language seems to attune their ears to pitch.

I like to imagine **an idyllic island in the Pacific**.

9. <u>It</u> is populated by an ancient tribe similar to the Neanderthals.
10. All of the people <u>there</u> have absolute pitch.

Choices in Crafting Adjective Clauses

While adjective clauses are quite common and easy to create, they can present some puzzles to writers and editors. Three questions are frequently asked about adjective clauses.

Who or Whom?

The *who/whom* distinction is rarely observed in speech or informal writing. However, the distinction hasn't disappeared entirely. Here's the rule: When the relative pronoun is a subject, replacing a word like *he, she,* or *they,* choose *who.* When the relative pronoun is an object, replacing a word like *him, her,* or *them,* choose *whom.*

These sentences illustrate the rule:

Grandmother worried about Kai-fong. He had become more proficient in English than in Cantonese.

Grandmother worried about Kai-fong, who had become more proficient in English than in Cantonese.

Grandmother worried about Kai-fong. She no longer understood him.

Grandmother worried about Kai-fong, whom she no longer understood.

Kai-fong became estranged from his parents. They worked long hours.

Kai-fong became estranged from his parents, who worked long hours.

Kai-fong became estranged from his parents. He rarely saw them.

Kai-fong became estranged from his parents, whom he rarely saw.

In speech, most of us would choose *who* every time, violating the rule in the second and fourth sentences. When writing, then, we have to choose whether to comply with the rule or to follow the everyday practice of speakers. Choices like this are governed by the formality of the context. My own practice is this: in academic papers, I always follow the rule. In any other genre, I make a judgment call, weighing the danger of sounding incorrect against the danger of sounding stuffy.

If the relative pronoun follows a preposition, you'll use *whom*, and you won't face any question about it because *who* would sound truly peculiar. (For example, you'd write "boys with whom he played" rather than "boys with who he played.") If you place the preposition at the end of the sentence — which, by the way, you have every right to do when you please — then the range of choices expands. Arranged from most to least formal, the options are these:

He had a small group of friends, other immigrant boys with whom he played soccer.

He had a small group of friends, other immigrant boys whom he played soccer with.

He had a small group of friends, other immigrant boys who he played soccer with.

Most writers prefer *who* or *whom* to *that* when referring to people. But if *who* sounds like an error and *whom* sounds overly formal, *that* offers yet another option, and sometimes it's possible to omit the relative pronoun altogether:

> He had a small group of friends, other immigrant boys that he played soccer with.

> He had a small group of friends, other immigrant boys he played soccer with.

With or without Commas?

Adjective clauses come in two varieties: restrictive and nonrestrictive. If an adjective clause is essential to the meaning of a noun — if it makes it possible for the reader to pick out the person or thing, of all people and things in the world, that the noun is intended to name — then it's **restrictive**. (The terminology actually makes some sense: a restrictive adjective clause restricts the possible reference of the noun to one object.) If an adjective clause simply supplies extra information about the noun, then it's **nonrestrictive**.

In speech, we signal whether an adjective clause is restrictive or nonrestrictive by means of intonation, and in writing we signal with punctuation. Nonrestrictive adjective clauses and other nonrestrictive modifiers are set apart, usually by commas but sometimes by dashes or parentheses.

Read these sentences aloud:

> The professor who developed UC Berkeley's seminar in "First and Second Language Acquisition" retired in 2004.

> Lily Wong Fillmore, who developed UC Berkeley's seminar in "First and Second Language Acquisition," retired in 2004.

In the first sentence, the adjective clause is restrictive; it limits the reference of "professor" to the single professor who is under discussion, the one who developed the seminar in language acquisition. In the second sentence, the adjective clause is nonrestrictive. It's already clear which professor is under discussion — there's only one Lily Wong Fillmore — so the adjective clause simply provides additional information.

The use of punctuation can determine how a reader understands an adjective clause. Consider these sentences:

> The three Chen children who succeeded in school did so because they learned English quickly.
>
> The three Chen children, who succeeded in school, did so because they learned English quickly.

Because the first sentence, in the absence of punctuation, presents the adjective clause as restrictive, we understand that it identifies particular children from a larger group. The sentence implies that there are more than three Chen children; it makes a statement about just those three who succeeded in school. By contrast, the adjective clause in the second sentence is set off by commas, so we read it as nonrestrictive. We understand that there are three Chen children, and the statement is about all of them.

Notice that the presence of punctuation has the same effect with other modifiers. In the sentences below, the modifier is a prepositional phrase:

> My nieces from Hong Kong had trouble adjusting to American foods.
>
> My nieces, from Hong Kong, had trouble adjusting to American foods.

In the first sentence, the prepositional phrase is punctuated as a restrictive modifier, so it limits the meaning of "my nieces" to a subset: those who came from Hong Kong. The second sentence, with a nonrestrictive modifier, makes its assertion about all of my nieces.

While the punctuation mark usually used to set off a nonrestrictive modifier is the comma, writers do have other options. A modifier set off by a dash is highlighted, while one enclosed in parentheses is pushed into the background. Compare:

> Fluency in English — which, in the United States, identifies speakers as "Americanized" — can have profound psychological, social, and economic effects.
>
> Fluency in English (which, in the United States, identifies speakers as "Americanized") can have profound psychological, social, and economic effects.

Which or *That*—or Not?

Like the *who/whom* choice, the *which/that* choice is governed by a rule that writers usually follow but occasionally ignore. If I were foolhardy enough to predict the future evolution of the language, I would put my money on the *which/that* distinction lasting longer than the *who/whom* distinction because the rule is generally observed in speech as well as in writing. Specifically, the rule calls for *that* in restrictive adjective clauses and *which* in nonrestrictive adjective clauses:

> The song sounds correct to him only in the key that he originally heard it in.

> The song sounds correct to him only in the key of C-sharp minor, which he originally heard it in.

Like the *who/whom* choice, the *which/that* choice becomes easy if the relative pronoun follows a preposition. In that case, whether the clause is restrictive or nonrestrictive, you will use *which*—and you won't have to stop to think about it because *that* would sound unacceptable.

> The song sounds correct to him only in the key in which he originally heard it.

> The song sounds correct to him only in the key of C-sharp minor, in which he originally heard it.

In many adjective clauses, it's also possible to omit the relative pronoun altogether. Read these sentences aloud:

> For most of us, such an ability to recognize an exact pitch seems uncanny, almost like another sense, a sense which we can never hope to possess, such as infrared or X-ray vision.

> For most of us, such an ability to recognize an exact pitch seems uncanny, almost like another sense, a sense that we can never hope to possess, such as infrared or X-ray vision.

> For most of us, such an ability to recognize an exact pitch seems uncanny, almost like another sense, a sense we can never hope to possess, such as infrared or X-ray vision.

I'd be happy to have written any one of these sentences. In fact, Oliver Sacks wrote the third version, omitting the pronoun. The choice has no impact on the sentence's significance, but it has a subtle effect on the pace: *which* tends to slow a sentence down and create a more formal tone; the omission of a relative pronoun tends to speed a sentence up and set a conversational tone; and *that* occupies the middle ground.

EXERCISE 6C

Practice distinguishing between restrictive and nonrestrictive clauses by choosing the appropriate relative pronoun (*which* or *that*) to begin each underlined clause. If the clause is nonrestrictive, use *which*—and be sure to set off the clause with commas. If the clause is restrictive, use *that*.

You will probably find this exercise easier if you begin by trusting your ear. Which sounds better to you, *which* or *that?* Then test your understanding by explaining whether the clause is nonrestrictive or restrictive.

Examples

Languages _____ use unfamiliar sounds are especially difficult to learn.

English _____ has more words in its vocabulary than any other language is especially difficult to learn.

Suggested Responses

Languages that use unfamiliar sounds are especially difficult to learn.
The adjective clause is restrictive; it identifies the particular "languages" that the sentence is about.

English, which has more words in its vocabulary than any other language, is especially difficult to learn.
The adjective clause is nonrestrictive; it provides relevant information about "English" but does not define or restrict the meaning of the word.

1. Attitudes toward language are powerful forces shaping how people see and deal with one another, especially in states _____ have a heavy concentration of recent immigrants.

2. Attitudes toward language are powerful forces shaping how people see and deal with one another, especially in California _____ has a heavy concentration of recent immigrants.

3. A school _____ establishes programs to demonstrate respect for multilingualism and multiculturalism can strengthen children's family ties.

4. Wong Fillmore cites *Hunger of Memory* _____ tells the story of Richard Rodriguez's acculturation to illustrate the tensions in a Spanish-speaking immigrant family.

5. In Spanish, Mr. Rodriguez expressed ideas and feelings _____ he rarely revealed in English.

6. Wong Fillmore calls attention to the social and political forces _____ militate against the retention of minority languages.

Exercise 6C continued

7. Wong Fillmore is critical of Proposition 63 _____ banned the use of languages other than English in public life.

8. Compare Wong Fillmore's article to Amy Tan's "Mother Tongue" _____ addresses the experience of a bilingual family in a personal, reflective spirit.

Reducing Adjective Clauses

Adjective clauses are by no means the only structure that can appear after a noun to modify it. In fact, editors striving for conciseness often reduce adjective clauses, removing the subject and/or the verb to create other kinds of modifiers. Look, for example, at this pair:

> In this engaging essay, Amy Tan, who is best known for her novel *The Joy Luck Club*, writes about her mother's "broken" English.

> In this engaging essay, Amy Tan, best known for her novel *The Joy Luck Club*, writes about her mother's "broken" English.

Whether you want to reduce the clause will depend on the rhythm of the surrounding language and your judgment about the smoothness and clarity of the sentence. In general, I reduce adjective clauses if the subject-verb pair seems entirely superfluous (as is often the case for *who is, who are, which is, which are, that is, that are*); if I hear a string of adjective clauses; or if a profusion of *that*'s becomes distracting.

The sentences below, adapted from "Papa Blows His Nose in G," include adjective clauses that could be reduced. (Reducing them restores Sacks's original sentences.)

> It is this ability which Frank V. lost with the frontal lobe damage ~~which was~~ caused by the rupture of his cerebral aneurysm.

> He might be so conscious of the C-ness of the C and the F-sharpness of the F-sharp that he fails to notice that they form a tritone, ~~which is~~ a dissonance which makes most people wince.

> This sense of loss was clearly brought out by one of my patients, Frank V., ~~who is~~ a composer who suffered brain damage from the rupture of an aneurysm of the anterior communicating artery.

> So it is related in *The Oxford Companion to Music*; there are many tales about Mozart's ear, some ~~of which are~~ no doubt apocryphal.

Reducing adjective clauses produces other kinds of modifiers. In the first sentence above, the reduction creates a verbal phrase headed by the verbal *caused*. In the second and third sentences, the reduction creates noun phrases headed by the nouns *dissonance* and *composer*. In the fourth sentence, the modifier is an absolute. We'll return to these structures in the next two chapters.

EXERCISE 6D

The sentences below contain a lot of adjective clauses—too many, in my opinion. Reduce some (not all!) of the clauses to phrases. Then, compare your sentences to the originals as they were written by Oliver Sacks, Amy Tan, and Lily Wong Fillmore.

Examples
Language loss is the result of both internal and external forces that are operating on children. The internal factors have to do with the desire for social inclusion; the external forces are the sociopolitical ones that are operating in the society against outsiders, against differences, against diversity. (*See Wong Fillmore, para. 33.*)

Sample Response
Language loss is the result of both internal and external forces ~~that are~~ operating on children. The internal forces have to do with the desire for social inclusion; the external forces are the sociopolitical ones ~~that are~~ operating in the society against outsiders, against differences, against diversity.

1. Gordon B, who was a professional violinist who wrote to me about tinnitus, or ringing in his ears, remarked matter-of-factly that his tinnitus was "a high F-natural." (*See Sacks, para. 1.*)

2. They observed that there was a critical period for the development of absolute pitch, which is before the age of eight or so—which is roughly the age at which children find it much more difficult to learn the phonemes of another language. (*See Sacks, para. 17.*)

3. In musicians with absolute pitch (but not musicians without) there was an exaggerated asymmetry between the volumes of the right and left planum temporal, which are structures in the brain that are important for the perception of speech and music. (*See Sacks, para. 18.*)

4. I was giving a speech that was filled with carefully wrought grammatical phrases, that was burdened, it suddenly seemed to me, with nominalized

forms, past perfect tenses, conditional phrases, all the forms of standard English that I had learned in school and through books, which were the forms of English I did not use at home with my mother. (*See Tan, para. 3.*)

5. I do think that the language that is spoken in the family, especially in immigrant families which are more insular, plays a large role in shaping the language of the child. (*See Tan, para. 15.*)

6. I never did well . . . with word analogies, which were pairs of words in which you were supposed to find some sort of logical, semantic relationship. (*See Tan, para. 17.*)

7. Lately I've been asked, as a writer, why there are not more Asian Americans who are represented in American literature. Why are there few Asian Americans who are enrolled in creative writing programs? (*See Tan, para. 18.*)

8. The Chens arrived in the U.S. in 1989: Mother, Father, Uncle (Father's brother), Grandmother (Father's mother), and the children, who were Kai-Fong, who was age five at the time of arrival (now sixteen), and Chu-Mei, who was age four (now fifteen). Once settled, the family quickly added two more children—the "ABC" ("American born Chinese") members of the Chen family, both of whom are girls, Chu-Wa (who is now ten) and Allison (who is now nine years old). (*See Wong Fillmore, para. 6.*)

Adjective Phrases

An adjective or cluster of adjectives that stands outside the noun phrase is called an **adjective phrase**.

My grandmother's cat, <u>sleek and black</u>, peers at the world through narrow yellow eyes.

<u>Sleek and black</u>, my grandmother's cat peers at the world through narrow yellow eyes.

Oliver Sacks's description of absolute pitch, <u>appreciative and even envious</u>, is clearly the work of a musician.

<u>Appreciative and even envious</u>, Oliver Sacks's description of absolute pitch is clearly the work of a musician.

When an adjective is simple — like *sleek* or *black* — it can reside happily either within the noun phrase or outside it:

My grandmother's <u>sleek</u>, <u>black</u> cat . . .
The adjectives are embedded in a noun phrase.

My grandmother's cat, <u>sleek and black</u> . . .
An adjective phrase follows the noun phrase.

<u>Sleek and black</u>, my grandmother's cat . . .
An adjective phrase precedes the noun phrase.

For a long string of adjectives, or for a description that can't be expressed simply, the adjective phrase is likely to be more graceful. Compare:

Oliver Sacks's <u>medically significant</u>, <u>carefully crafted</u>, and <u>accessible to a wide audience</u> case studies have made him America's most distinguished science writer.
The adjectives are embedded in the noun phrase — and the sentence is almost unreadable.

Oliver Sacks's case studies, <u>medically significant, carefully crafted, and accessible to a wide audience</u>, have made him American's most distinguished science writer.
An adjective phrase follows the noun phrase.

<u>Medically significant, carefully crafted, and accessible to a wide audience</u>, Oliver Sacks's case studies have made him America's most distinguished science writer.
An adjective phrase precedes the noun phrase.

EXERCISE 6E

Modify the noun phrase in boldface with several adjectives. First, place the adjectives within the noun phrase, immediately before the noun. Then craft an adjective phrase and experiment with its location in the sentence.

Example
My parents asked me to translate the doctor's questions.

Sample Responses
My <u>exhausted</u>, <u>frustrated</u>, <u>embarrassed</u> parents asked me to translate the doctor's questions.
adjectives before the noun

My parents, <u>exhausted, frustrated, and embarrassed</u>, asked me to translate the doctor's questions.
adjective phrase after the noun phrase

<u>Exhausted, frustrated, and embarrassed</u>, my parents asked me to translate the doctor's questions.
adjective phrase before the noun phrase

1. **The nurse** could not locate the CAT scan.
2. **My mother** asked me to call her stockbroker.
3. **The stockbroker's office** was in a brick building on Wall Street.
4. **The streets of Chinatown** still feel like home to me.
5. **The fog** hovers over the Golden Gate Bridge.

CHAPTER 7

Adding Action with Verbal Phrases

WATCH HOW HENRY LOUIS GATES JR. manages the action in this episode from his memoir ("Sin Boldly," p. 190). The scene is the Swordfish, a nightclub where students from Potomac State enjoy dancing to a live band on weekend nights. The year is 1969; the Swordfish does not admit African Americans. The Fearsome Foursome — Gates and three of his friends — decide that it's time to integrate the club.

> We parked the car and strolled up the stairs to the Swordfish. Since there was no cover charge, we walked straight into the middle of the dance floor. That's when the slo-mo started, an effect exacerbated by the strobe lights. Everybody froze: the kids from Piedmont and Keyser who had grown up with us; the students from Potomac State; the rednecks and crackers from up the hollers, the ones who came to town once a week all dressed up in their Sears, Roebuck perma-pressed drawers, their Thom McAn semi-leather shoes, their ultimately *white* sox, and their hair slicked back and wet-looking. The kids of rednecks, who liked to drink gallons of 3.2 beer, threaten everybody within earshot, and puke all over themselves—they froze, too, their worst nightmare staring them in the face.
>
> After what seemed like hours but was probably less than a minute, a homely white boy with extra-greasy blond hair recovered and began to shout "Niggers" as his face assumed the ugly mask of hillbilly racism.

I stared at this white boy's face, which turned redder and redder as *he* turned into the Devil, calling on his boys to kick our asses: calling us niggers and niggers and niggers to help them summon up their courage. White boys started moving around us, forming a circle around ours. Our good friends from Keyser and Potomac State were still frozen, embarrassed that we were *in* there, that we had violated their space, dared to cross the line. No help from them. (I lost lots of friends that night.) Then, breaking through the circle of rednecks, came the owner, who started screaming: Get out of here! Get out of here! And picked up Fisher and slammed his head against the wall.

There is much to be said about this passage, especially about its telling picture of race relations in the 1960s. But for now, I'd like to call your attention to the pacing—specifically, to the way Gates stops the action in the first paragraph, as "everybody froze," then starts it up in the second paragraph as the club's patrons begin to circle around the foursome.

Here are three key sentences from the first paragraph again, outlined so that you can see the clauses and modifiers:

That's when the slo-mo started,

an **effect** exacerbated by the strobe lights.

Everybody froze:

the **kids** from Piedmont and Keyser who had grown up with us;

the **students** from Potomac State;

the **rednecks and crackers** from up the hollers,

the **ones** who came to town once a week all dressed up in their Sears, Roebuck perma-pressed drawers, their Thom McAn semi-leather shoes, their ultimately *white* sox, and their hair slicked back and wet-looking.

The **kids** of rednecks,

who liked to drink gallons of 3.2 beer, threaten everybody within earshot, and puke all over themselves —

they froze too,

their worst **nightmare** staring them in the face.

Beginning with the first sentence above, when time slips off its track, Gates relies on noun phrases as modifiers. The sentences present us with a series of still shots, one picture after another, first this group of people, then the next group.

It's in the next paragraph that the action begins. Notice the modifiers here:

> I stared at this white boy's face,
>> which turned redder and redder
>>> as *he* turned into the Devil,
>>>> **calling** on his boys to kick our asses:
>>>> **calling** us niggers and niggers and niggers to help them summon up their courage.
>
> White boys started moving around us,
>> **forming** a circle around ours.
>
> Then,
>> **breaking** through the circle of rednecks,
>
> came the owner,
>> who started screaming: Get out of here! Get out of here!

In this paragraph, many of the modifiers are **verbal phrases** headed by the *-ing* form of verbs. Gates could have described these actions in clauses of their own (for example, "As the white boys started moving around us, they formed a circle around ours" or "Then came the owner, who broke through the circle of rednecks"), but by presenting them in phrases, he creates a dense cluster of simultaneous actions. To me, the paragraph feels tense, almost dizzying, as violence threatens and finally erupts.

Functions of Verbal Phrases

The headword of a verbal phrase is a **verbal**, a word derived from a verb but performing some other function — behaving like a noun, an adjective, or an adverb. Verbals come in three varieties: the present participle (*-ing*), past participle (*-ed* or irregular form), and infinitive (*to*) forms:

attending college

enrolled in the university; **hidden** from view

to earn a college degree

Verbals with these forms can be used in many ways—some so common and easy that you could write them in your sleep, others worthy of some attention and practice.

Among the common, easy uses of verbals are these:

SUBJECT

Attending Potomac State College was a big step for the young Gates.

At one time, to earn a college degree was to secure a ticket to professional, middle-class employment.

OBJECT OF A VERB

Gates loved studying literature with Professor Duke Whitmore.

Professor Whitmore wanted to reward Gates for his audacity.

OBJECT OF A PREPOSITION

During the break, students will have lots of time for playing Frisbee.

COMPLEMENT

At one time, to earn a college degree was to secure a ticket to professional, middle-class employment.

ONE-WORD ADJECTIVES

Most students prefer to take challenging classes.

Only enrolled students with stamped identification cards are permitted to use the university library.

For the remainder of this chapter, we'll be concentrating on verbal phrases like those in Gates's second paragraph—more complex phrases that function as modifiers, attached to but not grammatically integrated into a clause.

Phrases beginning with an *-ing* verbal usually describe an action, often one occurring simultaneously with the action described by the attached clause.

We dragged Fisher to the car, ducking the bottles and cans as we sped away.

Back home, we had sneaked around at first, hiding in cemeteries and in a crowd of friends, almost never being seen together in public alone.

"Sin boldly," he would tell me later, citing Martin Luther.

Phrases beginning with an *-ed* verbal usually function as adjectives.

> Our good friends from Keyser and Potomac State were still frozen, <u>embarrassed that we were *in* there</u>.

> And that is why the Swordfish nightclub is now Samson's Family Restaurant, <u>run by a very nice Filipino family</u>.

> I stayed out of Keyser on the day of the election, <u>terrified that I'd already caused Maura's father to lose</u>.

Verbal phrases in the *to* form describe a purpose; they may begin with *to, just to,* or *in order to.*

> I searched the audience for Miss Twigg's face, <u>just to see her expression when I read the speech!</u>

> I would attend [Potomac State] too, then go off to "the university"—in Morgantown—<u>to become a doctor</u>.

> I started parking my car on red lines and in front of fire hydrants, <u>just to test her assertion</u>.

Verbal phrases can appear early in the sentence as well. Any of these variations would sound perfectly natural:

> <u>Citing Martin Luther</u>, he told me to "sin boldly."

> <u>Terrified that I'd already caused Maura's father to lose</u>, I stayed out of Keyser.

> <u>Just to test her assertion</u>, I started parking my car on red lines and in front of fire hydrants.

EXERCISE 7A

Read the passages below, adapted from "Sin Boldly." Underline the verbal phrases used as modifiers. I count seven: five with an *-ing* verbal, one with an *-ed* verbal, and one with a *to* verbal.

> On weekends during the summer of 1969, I'd drive over to Rehoboth Beach, in Delaware, to see Maura, who was working as a waitress at the Crab Pot. I'd leave work on Friday at about four o'clock, then drive all the way to Delaware, arriving at Rehoboth before midnight, with as much energy as if I had just awakened. We'd get a motel room after her shift ended, and she'd bring a bushel of crabs, steamed in hot spice. We'd

Exercise 7A continued

get lots of ice-cold Budweiser and we'd have a feast, listening to Junior Walker play "What Does It Take" over and over and over again.

It was because of 'Bama's new office that I learned that the West Virginia State Police had opened a file on me in Mineral County, identifying me for possible custodial detention if and when race riots started. Maura gave me the news late one night, whispering it over the phone. Old 'Bama, feeling magnanimous after his victory, had wanted me to know and to be warned.

EXERCISE 7B

Combine the sentences in each group by transforming the sentences in bold-face into –*ing* verbal phrases. When you've completed the exercise, compare your sentences to the originals by David Sedaris ("Genetic Engineering," p. 246) and Tim O'Brien ("On the Rainy River," p. 211.)

Example
I'd heard once that if a single bird were to transport all the sand, grain by grain, from the eastern seaboard to the coast of Africa, it would take . . . I didn't catch the number of years. **I preferred to concentrate on the single bird chosen to perform this thankless task.** (*See Sedaris, para. 10.*)

I'd heard once that if a single bird were to transport all the sand, grain by grain, from the eastern seaboard to the coast of Africa, it would take . . . I didn't catch the number of years, preferring to concentrate on the single bird chosen to perform this thankless task.

1. I tried to creep by unnoticed, but he stopped me. **He claimed that I was just the fellow he'd been looking for.** (*See Sedaris, para. 9.*)
2. "Let me ask a little something," one of the men said. **He spat his spent cigarette butt into the surf.** (*See Sedaris, para. 13.*)
3. He moved several yards down the beach and began a new equation. **He captivated his audience with a lengthy explanation of each new and complex symbol.** (*See Sedaris, para. 15.*)
4. For more than twenty years I've had to live with it. **I felt the shame. I tried to push it away.** (*See O'Brien, para. 1.*)

Exercise 7B continued

5. Nothing radical, no hothead stuff. **I just rang a few doorbells for Gene McCarthy. I composed a few tedious, uninspired editorials for the campus newspaper.** (*See O'Brien, para. 3.*)

6. In the evenings I'd sometimes borrow my father's car and drive aimlessly around town. **I felt sorry for myself. I thought about the war and the pig factory and how my life seemed to be collapsing toward slaughter.** (*See O'Brien, para. 8.*)

EXERCISE 7C

Write sentences using each of the three kinds of verbal phrases based on the verbs *force, write,* and *earn.* Remember, you're not being asked to use the given verb in the independent clause; instead, create verbal phrases as in the example.

Example

Discover

-ing: Discovering that the nightclub owner is stubborn, the human rights commissioner threatens to shut down the club.

-ed: Her manuscript, discovered beneath the floorboards of the college library, is now being auctioned on eBay.

to: The main character had to travel across Nigeria to discover the truth her family had hidden from her for so many years.

Force

-ing:

ed:

to:

Write

-ing:

-en:

to:

Earn

-ing:

-ed:

to:

Managing Emphasis with Verbal Phrases

Verbal phrases, like other modifiers, create an opportunity for writers to manipulate emphasis. Compare these sentences:

> I gave the valedictory address at graduation, defying convention by writing my own speech.

> Giving the valedictory address at graduation, I defied convention by writing my own speech.

In the first sentence, the main point is that Gates gave the valedictory address. The sentence informs us that he was defying convention, but because that information appears in a modifier, we read it as an elaboration. In the second sentence, the defiance of convention has earned a promotion. When it occupies the independent clause, we read Gates's claim to have defied convention as the main point.

The order of information affects emphasis, too. As a general rule, you can highlight material by placing it at the end of the sentence.

> Just to see her expression when I read the speech, I searched the audience for Miss Twigg's face.

> I searched the audience for Miss Twigg's face, just to see her expression when I read the speech.

In both sentences, "just to see her expression" is a modifier, and in the first one it is, as you would expect, de-emphasized, setting the stage for the independent clause about looking for Miss Twigg. But in the second sentence, the emphasis is reversed simply because the modifier comes at the end. Verbal phrases, like other modifiers, tend to be read as background information in periodic sentences and to get more attention in cumulative sentences.

Because there are so many ways to emphasize one element in a sentence — using strong language or a striking image, rephrasing or repeating, adjusting sentence length, playing with punctuation — no single principle can predict which part of a sentence will be stressed. Still, these are useful generalizations: you can stress material by placing it in an independent clause (reducing other material to modifiers like verbal phrases) or by placing it at the end of the sentence.

Notice how Tim O'Brien controls the emphasis in this sentence from "On the Rainy River." The sentence describes a key moment in the story; in a boat, close enough to the Canadian shoreline to swim for it, the narrator suddenly realizes that he does not have the courage to do what he believes to be right.

> Bobbing there on the Rainy River, looking back at the Minnesota shore, I felt a sudden swell of helplessness come over me, a drowning sensation, as if I had toppled overboard and was being swept away by the silver waves.

The significant action here is internal: the narrator must abandon his self-image as "a man of conscience and courage" to acknowledge that he cannot resist the expectations of others. This transformation is expressed in a series of images that reach their dramatic height in the main clause. The first verbal phrase establishes the theme: "bobbing" on the river, the narrator is at the mercy of the waves. In the main clause, he is overcome by a "sudden swell" of helplessness — an image that encapsulates the point of the passage and, it could be argued, of the whole story. The end modifiers sustain the dramatic pitch, reinforcing the theme of helplessness with images of drowning.

EXERCISE 7D

Combine the material into a single sentence, using one sentence as the independent clause and transforming the others to -ing verbal phrases. Then, try a different combination, placing different material in the independent clause. (Feel free to switch the order of the information, too.)

Example
Maura and I sneaked around.

Maura and I hid in cemeteries and in a crowd of friends.

Maura and I were almost never seen together in public alone.

Sample Responses
Maura and I sneaked around, hiding in cemeteries and in a crowd of friends, almost never being seen together in public alone.

Sneaking around, hiding in cemeteries and in a crowd of friends, Maura and I were almost never seen together in public alone.

1. Her father had hidden behind a tree.
   Her father had watched her climb into my car.
2. The police followed us around town.
   The police dared us to go even one mile over the speed limit.

Exercise 7D continued

3. Eugene would make up words as he went along.
   Eugene used sounds similar to those he could not remember.
   Eugene made no sense.

4. We spruced up the Soul Mobile for the occasion.
   We replaced the old masking tape over the holes in the roof.

5. Maura's father had lived in Keyser all his life.
   Maura's father worked for the post office.
   Maura's father visited with just about everyone in town.

EXERCISE 7E

In general, material in a sentence is stressed when it appears in a clause rather than a phrase or when it appears at the end of a sentence. Like other generalizations about emphasis, these have limited application; they can inform a writer's judgment but cannot substitute for it.

Look closely at each pair of sentences that you created in Exercise 7D. When you place first one idea into a verbal phrase and then the other, what happens? Does the emphasis shift? Which sentence sounds better to your ear? What other factors affect the emphasis?

On the whole, do your sentences confirm the generalizations or complicate them? Be prepared to explain your impressions to classmates.

Reducing Clauses to Create Verbal Phrases

Back in Chapter 6, you reduced adjective clauses to phrases by eliminating the subject and/or the verb. In some sentences, the reduction changed an adjective clause to a verbal phrase—so that, for example, "the language *that is spoken in the family*" became "the language *spoken in the family*." Similarly, "sociopolitical forces *that operate in the society*" became "sociopolitical forces *operating in the society*."

Adverb clauses can sometimes be reduced to verbal phrases as well:

When he prepared for Duke Whitmore's class, Gates discovered the pleasures of literary scholarship.

Preparing for Duke Whitmore's class, Gates discovered the pleasures of literary scholarship.

After he finished his undergraduate degree, Gates studied English and American literature in Cambridge.

After finishing his undergraduate degree, Gates studied English and American literature in Cambridge.

In the first pair, the subordinator *when* disappears, while in the second pair, the subordinator *after* is retained. In both cases, the subject is eliminated and the verb changes to an *-ing* verbal.

As you edit your prose, you may sometimes decide that, for the sake of conciseness, clarity, rhythm, or emphasis, you wish to reduce a subordinate clause to a verbal phrase.

EXERCISE 7F

The passages below are adapted from Drew Gilpin Faust's "We Should Grow Too Fond of It" (p. 175) and Tim O'Brien's "On the Rainy River" (p. 211). After reading each passage, reduce the underlined clause to a verbal phrase. (Remember that, even when restricted to verbal phrases, you have several options: *-ing*, *-ed*, and *to*.) What do you think? Does the revised passage strike you as more or less effective than the original?

Example
Scholars saw in Civil War history the possibility of reaching across this divide not only because they wanted to sell books but also because they wished to add important considerations to wider American public discourse.

Scholars saw in Civil War history the possibility of reaching across this divide not only ~~because they wanted~~ to sell books but also ~~because they wished~~ to add important considerations to wider American public discourse.

1. Lee's remark, which was uttered in the very midst of battle's horror and chaos, may be his most quoted—and misquoted—statement.

2. If Maris Vinovskis worried in 1989 that social historians had lost the Civil War, they had by the end of the next decade certainly found it, as they connected home and battle fronts and as they situated the Civil War battlefield decisively in the larger context of nineteenth-century American life.

3. When we are caught in war's allure, we ignore its destructiveness—not just of others but of ourselves. . . . Are we as historians part of the problem or part of the solution? If we are attracted by the potential narrative coherence of war, we also create and reinforce it.

Exercise 7F continued

4. When I drove up Main Street, past the courthouse and the Ben Franklin store, I sometimes felt the fear that was spreading inside me like weeds.

5. When I look back after twenty years, I sometimes wonder if the events of that summer didn't happen in some other dimension, a place where your life exists before you've lived it, and where it goes afterward. None of it ever seemed real. During my time at the Tip Top Lodge I had the feeling that I'd slipped out of my own skin, that I hovered a few feet away while some poor yo-yo with my name and face tried to make his way toward a future he didn't understand and didn't want.

6. I went through whole days when I felt dizzy with sorrow. I couldn't sleep; I couldn't lie still. At night I'd toss around in bed, half awake, half dreaming, as I imagined how I'd sneak down to the beach and quietly push one of the old man's boats out into the river.

Editing Dangling Modifiers

There is probably no grammar term that evokes such apprehension, or such ridicule, as **dangling modifier**. When you imagine Miss Grundy — that stereotype of fussy English teachers, with stiff posture, pursed lips, and an obsession for grammatical purity — what is she doing? She's smacking a ruler on the desk of a red-faced child, and she's exclaiming "Dangling Modifier!" The other children feel sorry for the mortified young writer, but they can't help snickering as they think about how to deploy the word *dangling* during recess.

Because modifiers are separate from the essential structure of the clause, they can be more or less firmly attached to the clause. If a modifier is not attached carefully — if there's some ambiguity about what it modifies — it is said to dangle. Since verbal phrases are especially prone to dangling, it's worth taking time during proofreading to double-check verbal phrases, making sure they're firmly tethered.

The sentence below illustrates a dangling modifier:

Reading *The Things They Carried*, the alienation of Vietnam veterans was easier to understand.

Who read *The Things They Carried?* Alienation? That can't be what the writer meant to say. To edit the sentence, insert a noun (or pronoun) that identifies the reader immediately after the verbal phrase, or change the verbal phrase to a different sort of structure—for example, an adverb clause. Because an adverb clause has its own subject-verb pair, there can be no confusion about who's doing what.

Reading *The Things They Carried*, I began to understand the alienation of Vietnam veterans.
edited by inserting the appropriate noun (here, a pronoun) right after the verbal phrase

After I read *The Things They Carried*, the alienation of Vietnam veterans was easier to understand.
edited by changing the verbal phrase to a clause

Writers, editors, grammarians, and other lovers of language sometimes disagree about whether a dangling modifier really causes ambiguity, whether it really requires editing. A hard-liner might object to the sentence below:

When learning a new language, it may be necessary to risk social embarrassment in order to interact with native speakers.

Who is learning a new language? It? That doesn't make much sense. And yet . . . any reader would understand this sentence easily enough, and there might be good reason to avoid using words such as *you* or *language learners* in the independent clause. Choices about editing dangling modifiers, like so many other choices writers and editors make, require not just attention to structure but good judgment.

EXERCISE 7G

In each of the sentences below (loosely based on the story "Genetic Engineering"), the verbal phrase is a dangling modifier. Revise the sentence, either by inserting an appropriate noun or pronoun right after the verbal phrase or by changing the verbal phrase to a clause.

Example
To test my complex theories of suspended animation, a colony of slugs was placed in the basement freezer.

Edited (option 1)
To test my complex theories of suspended animation, I placed a colony of slugs in the basement freezer.

Exercise 7G continued

Edited (option 2)
Because I wanted to test my complex theories of suspended animation, a colony of slugs was placed in the basement freezer.

1. Soon after repairing my record player, the rubber band snapped and the damned thing broke all over again.
2. Choosing between their mother's interest in tanning and their father's interest in science, it was no problem for the Sedaris kids.
3. After visiting my father's office, there was comfort in knowing he had some colleagues who shared his interests.
4. Once completed, the young scientist wished he could redesign his experiment.
5. Having sold their homes on the beach, the engineer's comments about the value of sand were interesting to the fishermen.
6. After selling their homes to retirees from out of state, the property value went up.

Punctuation also affects a reader's understanding of verbal phrases. Any verbal phrase set off by a comma, whether it appears at the beginning or the end of a clause, will be understood to modify the clause's subject:

Using a magnifying glass, I studied an old photograph of my father.

I studied an old photograph of my father, using a magnifying glass.

I studied an old photograph of my father using a magnifying glass.

Who was using the magnifying glass? Readers will understand the first two sentences to mean same thing — that the narrator used a magnifying glass to study a photograph. In the last sentence, the absence of the comma makes a big difference. Now, the narrator studies an image in which his father has a magnifying glass in hand.

Rather than close this chapter with warnings about errors or advice about punctuation, I'd like to return to the main point. Verbal phrases are a versatile syntactic structure, often underused in the work of undergraduate writers but common in published prose. I urge you to experiment with them in your writing.

EXERCISE 7H

Write sentences whose structure imitates the models by Tim O'Brien.

Example

On two or three afternoons, to pass some time, I helped Elroy get the place ready for winter, sweeping down the cabins and hauling in the boats, little chores that kept my body moving.

Sample Response

On the day before Christmas,
phrase establishing the time

to make a contribution I could afford,
"to" verbal phrase

I baked cinnamon rolls,
independent clause

preparing them from scratch and presenting them fresh from the oven,
"-ing" verbal phrases joined by and

a gift to the whole family.
noun phrase

To remove the stuff, I used a kind of water gun. The trick was to maneuver the gun with your whole body, not lifting with the arms, just letting the rubber cord do the work for you.

1. Describe a complex action, something you do well:

_____
"to" verbal phrase

_____
independent clause

The trick _____
independent clause

_____
"-ing" verbal phrase

_____
"-ing" verbal phrase

Bending down, he opened up his tackle box and busied himself with a bobber and a piece of wire leader, humming to himself, his eyes down.

2. Describe a person engaged in an everyday activity.

_____
"-ing" verbal phrase

_____
Independent clause

_____
"-ing" verbal phrase

_____
another modifier describing the person

I remember packing a suitcase and carrying it out to the kitchen, standing very still for a few minutes, looking carefully at the familiar objects all around me.

3. Recall a significant moment; describe your actions at the time, creating a somber, reflective mood.

I remember _____
independent clause

_____
"-ing" verbal phrase

_____
"-ing" verbal phrase

4. Recall a significant moment; describe your actions at the time, creating a joyful mood.

I remember _____
independent clause

_____
"-ing" verbal phrase

_____
"-ing" verbal phrase

Layering Meaning with Appositives and Absolutes

WHAT'S NOT TO LOVE about apposition? Appositives are easy to write, extremely versatile, and risk-free — you rarely see a dangling, misplaced, or otherwise misguided appositive. To the wise writer, appositives are staples, the salt and pepper of modification.

This chapter discusses three kinds of modifiers that belong in every writer's repertoire: noun phrases in apposition, other structures in apposition, and absolute phrases.

Noun Phrases in Apposition

An **appositive** is a noun phrase that appears in a sentence next to another noun phrase referring to the same person or thing. In everyday speech, appositives sometimes appear in introductions, as in "This is my brother-in-law, *Jerry Allen*" or "I'd like you to meet Jerry Allen, *my brother-in-law from Texas*." The two noun phrases "Jerry Allen" and "my brother-in-law from Texas" have the same **referent** — that is, they refer to the same person — but there is informational value in naming the person both ways. Similarly, an appositive might be placed next to other proper nouns (Thomas Edison Elementary, *my children's school*) or, perhaps, used to explain a term (a spiral, *the long glide that Michelle Kwan does so beautifully*).

Like verbal phrases, appositives can be thought of as supplements—extra information added to the clause—or as reductions of separate sentences. Compare the sentences below:

I'd like you to meet Jerry Allen.

I'd like you to meet Jerry Allen. He is my brother-in-law from Texas.

I'd like you to meet Jerry Allen, who is my brother-in-law from Texas.

I'd like you to meet **Jerry Allen,** my brother-in-law from Texas.

In the final sentence, the appositive "my brother-in-law from Texas" serves as a modifier, restating the initial noun phrase, "Jerry Allen." The use of an appositive makes the final sentence more informative than the first, more concise than the second or third.

In published writing, appositives are quite common. They perform several functions, illustrated below with sentences from Drew Gilpin Faust's "We Should Grow Too Fond of It" (p. 175), Oliver Sacks's essay "Papa Blows His Nose in G" (p. 236), and Louise Erdrich's short story "Shamengwa" (p. 159).

Identifying People

Appositives are often paired with proper nouns, providing identifying information so that readers will understand the significance of a name. Normally the name comes first, then the identification—but, as you see in some of the examples below, the order can be reversed:

Judah P. Benjamin, attorney general of the new Confederacy, reassured a New Orleans crowd in the winter of 1861 that war was far from an "unmixed evil."

Sir Frederick Ouseley, a former professor of music at Oxford, for example, "was all his life remarkable for his sense of absolute pitch."

This sense of loss was brought out by **one of my patients,** Frank V., a composer who suffered brain damage from the rupture of an aneurysm of the anterior communicating artery.

Every few weeks, he had [his hair] carefully trimmed and styled by **his daughter,** Geraldine, who traveled in from the bush just to do it.

Defining Terms

A neurologist who writes about his research for a popular audience, Oliver Sacks often uses technical vocabulary. He frequently provides definitions of medical terms in appositives:

Gordon B, a professional violinist who wrote to me about **tinnitus,** or ringing in his ears, remarked matter-of-factly that his tinnitus was "a high F-natural."

The definition of "tinnitus" is helpful to a non-expert reader, and because it appears in an appositive, it doesn't slow the pace of the sentence. The addition of "or" makes it sound almost conversational.

A colleague recently told me that he likes to read Sacks's essays because they make him feel smart. Sacks's use of language signals his assumptions about his readers: he seems to imagine that we are intelligent, well educated, interested in the quirks of the human mind, prepared to understand a neurologist's insights. If he paused to provide extensive definitions, Sacks would highlight the difference between his own background knowledge and that of his readers; if he didn't define technical terms at all, he would leave us in the dark. By means of apposition, Sacks slips the definitions in unobtrusively:

A 1995 paper by Gottfried Schlaug and his colleagues showed that in musicians with absolute pitch (but not musicians without), there was an exaggerated asymmetry between the volumes of **the right and left planum temporal,** structures in the brain that are important for the perception of speech and music.

The neural correlates of absolute pitch have been illuminated by comparing the brains of musicians with and without absolute pitch using **a refined form of structural brain imaging** (MRI morphometry).

Sacks assumes a reader who knows (or who will look up) words like "asymmetry" and "correlates." But no reader without a background in science could be expected to know "planum temporal" or "MRI morphometry" — so Sacks sets the terms side by side with their definitions. In academic writing, appositives often perform this function.

Filling in Examples

Appositives can also pin down the meaning of a word or phrase by providing a concise series of examples.

The pitch is bundled in with **other attributes of the note**—its timbre (very importantly), its loudness, and so on.

Deutsch et al. have also showed very dramatic difference in the incidence of absolute pitch in **two populations of first-year music students:** one at the Eastman School of Music in Rochester, New York, and the other at the Central Conservatory of Music in Beijing.

Historians' work in uncovering and documenting the lives of **groups once labeled "inarticulate"**—workers, slaves, women—had embodied a fundamental commitment to giving these new subjects of historical inquiry both voice and agency.

In each case, the clause contains a term that begs to be unpacked— what other attributes? what two populations? what groups?—and the appositive supplies the specifics.

Occasionally an appositive listing specifics will begin the sentence. In the sentence below, the list is, conceptually, the subject of the sentence. But long noun phrases make awkward sentence subjects. By presenting the list in an appositive, then using a simple pronoun as the grammatical subject, Erdrich makes the sentence easy to process:

Her strong arms, her kisses, the clean soap smell of her face, her voice calming me—all of this was gone.

Compare: Her strong arms, her kisses, the clean soap smell of her face, and her voice calming me were gone.

Renaming with a Twist

Perhaps the most important use of appositives in writing is to rename a person or thing, or to restate an idea, in words that get the reader to see it in a new light. The title of Drew Gilpin Faust's article about Civil War scholarship comes from a remark by Robert E. Lee. If war were not so terrible, he said, "we should grow too fond of it." In her opening paragraph, Faust reflects on the observation and on the man who made it:

> **Lee,** the romantic hero of his own time and the marble man of ages that followed, displays here **a complexity,** an ambivalence, a capacity for irony that suggests cracks in the marble.

The appositive after "Lee" does not identify him — that is hardly necessary for an audience of historians. Instead, it presents an idealized, one-dimensional characterization of Lee, a characterization called into question by his remark about the seductiveness of war. The other appositives are, from a grammatical point of view, intriguing. "A complexity, an ambivalence, a capacity for irony" — is that simply a series? But no, Lee doesn't display three qualities; he displays one, which Faust chooses to name three ways. The first noun phrase, "a complexity," names the quality, and the appositives offer additional shades of meaning.

In the examples below, the appositives work in a similar way, restating the ideas so that we look at them from a slightly different angle:

> Fought in April 1862, Shiloh marked **a new departure in warfare,** a level of death and destruction previously unknown and unimagined.

> **More than 60,000 volumes** of Civil War history had appeared by the end of the twentieth century, more than a book a day since Appomattox.

> And the accumulation of **these many narratives,** these thousands and thousands of deaths into the Civil War's massive death toll, have given the conflict, as James McPherson has written, **a "horrifying but hypnotic fascination,"** a fascination I would suggest is almost pornographic in its combination of thrill and terror.

EXERCISE 8A

1. Underline six appositives in the paragraph below.

"Shamengwa," a short story by Louise Erdrich, is narrated by a tribal judge, a character whose name we never learn but whose voice we immediately trust. The narrator offers a loving description of Shamengwa, an elder in the village who is known for his talent playing the violin. When Shamengwa's violin is stolen, suspicion falls on Corwin Peace, a young man with a record of criminal activity. Corwin is caught in Spirit Lake, a neighboring town, where he is entertaining the crowd at the mall by pretending to play the violin. The judge sentences him to violin

Exercise 8A continued

lessons. As the months go by, Shamengwa and Corwin, the master and the apprentice, learn to understand each other.

2. Think of a novel, film, or television program in which the characters are particularly well drawn. Write a paragraph describing the characters, providing an initial identification of each in an appositive. Include at least six appositives; check to be sure that each is a noun phrase set beside another noun phrase with the same referent.

EXERCISE 8B

Combine the sentences in each group by creating appositives. Leave the first sentence as is, and transform what follows into one or more appositives. When you've completed the exercise, compare your sentences to the originals.

Example
For most of us, such an ability to recognize exact pitch seems uncanny, almost like another sense. It is like a sense we can never hope to possess, such as infrared or X-ray vision. (*See Sacks, para. 3.*)

Sample Response
For most of us, such an ability to recognize exact pitch seems uncanny, almost like another sense, a sense we can never hope to possess, such as infrared or X-ray vision.

1. He might be so conscious of the C-ness of the C and the F-sharpness of the F-sharp that he fails to notice that they form a tritone. A tritone is a dissonance which makes most people wince. (*See Sacks, para. 9.*)

2. Previously every note and every key had had a distinctive flavor for him. Each note had had a character uniquely its own. (*See Sacks, para. 11.*)

3. He even won awards. He won prizes of the cheap sort given at local musical contests. They were engraved plaques and small tin cups set on plastic pedestals. (*See Erdrich, para. 4.*)

4. My true friend was my fiddle, anyway. It was the only friend I really needed. (*See Erdrich, para. 28.*)

5. His was a peaceful death. It was the sort of death we used to pray to Saint Joseph to give us all. (*See Erdrich, para. 48.*)

Exercise 8B continued

6. The war serves as a moment of truth. It serves as a moment when individuals have to define their deeply held priorities and act on them. (*See Faust, para. 20.*)

7. Writers and historians are critical to defining and elaborating the narratives that differentiate war from purposeless violence. They define the stories that explain, contextualize, construct, order, and rationalize what we call war. (*See Faust, para. 28.*)

8. A considerable proportion of the scholars who began to direct their attention to the Civil War were children of the Vietnam era. These scholars were individuals struck by the changed political atmosphere of the 1980s. They were individuals who had lived through a period when war was at the heart of American public life and discourse in the late 1960s and 1970s. They were individuals who wanted to understand the historic roots of America's relationship with war as they now witnessed its late-century return to respectability. (*See Faust, para. 17.*)

EXERCISE 8C

Add an appositive after the noun phrase in boldface.

Example
Corwin learned to play the violin.

Sample Responses
Corwin, a troubled young man who had been searching for beauty and purpose in his life, learned to play the violin.

Corwin, a lifelong troublemaker and thief, learned to play the violin.

As you develop sentences 1–3, create a positive image of your piano lessons.

1. I'll never forget the day I met **my piano teacher.**
2. She gave lessons in **her living room.**
3. She had **a large, grey cat.**

As you develop sentences 4–6, create a negative image of your piano lessons.

4. I'll never forget the day I met **my piano teacher.**
5. She gave lessons in **her living room.**
6. She had **a large, grey cat.**

You have probably noticed that writers punctuate appositives with a variety of marks. Commas are the default punctuation. But, especially if the appositive is long and complex, containing commas of its own, it's helpful to set it off with more emphatic punctuation such as a colon or dash.

In fiction, you'll sometimes even see appositives punctuated with periods. Here's one of my favorite passages from "Shamengwa":

> The music was more than music—at least, more than what we are used to hearing. The sound connected instantly with **something deep and joyous.** Those powerful moments of true knowledge which we paper over with daily life. The music tapped **our terrors,** too. Things we'd lived through and wanted never to repeat. Shredded imaginings, unadmitted longings, fear, and also surprising pleasures. We can't live at that pitch. But every so often, something shatters like ice, and we fall into the river of our own existence. We are aware. This realization was in the music somehow, or in the way Shamengwa played it.

Other Structures in Apposition

Though the term *appositive* is usually reserved for noun phrases, many structures can be placed in apposition—that is, placed alongside a clause or phrase of the same type, with the same referent. Then the second clause or phrase will be read as a modifier, restating or elaborating on the first.

The sentences below illustrate structures that are frequently placed in apposition.

Dependent Clauses

> Yet the war intrigues us **not simply because we identify with its central issues,** not just because it seems curiously modern.

> Faust suggests **that the idea of war helps us make sense of chaotic events,** that the familiar narrative of attack and defense enables us to come to terms with violence.

> **When the nation is at war,** when we understand that the stakes are high, Americans can be persuaded to make sacrifices—even the sacrifice of our sons and daughters.

Sacks explains **that perfect pitch is more likely under certain conditions,** that it appears with greater frequency among those who speak tonal languages and those who receive musical training from an early age.

When I was four, my older sister discovered **that I had perfect pitch,** that I could instantly identify any note across the keyboard without looking.

Verb Phrases

When I was four, my older sister discovered that I **had perfect pitch**— could instantly identify any note across the keyboard without looking.

The war, he suggests, **has in fact made us,** has set the agenda for the world we now inhabit.

As though her heart, too, were buried underneath that small white headstone in the Catholic cemetery, she **turned cold,** turned away from the rest of us.

Now that I am old and know the ways of grief, I understand that she **felt too much,** loved too much.

I might have **stayed that way,** joined my mother in the darkness from which she could not return.

Prepositional Phrases

The Civil War, **with its decisive events in the realms both of battle and of national policy,** with its clearly defined moments of truth, offered unparalleled opportunities to explore, document, and highlight these examples of human agency.

Through its implicit and explicit conventions, through its rules, war limits and structures its violence; it imbues violence with a justification, a trajectory, and a purpose.

He simply ends his book with calls **for love,** for Eros in the face of Thanatos.

But always, no matter how hesitantly, it ended up advancing **straight toward the southern rock,** straight toward me.

I do my best to make the small decisions well, and I try not to hunger **for the greater things,** for the deeper explanations.

If you examine all of the sentences in this section carefully, you'll see that the structures placed in apposition fit into the same grammatical slot in the sentence. For example, you could choose either of Erdrich's verb phrases to complete the sentence below:

| I might have | stayed that way. |
| I might have | joined my mother in the darkness from which she could not return. |

Typically, structures in apposition are arranged so that the most general statement of the idea comes first, with the modifier adding specific detail. Look at the example below:

> People with absolute pitch must be able not only to perceive precise pitch differences, but **to label them,** to line them up with the notes or names of a musical scale.

The more general "to label them" naturally precedes the more specific "to line them up with the notes or names of a musical scale."

When the phrases are about equally specific, you can play with the order:

> *DeBow's Review* anticipated from war "**a sublime and awful beauty—** a fearful and terrible loveliness—that atones in deeds of high enterprise and acts of heroic valor for the carnage, the desolation, the slaughter."

> *DeBow's Review* anticipated from war "**a fearful and terrible loveliness**—a sublime and awful beauty—that atones in deeds of high enterprise and acts of heroic valor for the carnage, the desolation, the slaughter."

I'd like to stress two points: Apposition is easy. And it gives writers access to a wide range of choices for developing sentences with information, ideas, and images.

EXERCISE 8D

If you haven't already done so, read Louise Erdrich's short story "Shamengwa" (p. 159). Then develop each of the following sentences by adding at least one phrase in apposition to the phrase in boldface. The new phrase should echo the first one in structure and meaning; it should contain virtually the same content, reworded so that the reader sees it in a new light. Take

Exercise 8D continued

your time with this exercise, writing sentences consistent with the meaning and the mood of Erdrich's story.

Examples

Shamengwa's music was **extraordinary.**

Shamengwa's music could make listeners aware **of joys and grief that lay buried in their hearts.**

People's emotions often turn on them.

Sample Responses

Shamengwa's music was extraordinary, hauntingly beautiful.

Shamengwa's music could make listeners aware of joys and grief that lay buried in their hearts, of hidden hopes and secret fears, of memories they had tried to lock away.

People's emotions, their fears and resentments, even their love, often turn on them.

1. Shamengwa's arm was injured in **a childhood accident.**
2. Corwin drove a 1991 Impala **with all the signs of old age and hard use.**
3. The narrator is surprised to discover **how deeply he misses Shamengwa's music.**
4. At Geraldine's urging, Shamengwa tells the story of **how his fiddle came to him.**
5. After the death of her youngest child, Shamengwa's mother **fell into a state of numb despair.**
6. Corwin's sentence was **to study with Shamengwa.**
7. Shamengwa was **proud of Corwin.**
8. **When the moon slipped behind the clouds,** Billy applied pitch to Edwin's canoe.

Absolute Phrases

Especially in descriptive passages, writers sometimes use a modifier called an **absolute phrase.** Like an appositive, an absolute is headed by a noun, but instead of renaming the referent of another noun phrase, it introduces a new referent. While an absolute phrase may be most strongly linked to a particular word or phrase, it is usually understood to modify the sentence as a whole.

It was the middle of September on the reservation, the mornings chill, the afternoons warm, the leaves still green and thick in their final sweetness.

Corwin stood gazing at the coffin, the violin dangling from one hand.

Fickle gnomes control the weather, and an air conditioner is powered by a team of squirrels, their cheeks packed with ice cubes.

Gretchen's method of tanning involved baby oil and a series of poses that tended to draw crowds, the mothers shielding their children's eyes with sand-covered fingers.

The modifiers in these sentences are absolute phrases. If you study their structure, you will notice that each is headed by a noun ("mornings," "afternoons," "leaves," "violin," "cheeks," "mothers"). And each is *almost* a sentence on its own; although there is no subject-verb pair, it is easy to think of the absolutes as transformations of complete sentences.

In some cases, absolutes represent sentences that have been reduced to phrases by deletion of the verb *to be:*

It was the middle of September on the reservation. The mornings were chill. The afternoons were warm. The leaves were still green and thick in thier final sweetness.

It was the middle of September on the reservation, the mornings chill, the afternoons warm, the leaves still green and thick in their final sweetness.

Fickle gnomes control the weather, and an air conditioner is powered by a team of squirrels. Their cheeks are packed with ice cubes.

Fickle gnomes control the weather, and an air conditioner is powered by a team of squirrels, their cheeks packed with ice cubes.

Sometimes, absolute phrases retain the verb in its *-ing* form:

Corwin stood gazing at the coffin. The violin dangled from one hand.

Corwin stood gazing at the coffin, the violin dangling from one hand.

Gretchen's method of tanning involved baby oil and a series of poses that tended to draw crowds. The mothers shielded their children's eyes with sand-covered fingers.

Gretchen's method of tanning involved baby oil and a series of poses that tended to draw crowds, the mothers shielding their children's eyes with sand-covered fingers.

The linguist Martha Kolln[1] points out that absolutes can also be seen as alternatives to prepositional phrases headed by *with*:

> Corwin stood gazing at the coffin, <u>with</u> the violin dangling from one hand.

> Corwin stood gazing at the coffin, the violin dangling from one hand.

You'll often see absolutes in series, probably because the series permits a writer to break an image down into parts, zooming in for a close-up of one part, then another. For example, in several sentences in "Shamengwa," Erdrich uses absolute phrases in physical descriptions of people, calling our attention to arms and legs, right hand and left hand, shoulders and hands:

> So when Geraldine came to trim her father's hair one morning and found him on the floor, <u>his good hand bound behind his back,</u> <u>his ankles tied</u>, she was not surprised to see the lock of the cupboard smashed and the violin gone.

> She spent most of her time at the church, <u>her ivory-and-silver rosary draped over her right fist,</u> <u>her left hand wearing the beads smoother, smaller,</u> until I thought one day for sure they would disappear between her fingers.

> Corwin had been sitting in the back and now he walked up to the front, <u>his shoulders hunched,</u> <u>hands shoved in his pockets</u>.

EXERCISE 8E

Combine the sentences below by creating absolute phrases. Leave the first sentence as it is, and reduce the others to absolutes by eliminating a *to be* verb or by changing the verb to its *-ing* form.

Example
He was asleep. His violin was next to the bed. The covers were pulled to his chin.

Sample Response
He was asleep, his violin next to the bed, the covers pulled to his chin.

1. Shamengwa was disheveled. His shirt was buttoned wrong. His face was unshaven. His breath was sour.
2. He told his story in a measured voice. His hands rested in his lap. His listeners leaned forward to hear.

Exercise 8E continued

3. Shamengwa sat by the lake in silence. Flies buzzed around his face. The wind boomed in his ears. The sun slowly dropped toward the horizon.

4. There are many tales about Mozart's ear. Some are no doubt apocryphal.

5. To those with absolute pitch, every tone, every key seems qualitatively different. Each possesses its own character.

6. He had always had absolute pitch. His ear immediately discerned the frequency of musical notes and even everyday sounds.

7. Moral leaders expected the Civil War to improve the nation's character. Preachers referred to war's "chastening rod." Secular observers welcomed a new spirit of discipline and self-sacrifice.

8. Civilians visited the battlefields at Antietam and Gettysburg. Men, women, and even children looked on as soldiers carried off the wounded and buried the dead.

EXERCISE 8F

Develop each sentence by adding at least two absolute phrases. Visualize an image, then render it for your reader, part by part.

Example
She was all decked out for the prom.

Sample Response
She was all decked out for the prom, her body sheathed in a silky, floor-length gown, hair pulled into an elegant chignon, feet adorned in fashionable sandals, a glittery little purse hanging from her shoulder.

1. I was prepared for my new job.

2. The vampire entered the bedroom.

3. The cottage appeared to be uninhabited.

4. The waiter brought us a hamburger. (*Make the hamburger sound tempting.*)

5. The waiter brought us a hamburger. (*Make the hamburger sound unappetizing.*)

CHAPTER 8 NOTE

[1]Martha Kolln, *Understanding English Grammar* (New York: Macmillan Publishing Company, 1990).

CHAPTER 9

Special Effects

Expectations and Exceptions

LINGUISTS AND EDUCATIONAL researchers have studied how the mind processes language. They have observed the order in which syntactic structures are acquired (which structures children master first, which ones take longer) and the speed with which children and adults comprehend sentences. The insights of these researchers can explain why some texts strike us as reader-friendly while others require a hard slog.

Readers want sentences to be easy to process; they want subjects and verbs to behave like subjects and verbs, sentences to be clear and complete, paragraphs to flow smoothly. These are reasonable expectations, and writers comply with them because we wish to be understood and, perhaps, to give pleasure.

But occasionally, we don't give readers quite what they expect. Occasionally, we can communicate what we mean more powerfully or more beautifully if we take readers by surprise. This chapter describes readers' expectations primarily in order to recommend that you meet them — stopping along the way to point out some examples of special effects achieved by breaking with convention.

Focus on the Subject

If you've read Chapter 3, you know all about focus. Writers create well-focused sentences by placing actors — often, human actors — in the subject position of sentences. Well-focused sentences are easy for English speakers to process because they follow the familiar SVO (subject-verb-object) pattern. A well-focused sentence strikes readers as clear and easy to read precisely because it gives them what they expect, what they intuitively accept as the norm.

The sentences below are simple, straightforward examples of the subject-verb-object order, with the actor and action appearing right up front in the subject-verb positions:

Elroy fixed breakfast for me.

I took my suitcase out to the car.

Now, consider another option. In a passive-voice construction, the actor is removed from the subject position:

ACTIVE VOICE	PASSIVE VOICE
Elroy fixed breakfast for me.	Breakfast was fixed for me by Elroy.
I took my suitcase out to the car.	My suitcase was taken out to the car by me.

Why might a writer use the passive voice? Writers sometimes make this choice for the sake of paragraph continuity; for example, imagine a paragraph about the three meals:

Breakfast was fixed for me by Elroy. Lunch was Mary Lou's responsibility, and dinner was prepared by Jonathan.

And writers sometimes choose the passive voice in order to create that *by* phrase at the end, giving the actor even more stress than he or she would get in the subject position:

My suitcase was taken out to the car by me! (Where in hell was the bellhop?)

A structure called the *it*-cleft provides yet another option for manipulating emphasis.

ACTOR-ACTION WORD ORDER	*IT*-CLEFT
Elroy fixed breakfast for me.	It was Elroy who fixed breakfast for me.
I took my suitcase out to the car.	It was I who took my suitcase out to the car.

The *it*-cleft highlights the noun phrase immediately following the subject (*it*) and the verb (a form of *be*). The sentences above stress that "it was Elroy" and nobody else who fixed my breakfast; "it was I" and nobody else who carried the suitcase.

Placing a different noun phrase after the subject and verb shifts the stress:

ACTOR-ACTION WORD ORDER	*IT*-CLEFT
Elroy fixed breakfast for me.	It was breakfast that Elroy fixed for me.
I took my suitcase out to the car.	It was my suitcase that I took out to the car.

In this iteration, the first sentence tells us that "it was breakfast" and no other meal that Elroy fixed, the second that "it was my suitcase" and nothing else (or my suitcase and nobody else's) that I took to the car.

A similar effect can be achieved with the *what*-cleft.

ACTOR-ACTION WORD ORDER	*WHAT*-CLEFT
Elroy fixed breakfast for me.	What Elroy fixed for me was breakfast.
I took my suitcase out to the car.	What I took out to the car was my suitcase.

The *what*-cleft structure stresses a noun phrase—"breakfast," "my suitcase"—by pushing it to the end of the sentence.

The clauses I've been playing with are taken from Tim O'Brien's story "On the Rainy River" where, in fact, he placed the actor in the subject position. If you read the surrounding sentences, you'll see that this is a sober, quiet moment in the story:

> I don't remember saying goodbye. The last night we had dinner together, and I went to bed early, and in the morning Elroy fixed breakfast for me. . . .
>
> At some point later in the morning, it's possible that we shook hands—I just don't remember—but I do know that by the time I'd finished packing the old man had disappeared. Around noon, when I took my suitcase out to the car, I noticed that his old black pickup truck was no longer parked in front of the house. . . . I washed up the breakfast dishes, left his two hundred dollars on the kitchen counter, and drove south toward home.

At this point, O'Brien writes the lean, clear prose that most of us strive for on most occasions.

By contrast, let's look at some special occasions. Here is the first sentence of "On the Rainy River":

> This is one story I've never told before.

O'Brien opens his story with a sentence that, like the *it*-cleft and *what*-cleft, violates our expectations for word order. If the sentence began with the actor as subject, it would read "I've never told this story before." To my mind, O'Brien's version is more effective because it stresses the story rather than the storyteller; it promises that this story to which I'm about to commit my time is something special. This effect is heightened in the sentences that follow:

> This is one story I've never told before. Not to anyone. Not to my parents, not to my brother or sister, not even to my wife.

The story is a long-held secret — and he's telling it to me! "This is one story" . . . this is some story. I'm hooked.

Louise Erdrich's story "Shamengwa" also opens with a sentence that alters the SVO pattern. The word order is inverted, the verb appearing before the subject:

> At the edge of our reservation settlement there lived an old man whose arm was twisted up winglike along his side, and who was for that reason named for a butterfly — Shamengwa.

If Erdrich had begun her sentence with the actor as subject, it would read:

> An old man whose arm was twisted up winglike along his side, and who was for that reason named for a butterfly—Shamengwa—lived at the edge of our reservation settlement.

That will never do. The noun phrase, modified as it is by two adjective clauses, is just too long to occupy the subject position; the reader has to wait too long to reach the verb. How about this one:

> An old man lived at the edge of our reservation settlement. His arm was twisted up winglike along his side, and he was for that reason named for a butterfly—Shamengwa.

Better, I think, but still not as effective as Erdrich's sentence. With "there lived an old man," she evokes a familiar storytelling convention ("once upon a time, there lived a beautiful princess"), drawing us into her fictional world.

The point is this. The injunction to name the actor and action early in a sentence, in the subject-verb position, is a reliable guideline, and writers comply with it most of the time. "Except," as Dr. Seuss might say, "when they don't. Because, sometimes, they won't."

EXERCISE 9A

Practice the *it*-cleft and *what*-cleft constructions by revising these sentences. Use the unconventional word order to stress the phrase in boldface.

Example
it-cleft

My mother lost a baby boy to diphtheria when I was but four years old, and **that loss** turned my mother to the Church.

Sample Response
My mother lost a baby boy to diphtheria when I was but four years old, and it was that loss that turned my mother to the Church.

Example
what-cleft

Diphtheria took her youngest child from her.

Sample Response
What took her youngest child from her was diphtheria.

1. *it*-cleft
   About that time, I received a terrible kick from the cow.
2. *it*-cleft
   The cow's kick injured Shamengwa's arm.
3. *what*-cleft
   The cow's kick injured Shamengwa's arm.
4. *it*-cleft
   On the first hot afternoon in early May, I opened my window.
5. *it*-cleft
   I heard **the sound of Corwin's music.**
6. *what*-cleft
   I heard **the sound of Corwin's music.**

Exercise 9A continued

7. *it*-cleft
The narrator finally learned the story of the violin's past.

8. *what*-cleft
The date on the letter, 1897, stuck in my mind, woke me in the middle of the night.

EXERCISE 9B

Examine these sentences from "On the Rainy River" and "Shamengwa." First, you see the sentence with conventional SVO word order; then, you see it as it appears in the story. Read each sentence in its context. Try to account for the writer's choice, whether by speculating about the reason(s) that may have motivated the writer or by describing the effect of the sentence on you as you read. Attend to such matters as emphasis and paragraph continuity.

Example
I've told most of this before, or at least hinted at it, but I have never told the full truth.

Most of this I've told before, or at least hinted at, but what I have never told is the full truth. (*See O'Brien, para. 13.*)

Sample Analysis
The first clause, "most of this I've told before," is very close to "this is one story I've never told before," the opening sentence in "On the Rainy River." Consequently, it echoes the first sentence and weaves the theme of speech vs. silence into the story. The second clause uses the *what*-cleft to stress both "I have never told" and "the full truth." This promises that what's coming is the full truth.

1. The raw fact of terror was beyond all this, or at the very center.
   Beyond all this, or at the very center, was the raw fact of terror. (*See O'Brien, para. 9.*)

2. The Rainy River, wide as a lake in places, was off to my right, and Canada was beyond the Rainy River.
   Off to my right was the Rainy River, wide as a lake in places, and beyond the Rainy River was Canada. (*See O'Brien, para. 16.*)

Exercise 9B continued

3. Elroy must've understood some of this.

   Some of this Elroy must've understood (*O'Brien, para. 29*).

4. A black case of womanly shape that fastened on the side with two brass locks was there, lashed to a crosspiece in the bow.

   There, lashed to a crosspiece in the bow, was a black case of womanly shape that fastened on the side with two brass locks (*Erdrich, para. 36*).

5. And that is why I will play no other fiddle.

   And that is why no other fiddle will I play (*Erdrich, para. 37*).

Completeness and Explicitness

Readers find sentences easy to understand if every syntactic unit (every clause or phrase) is grammatically complete and explicitly marked, its structure immediately identifiable. For example, of the two sentences below, the second is easier to process:

> The stories you read in childhood shape your personality.

> The stories <u>that</u> you read in childhood shape your personality.

In this sentence, the relative pronoun *that* is optional; both sentences are perfectly correct, and you'll see sentences just like them everywhere in published prose. But readers grasp the second more easily, presumably because the presence of the function word *that* signals the adjective clause, indicating how to piece the sentence together.

The same phenomenon can be observed when *that* introduces other structures, in this case a noun clause:

> I noticed his old black pickup truck was no longer parked in front of the house.

> I noticed <u>that</u> his old black pickup truck was no longer parked in front of the house.

In this pair, it's easier to see why the absence of *that* slows processing. As you read the first sentence, you would certainly understand "I noticed" as the subject and verb, and you might well interpret the next noun phrase, "his old black pickup truck," as the object. But you'd be wrong: the object is the whole clause. (What did I notice? That the pickup truck was gone.) In the second sentence, the presence of *that* signals that a whole clause will occupy the subject position, so there's no risk of a misreading.

As I pointed out in Chapter 3, function words can be similarly helpful in pairs and series. Lily Wong Fillmore's article about language loss in immigrant families illustrates this effect:

> They call Grandmother "Ah Yin-Yin," but they do not know how to say much else in Cantonese to their grandmother or their parents.

> Father and Uncle have begun to pick up a little English from coworkers and from the Americans they see occasionally.

> The three Chen children who can be described as successful students are so because they have learned English quickly and have made progress in school.

The sentences would be clear enough if Wong Fillmore had chosen not to repeat the determiner in the first sentence (that is, if she had written "to their grandmother or parents"), the preposition in the second ("from coworkers and the Americans they see occasionally"), or the auxiliary verb in the third ("they have learned English quickly and made progress in school"). But the repetition is helpful, ensuring that readers can immediately see the structure of each pair.

The passage below contains two lists, both headed by prepositions:

> Language loss is the result of both internal and external forces operating on children. The internal factors have to do with the desire for social inclusion, conformity, and the need to communicate with others. The external forces are the sociopolitical ones operating in the society against outsiders, against differences, against diversity.

The first preposition, "for," appears just once. But "against" appears three times. One effect of this repetition is to emphasize the meaning: sociopolitical forces operate *against* the interests of immigrant children. Another effect is to promote easy processing. In short, to accommodate readers, writers usually make grammatical structures complete and explicit, using function words to signal syntactic relationships.

Because complete grammatical units are the norm, sentences that omit an expected word or phrase can be quite striking. Here, in three grammatically complete sentences, is the opening to "On the Rainy River":

> This is one story I've never told before. I haven't told it to anyone. I haven't told it to my parents, to my brother or sister, or even to my wife.

And here, again, is the opening as it appears in print:

> This is one story I've never told before. Not to anyone. Not to my parents, not to my brother or sister, not even to my wife.

O'Brien repeats the function word *not* — but he omits the grammatical core of the second and third sentences, writing just prepositional phrases punctuated with periods. He violates the expectation of explicitness and completeness, leaving it to the reader to find a grammatical home for the prepositional phrases by linking them to the first sentence.

O'Brien's second and third sentences are **fragments**, units punctuated as sentences but missing an independent clause. Fragments call attention to themselves; readers notice them, and reactions can range from puzzlement to admiration. To my ear, O'Brien's fragments make his prose sound like a speaking voice, especially in passages like these:

> In June of 1967, a month after graduating from Macalester College, I was drafted to fight a war I hated. I was twenty-one years old. <u>Young, yes, and politically naïve</u>, but even so the American war in Vietnam seemed to me wrong.

> In any case those were my convictions, and back in college I had taken a modest stand against the war. <u>Nothing radical, no hothead stuff, just ringing a few doorbells for Gene McCarthy, composing a few tedious, uninspired editorials for the campus newspaper.</u>

O'Brien also favors fragments in passages describing emotional turmoil, where the scraps of language recreate the turbulent current of the narrator's thoughts and feelings:

> I remember a sound in my head. It wasn't thinking, just a silent howl. <u>A million things all at once</u>—I was too good for this war. <u>Too smart, too compassionate, too everything</u>. It couldn't happen. . . . <u>A mistake, maybe</u>—a foul-up in the paperwork.

Fragments appear in all genres of writing. They are infrequent in academic writing because its purposes are best served by explicitness and because, for better or worse, academic writers maintain a formal tone. Fragments are more frequent in fiction, where we value the artfulness of special effects.

EXERCISE 9C

In the paragraph below, Louise Erdrich describes the character Corwin Peace. Read the paragraph carefully, then work with it.

> Corwin was one of those I see again and again. A bad thing waiting for a worse thing to happen. A mistake, but one that we kept trying to salvage, because he was so young. Some thought he had no redeeming value whatsoever. A sociopath. A clever manipulator, who drugged himself dangerous each weekend. Others pitied him and blamed his behavior on his mother's drinking. F.A.E. F.A.S. A.D.D. He wore those initials after his name the way educated people append their degrees. Still others thought they saw something in him that could be saved—perhaps the most dangerous idea of all. . . . He was, unfortunately, good-looking, with the features of an Edward Curtis subject, though the crack and vodka were beginning to make him puffy.

1. Underline the fragments.
2. Rewrite the paragraph so that it contains only complete grammatical sentences, retaining the meaning as much as possible. What do you think? Are there places where your revisions improve the paragraph?

EXERCISE 9D

This passage is adapted from Tim O'Brien's "On the Rainy River" (p. 211). It continues the description of the narrator's reaction to receiving a draft notice.

> I was a *liberal,* for Christ sake: If they needed fresh bodies, why not draft some back-to-the-stone-age hawk? Why not draft some dumb jingo in his hard hat and Bomb Hanoi button, or one of LBJ's pretty daughters, or Westmoreland's whole handsome family—nephews and nieces and baby grandson. There should be a law, I thought. If you support a war, if you think it's worth the price, that's fine, but you have to put your own precious fluids on the line. You have to head for the front and hook up with an infantry unit and help spill the blood. And you have to bring along your wife, or your kids, or your lover. There should be a law, I thought.

1. Rewrite the passage so that it has at least three fragments, using the material provided but cutting some units loose from their grammatical mooring in the sentences.
2. What do you think? Are there places where your revisions improve the passage? Compare your choices to O'Brien's. (*See para. 4.*)

Sentence Variety

Prose flows. It has a pace, a rhythm — and readers find it most pleasing when the rhythm is varied, with the pace speeding up or slowing down at appropriate points, the reader's voice sometimes rising, sometimes falling. Virginia Woolf said that when she wrote, she heard the rhythm first, and she filled in words to keep up with it.

The passage below appears about halfway through "On the Rainy River." These are not the kind of paragraphs that will echo in your mind for the rest of the afternoon; they don't come from a turning point in the story, they don't offer high drama. But they flow easily, as you'll hear if you read them aloud:

> We spent six days together at the Tip Top Lodge. Just the two of us. Tourist season was over, and there were no boats on the river, and the wilderness seemed to withdraw into a great permanent stillness. Over those six days Elroy Berdahl and I took most of our meals together. In the mornings we sometimes went out on long hikes into the woods, and at night we played Scrabble or listened to records or sat reading in front of his big stone fireplace. At times I felt the awkwardness of an intruder, but Elroy accepted me into his quiet routine without fuss or ceremony. He took my presence for granted, the same way he might've sheltered a stray cat — no wasted sighs or pity — and there was never any talk about it. Just the opposite. What I remember more than anything is the man's willful, almost ferocious silence. In all that time together, all those hours, he never asked the obvious questions: Why was I there? Why alone? Why so preoccupied? If Elroy was curious about any of this, he was careful never to put it into words.
>
> My hunch, though, is that he already knew. At least the basics. After all, it was 1968, and guys were burning draft cards, and Canada was just a boat ride away. Elroy Berdahl was no hick. His bedroom, I remember, was cluttered with books and newspapers. He killed me at the Scrabble board, barely concentrating, and on those occasions when speech was necessary he had a way of compressing large thoughts into small, cryptic packets of language. One evening, just at sunset, he pointed up at an owl circling over the violet-lighted forest to the west.
>
> "Hey, O'Brien," he said. "There's Jesus."

Analyzing the paragraphs for sentence variety, you immediately notice the wide range of sentence lengths. The shortest sentences — "Why alone?" "There's Jesus" — contain just 2 words; the longest (beginning

"In the mornings we sometimes went out") contains 33. There is no unbroken sequence of long sentences (more than 25 words), and the only extended sequence of short sentences (fewer than 15 words) is the one that ends the first paragraph.

We'll return to sentence length in a moment. But first, I'd like to point out two other kinds of variation. One way of classifying sentences is to note their functions. Sentences fall into four categories: declaratives (statements), interrogatives (questions), imperatives (commands), and exclamations. The previous passage, like most prose, relies primarily on declarative sentences. But the string of declaratives is interrupted by questions near the end of the first paragraph and by the quoted exclamation in the last.

Another way to classify sentences is to consider the complexity of their structure, observing the mix of independent clauses, dependent clauses, and modifiers. Here's how the first paragraph shakes out:

We spent six days together at the Tip Top Lodge.	*one independent clause*
Just the two of us.	*fragment*
Tourist season was over, and there were no boats on the river, and the wilderness seemed to withdraw into a great permanent stillness.	*three independent clauses joined by* and
Over those six days Elroy Berdahl and I took most of our meals together.	*one independent clause*
In the mornings we sometimes went out on long hikes into the woods, and at night we played Scrabble or listened to records or sat reading in front of his big stone fireplace.	*two independent clauses joined by* and; *the second clause contains a coordinate series*
At times I felt the awkwardness of an intruder, but Elroy accepted me into his quiet routine without fuss or ceremony.	*two independent clauses joined by* but
He took my presence for granted, the same way he might've sheltered a stray cat—no wasted sighs or pity—and there was never any talk about it.	*two independent clauses joined by* and; *the first clause is modified by two noun phrases*
Just the opposite.	*fragment*
What I remember more than anything is the man's willful, almost ferocious silence.	*one independent clause;* what-*cleft*

In all that time together, all those hours, he never asked the obvious questions:	one independent clause; introductory prepositional phrase contains an appositive
Why was I there?	one independent clause
Why alone?	fragment
Why so preoccupied?	fragment
If Elroy was curious about any of this, he was careful never to put it into words.	one dependent clause, one independent clause

The second paragraph is equally varied in terms of the sentences' complexity.

It may well be that O'Brien, like Woolf, writes with his ear, producing sentences that vary in length, function, and complexity in response to an intuitive sense of what sounds right. Actually, I suspect that most of us write that way. We hear the music of language around us every day from birth — perhaps before birth — so that, as we write, we reach for words that will capture the right sound as well as the right meaning.

EXERCISE 9E

Analyze sentence variety in this passage from "Shamengwa."

Shamengwa was a man of refinement, who prepared himself carefully to meet life every day. In the Ojibwa language that is spoken on our reservation, *owehzhee* is the way men get themselves up—pluck stray hairs, brush each tooth, make a precise part in their hair, and, these days, press a sharp crease down the front of their blue jeans—in order to show that, although the government has tried in every way possible to destroy their manhood, they are undefeatable. *Owehzhee.* We still look good and we know it. The old man was never seen in disarray, and yet there was more to it.

He played the fiddle. How he played the fiddle! Although his arm was so twisted and disfigured that his shirts had to be carefully altered and pinned to accommodate the gnarled shape, he had agility in that arm, even strength. Ever since he was very young, Shamengwa had, with the aid of a white silk scarf, tied his elbow into a position that allowed the elegant hand and fingers at the end of the damaged arm full play across the fiddle's strings. With his other hand, he drew the bow.

Exercise 9E continued

1. How many words are in the shortest sentence?
2. How many words are in the longest sentence?
3. How many sentences are short, with fewer than 15 words?
4. How many are long, with more than 25 words?
5. Are there sequences of three or more very short sentences in a row?
6. Are there sequences of long sentences?
7. Where does Erdrich use something other than declarative sentences—questions, commands, exclamations, or fragments? (Think about the effect of these sentences, considering why she may have chosen to set them apart.)

EXERCISE 9F

If you'd like to examine sentence variety in an essay rather than a short story, work with this passage from Lily Wong Fillmore's article "Loss of Family Languages" (p. 259).

> The three Chen children who can be described as successful students are so because they have learned English quickly and have made progress at school. They are acquiring the skills and information they need for educational advancement and participation in the work world. But is that all that is important? Can school provide children with everything they need to learn through the formal educational process?
>
> I contend that the school cannot provide children what is most fundamental to success in life. The family plays a crucial role in providing the basic elements for successful functioning. These include: a sense of belonging; knowledge of who one is and where one comes from; an understanding of how one is connected to the important others and events in one's life; the ability to deal with adversity; and knowing one's responsibility to self, family, community. Other elements could be added to the list, but the point is that these are things the family must provide children at home while they are growing up. They cannot be taught at school. The content differs from family to family, but this is the curriculum of the home—what parents and other family members teach and inculcate in children in the socialization process.

1. How many words are in the shortest sentence?
2. How many words are in the longest sentence?

Exercise 9F continued

3. How many sentences are short, with fewer than 15 words?
4. How many are long, with more than 25 words?
5. Are there sequences of three or more very short sentences in a row?
6. Are there sequences of long sentences?
7. Where does Wong Fillmore use something other than declarative sentences—questions, commands, exclamations, or fragments? (Think about the effect of these sentences, considering why she may have chosen to set them apart.)

EXERCISE 9G

Choose a passage of about 200 words in a text you have recently written. Analyze the passage for sentence variety, asking the seven questions printed in Exercises 9E and 9F. How does your prose compare to that of published writers? Can you make it smoother or stronger by revising the sentences to introduce more variety?

Sentence length is always a topic of interest to writers, editors, and teachers. Short sentences have much to recommend them: they are easy for readers to process, and they are easy for writers to produce. For very young or unskilled writers, short sentences seem a safe choice because they don't present many opportunities for error. And some professional writers, especially those who create technical documents, prefer short sentences, seeking an average sentence length of 15 to 20 words.

Long sentences have their virtues as well. If you have read Chapters 5 through 8, you have seen that the use of modifiers makes it possible for a writer to be specific and precise — and of course, the more modification, the longer the sentence. And there is a relationship between sentence length and intellectual sophistication. Children write short sentences; as they mature, the average sentence length in their writing moves steadily upward. In some publications, especially academic journals and high-prestige magazines like *Granta* and *The New Yorker*, average sentence length climbs toward 25 words.

But in the end, we come back to the importance of variety. Even in a genre where generally short-ish sentences and a low words-per-sentence average are preferred, it's risky to write one short sentence after another after another: the prose is likely to sound choppy and childlike. Even in a genre where generally long-ish sentences and a high words-per-sentence average are preferred, it's risky to write an unbroken sequence of long sentences or to let a sentence extend beyond, say, 60 words: the prose is likely to strike readers as dense and difficult.

Let's have a look at some passages in which Louise Erdrich and Tim O'Brien have taken the risk.

In the following passage, Erdrich renders a pivotal moment in Shamengwa's story, relying heavily on very short sentences:

> The dream was simple. A voice. *Go to the lake and sit by the southern rock. Wait there. I will come to you.*
>
> I decided to follow these instructions. I took my bedroll, a scrap of jerky, and a loaf of bannock, and sat myself down on the crackling lichen of the southern rock. That plate of stone jutted out into the water, which dropped off from its edges into a green-black depth. From that rock, I could see all that happened on the water. I put tobacco down for the spirits. All day I sat there waiting. Flies bit me. The wind boomed in my ears. Nothing happened. I curled up when the light left and I slept. Stayed on the next morning. The next day, too. It was the first time that I had ever slept out on the shores, and I began to understand why people said of the lake that there was no end to it, even though it was bounded by rocks.

Sentence length in this passage ranges from 2 words in the second sentence to 39 words in the last sentence. Still, the short sentences stand out because there are so many of them and because they are so very short. The passage has two series of short sentences, one describing the dream and the other describing the young Shamengwa's experience sitting beside the lake. Erdrich tells us how to read the first set of short sentences: they are a dream. And so we know how to read the second set as well. As I read about Shamengwa sitting on the southern rock, I imagine his frame of mind — dreamlike, surreal. Shamengwa is prepared — and by the rhythm of the prose, the reader is prepared — to accept a boat without an oarsman, floating across the lake with the gift of a violin.

Very short or very long sentences also indicate an altered consciousness in several passages of "On the Rainy River." The final crisis, the moment when the narrator's struggle with his conscience finally tears him apart, takes place as he sits in a boat on the river, the Canadian shore just twenty yards away:

> My whole life seemed to spill out into the river, swirling away from me, everything I had ever been or ever wanted to be. I couldn't get my breath; I couldn't stay afloat; I couldn't tell which way to swim. A hallucination, I suppose, but as real as anything I would ever feel. . . . A squad of cheerleaders did cartwheels along the banks of the Rainy River; they had megaphones and pompoms and smooth brown thighs. The crowd swayed left and right. A marching band played fight songs. All my aunts and uncles were there, and Abraham Lincoln, and Saint George, and a nine-year-old girl named Linda who had died of a brain tumor back in fifth grade, and several members of the United States Senate, and a blind poet scribbling notes, and LBJ, and Huck Finn, and Abbie Hoffman, and all the dead soldiers back from the grave, and the many thousands who were later to die—villagers with terrible burns, little kids without arms or legs—yes, and the Joint Chiefs of Staff were there, and a couple of popes, and a first lieutenant named Jimmy Cross, and the last surviving veteran of the American Civil War, and Jane Fonda dressed up as Barbarella, and an old man sprawling beside a pigpen, and my grandfather, and Gary Cooper, and a kind-faced woman carrying an umbrella and a copy of Plato's Republic, and a million ferocious citizens waving flags of all shapes and colors—people in hard hats, people in headbands—they were all whooping and chanting and urging me toward one shore or the other.

O'Brien follows this remarkable kaleidoscope of images with a return to the aluminum boat, rocking on the river. Elroy Berdahl "remained quiet. He kept fishing. . . . He made it real." The final paragraphs describing Berdahl's patient watchfulness and then the narrator's preparations to return home bring the reader back to earth with a conventional blend of sentences, varied in length but no longer extreme.

Very short sentences in sequence, or very long sentences, create special effects. Readers are surprised to see them. Brought up short, they read with special attention—and the writer has an opportunity to heighten the impact of words describing something frightening, something tumultuous, something magical.

EXERCISE 9H

Select a paragraph that you've recently written, perhaps the introduction to an essay, a snippet from a story, or an entry in your journal. (If you can't think of a suitable paragraph, write one: in 100 to 200 words, describe a recent dream.) Write two more versions of your paragraph, keeping the content essentially the same, but experimenting with sentence variety.

1. Minimize sentence variety. Write every sentence in one or two clauses, and don't let the sentence length drop below 10 words or rise above 15. Try to make the prose sound dull, plodding, or singsong.

2. Maximize sentence variety. Experiment with different sentence types (questions, commands, exclamations) and with extreme sentence lengths—very short sentences and/or an ultra-long sentence like O'Brien's. Be as artful as you can, using the unconventional sentences to heighten the paragraph's effect.

ANTHOLOGY

Model Texts
for Writers

Shamengwa

LOUISE ERDRICH was born in 1954 into a family of story-tellers. With the encouragement of her parents, who were teachers in Wahpeton, North Dakota, she began writing as a child, and she developed the storyteller's habit of observing the people around her closely, listening for the rhythms of everyday speech. In 1972, she enrolled in Dartmouth College as part of the college's first class to include women. During her undergraduate years, she published several poems, and her first book was a poetry collection. But she soon returned to storytelling, and today she is best known for her short stories and novels.

While at Dartmouth, Erdrich studied English and creative writing. She also took classes in the Native American Studies program directed by Michael Dorris, a young anthropologist who would later become her husband and coauthor. Her studies prompted her to explore the Ojibwa heritage of her mother's family. After graduating from Dartmouth, Erdrich enrolled in a program in creative writing at Johns Hopkins, earning her M.A. in 1979. She now lives in Minneapolis, Minnesota, where she owns Birchbark Books.

Many of Erdrich's stories take place among the Ojibwa people of North Dakota and Minnesota. "Shamengwa" is typical of her fiction, telling the stories of several characters—an aging musician, a young ruffian who steals his violin, two brothers who played the same violin long ago—presenting them as individuals but embedding them in a network of relationships and a series of events by which they are bound together. The theme of relationships being ruptured and repaired is echoed by the story's structure: it is told from multiple points of view, but it begins and ends in the voice of a tribal judge whose purpose is to preserve the community. Storytelling itself has the function of preserving community: the narrator's responsibility, he says, is "to keep watch over this little patch of earth, to judge its miseries and tell its stories."

Louise Erdrich is widely admired for her skill as a stylist. Crit-
ics often describe her writing as "lyrical": even when she is writing
prose, the language is poetic, with a gentle rhythm, striking images,
and frequent use of metaphor. Erdrich's thirteen novels include
Love Medicine (1984), which won the National Book Critics Circle
Award, and *The Plague of Doves* (2008), a finalist for the Pulitzer
Prize. She has also published several children's books; *The Blue
Jay's Dance: A Birthyear* (1995), a memoir of motherhood; and *The
Red Convertible* (2010), a collection of short stories.

"Shamengwa" was published in *The New Yorker* in December
2002 and reprinted in *The Best American Short Stories of 2003*.

I

At the edge of our reservation settlement there lived an old
man whose arm was twisted up winglike along his side, and
who was for that reason named for a butterfly — Shamengwa.
Other than his arm, he was an extremely well-made person. Anyone
could see that he had been handsome, and he still cut a graceful figure,
slim and of medium height. His head was covered with a startling thick
mane of white hair, which he was proud of. Every few weeks, he had it
carefully trimmed and styled by his daughter, Geraldine, who travelled
in from the bush just to do it.

Shamengwa was a man of refinement, who prepared himself carefully to meet life every day. In the Ojibwa language that is spoken on
our reservation, *owehzhee* is the way men get themselves up — pluck
stray hairs, brush each tooth, make a precise part in their hair, and,
these days, press a sharp crease down the front of their blue-jeans — in
order to show that, although the government has tried in every way
possible to destroy their manhood, they are undefeatable. *Owehzhee.*
We still look good and we know it. The old man was never seen in
disarray, and yet there was more to it.

He played the fiddle. How he played the fiddle! Although his arm
was so twisted and disfigured that his shirts had to be carefully altered
and pinned to accommodate the gnarled shape, he had agility in that
arm, even strength. Ever since he was very young, Shamengwa had,
with the aid of a white silk scarf, tied his elbow into a position that
allowed the elegant hand and fingers at the end of the damaged arm
full play across the fiddle's strings. With his other hand, he drew the

bow. When I try to explain the sound he made, I come to some trouble with words. Inside became outside when Shamengwa played music. Yet inside to outside does not half sum it up. The music was more than music — at least, more than what we are used to hearing. The sound connected instantly with something deep and joyous. Those powerful moments of true knowledge which we paper over with daily life. The music tapped our terrors, too. Things we'd lived through and wanted never to repeat. Shredded imaginings, unadmitted longings, fear, and also surprising pleasures. We can't live at that pitch. But, every so often, something shatters like ice, and we fall into the river of our own exis tence. We are aware. This realization was in the music, somehow, or in the way Shamengwa played it.

Thus Shamengwa wasn't wanted at every party. The wild joy his jigs and reels brought forth might just as easily send people crashing onto the rocks of their roughest memories and they'd end up stunned and addled or crying in their beer. So it is. People's emotions often turn on them. Geraldine, a dedicated, headstrong woman who six years back had borne a baby, dumped its father, and earned a degree in education, sometimes drove Shamengwa to fiddling contests, where he could per-form in more of a concert setting. He even won awards, prizes of the cheap sort given at local musical contests — engraved plaques and small tin cups set on plastic pedestals. These he placed on a triangle scrap of shelf high in one corner of his house. The awards were never dusted, and sometimes, when his grandchild asked him to take them down for her to play with, they came apart. Shamengwa didn't care. He was, however, fanatical about his violin.

He treated this instrument with the reverence we accord our drums, which are considered living beings and require from us food, water, shelter, and love. He fussed over it, stroked it clean with a soft cotton handkerchief, laid it carefully away in the cupboard every night in a leather case that he kept as well polished as his shoes. The case was lined with velvet that had been faded by time from a heavy blood red to a pallid and streaked violet. I don't know violins, but his was thought to be exceptionally beautiful; it was generally understood to be old and quite valuable, too. So when Geraldine came to trim her father's hair one morning and found him on the floor, his good hand bound behind his back, his ankles tied, she was not surprised to see the lock of the cupboard smashed and the violin gone.

I am a tribal judge, and things come to me through the grapevine of the court system or the tribal police. Gossip, rumors, scuttlebutt, B.S., or just flawed information. I always tune in, and I even take notes on what I hear around. It's sometimes wrong, or exaggerated, but just as often it contains a germ of useful truth. In this case, for instance, the name Corwin Peace was on people's lips, although there was no direct evidence that he had committed the crime.

Corwin was one of those I see again and again. A bad thing waiting for a worse thing to happen. A mistake, but one that we kept trying to salvage, because he was so young. Some thought he had no redeeming value whatsoever. A sociopath. A clever manipulator, who drugged himself dangerous each weekend. Others pitied him and blamed his behavior on his mother's drinking. F.A.E. F.A.S. A.D.D. He wore those initials after his name the way educated people append their degrees. Still others thought they saw something in him that could be saved — perhaps the most dangerous idea of all. He was a petty dealer with a string of girlfriends. He was, unfortunately, good-looking, with the features of an Edward Curtis subject, though the crack and vodka were beginning to make him puffy.

Drugs now travel the old fur-trade routes, and where once Corwin would have sat high on a bale of buffalo robes and sung travelling songs to the screeching of an oxcart, now he drove a 1991 Impala with hubcaps missing and its back end dragging. He drove it hard and he drove it all cranked up, but he was rarely caught, because he travelled such erratic hours. He drove without a license — it had long ago been taken from him. D.U.I. And he was always looking for money — scamming, betting, shooting pool, even now and then working a job that, horrifyingly, put him on the other side of a counter frying Chinese chicken strips. He was one of those whom I kept track of because I imagined I'd be seeing the full down-arcing shape of his life's trajectory. I wanted to make certain that if I had to put him away I could do it and sleep well that same night. So far, he had confirmed this.

As the days passed, Corwin lay low and picked up his job at the deep fryer. He made one of those rallying attempts that gave heart to so many of his would-be saviors. He straightened out, stayed sober, and used his best manners, and when questioned was convincingly hopeful about his prospects and affable about his failures. "I'm a jackass," he admitted, "but I never sank so low as to rip off the old man's fiddle."

Yet he had, of course. And, while we waited for him to make his   10
move, there was the old man, who quickly began to fail. I had not realized how much I loved to hear him play — sometimes out on his
scrubby back lawn after dusk, sometimes at those little concerts, and
other times just for groups of people who would gather round. After weeks had passed, a dull spot opened and I ached with surprising
poignance for Shamengwa's loss, which I honestly shared, so that I had
to seek him out and sit with him as if it would help to mourn the absence of his music together. I wanted to know, too, whether, if the violin
did not turn up, we could get together and buy him a new, perhaps
even better instrument. So I sat in Shamengwa's little front room one
afternoon and tried to find an opening.

"Of course," I said, "we think we know who took your fiddle. We've
got our eye on him."

Shamengwa swept his hair back with the one graceful hand and
said, as he had many times, "I was struck from behind."

Where he'd hit the ground, his cheekbone had split and the white of
his eye was an angry red. He moved with a stiff, pained slowness, the
rigidity of a very old person. He lowered himself piece by piece into a
padded brown rocking chair and gazed at me, or past me, really. I soon
understood that although he spoke quietly and answered questions, he
was not fully engaged in the conversation. In fact, he was only half present, and somewhat disheveled, irritable as well, neither of which I'd ever
seen in him before. His shirt was buttoned wrong, the plaid askew, and
he hadn't shaved that morning. His breath was sour, and he didn't seem
at all glad that I had come.

We sat together in a challenging silence until Geraldine brought two
mugs of hot, strong, sugared tea and got another for herself. Shamengwa's hand shook as he lifted the cup, but he drank. His face cleared a bit
as the tea went down, and I decided that there would be no better time
to put forth my idea.

"Uncle," I said, "we would like to buy a new fiddle for you."   15

Shamengwa said nothing, but put down the cup and folded his
hands in his lap. He looked past me and frowned in a thoughtful way.

"Wouldn't he like a new violin?" I appealed to Geraldine. She shook
her head as if she were both annoyed with me and exasperated with
her father. We sat in silence. I didn't know where to go from there. Shamengwa had leaned back in his chair and closed his eyes. I thought he

might be trying to get rid of me. But I was stubborn and did not want to go. I wanted to hear Shamengwa's music again.

"Oh, tell him about it, Daddy," Geraldine said at last.

Shamengwa leaned forward and bent his head over his hands as though he were praying.

20   I relaxed now and understood that I was going to hear something. It was that breathless gathering moment I've known just before composure cracks, the witness breaks, the truth comes out. I am familiar with it, and although this was not exactly a confession, it was, as it turned out, something not generally known on the reservation.

II

My mother lost a baby boy to diphtheria when I was but four years old, Shamengwa said, and it was that loss that turned my mother to the Church. Before that, I remember my father playing chansons, reels, and jigs on his fiddle, but after the baby's death he put the fiddle down and took the Holy Communion. My mother out of grief became strict with my father, my older sister, and me. Where before we'd had a lively house that people liked to visit, now there was quiet. No wine and no music. We kept our voices down because our noise hurt, my mother said, and there was no laughing or teasing by my father, who had once been a dancing and hilarious man.

I don't believe my mother meant things to change so, but the sorrow she bore was beyond her strength. As though her heart, too, were buried underneath that small white headstone in the Catholic cemetery, she turned cold, turned away from the rest of us. Now that I am old and know the ways of grief, I understand she felt too much, loved too hard, and was afraid to lose us as she had lost my brother. But to a little boy these things are hidden. It only seemed to me that, along with that baby, I had lost her love. Her strong arms, her kisses, the clean soap smell of her face, her voice calming me — all of this was gone. She was like a statue in a church. Every so often we would find her in the kitchen, standing still, staring through the wall. At first we touched her clothes, petted her hands. My father kissed her, spoke gently into her ear, combed her hair into a shawl around her shoulders. Later, after we had given up, we just walked around her as you would a stump. My sister took up the cooking, and gradually we accepted that the lively, loving mother we had known wasn't going to return. We didn't try to coax her out. She spent most of her time at the church, her ivory-and-silver rosary draped over her right fist, her left hand wearing the beads smoother, smaller, until I thought one day for sure they would disappear between her fingers.

We lived right here then, but in those days trees and bush still surrounded us. There were no houses to the west. We pastured our horses where the Dairy Queen now stands. One day, while my family was in town and I was home with a cold, I became restless. I began to poke around, and soon enough I came across the fiddle that my mother had forced my father to stop playing. There it was. I was alone with it. I was only five or six years old, but I could balance a fiddle and I remembered how my father had used the bow. I got sound out of it all right, though nothing pleasing. The noise made my bones shiver. I put the fiddle back carefully, well before my parents came home, and climbed underneath my blankets when they walked into the yard. I pretended to sleep, not because I wanted to keep up the appearance of being sick but because I could not bear to return to the way things had been. Something had changed. Something had disrupted the nature of all that I knew. This deep thing had to do with the fiddle.

After that, I contrived, as often as I could, to stay alone in the house. As soon as everyone was gone I took the fiddle from its hiding place, and I tuned it to my own liking. I learned how to play it one string at a time, and I started to fit these sounds together. The sequence of notes made my brain itch. It became a torment for me to have to put away the fiddle when my family came home. Sometimes, if the wind was right, I sneaked the fiddle from the house and played out in the woods. I was always careful that the wind should carry my music away to the west, where there was no one to hear it. But one day the wind may have shifted. Or perhaps my mother's ears were more sensitive than my sister's and my father's. Because when I came back into the house I found her staring out the window, to the west. She was excited, breathing fast. Did you hear it? She cried out. Did you hear it? Terrified to be discovered, I said no. She was very agitated, and my father had a hard time calming her. After he finally got her to sleep, he sat at the table with his head in his hands. I tiptoed around the house, did the chores. I felt terrible not telling him that my music was what she'd heard. But now, as I look back, I consider my silence the first decision I made as a true musician. An artist. My playing was more important to me than my father's pain. It was that clear. I said nothing, but after that I was all the more sly and twice as secretive.

25   It was a question of survival, after all. If I had not found the music, I would have died of the silence. There are ways of being abandoned even when your parents are right there.

We had two cows, and I did the milking in the morning and evening. Lucky, because if my parents forgot to cook at least I had the milk. I can't say I really ever suffered from a stomach kind of hunger, but another kind of human hunger bit me. I was lonely. It was about that time that I received a terrible kick from the cow, an accident, as she was usually mild. A wasp sting, perhaps, caused her to lash out in surprise. She caught my arm and, although I had no way of knowing it, shattered the bone. Painful? Oh, for certain it was, but my parents did not think to take me to a doctor. They did not notice, I suppose. I did tell my father about it, but he only nodded, pretending that he had heard, and went back to whatever he was doing.

The pain in my arm kept me awake, and at night, when I couldn't distract myself, I moaned in my blankets by the stove. But worse was the uselessness of the arm in playing the fiddle. I tried to prop it up, but it fell like a rag doll's arm. I finally hit upon a solution. I started tying up my broken arm, just as I do now. I had, of course, no idea that it would heal that way and that as a result I would be considered a permanent cripple. I only knew that with the arm tied up I could play, and that playing saved my life. So I was, like most artists, deformed by my art. I was shaped.

School is where I got the name I carry now. Shamengwa, the black-and-orange butterfly. It was a joke on my "wing arm." Although a nun told me that a picture of a butterfly in a painting of Our Lady was meant to represent the Holy Spirit, I didn't like the name at first. My bashfulness about the shape of my arm caused me to avoid people even once I was older, and I made no friends. Human friends. My true friend was my fiddle, anyway, the only friend I really needed. And then I lost that friend.

My parents had gone to church, but there was on that winter's day some problem with the stove. Smoke had filled the nave at the start of Mass and everyone was sent straight home. When my mother and father arrived, I was deep into my playing. They listened, standing at the door rooted by the surprise of what they heard, for how long I do not know. I had not heard the door open and, with my eyes shut, had not seen the light thereby admitted. Finally, I noticed the cold breeze that swirled around me, turned, and we stared at one another with a shocked gravity that my father broke at last by asking, "How long?"

I did not answer, although I wanted to. *Seven years. Seven years!*   30

He led my mother in. They shut the door behind them. Then he said, in a voice of troubled softness, "Keep on."

So I played, and when I stopped he said nothing.

Discovered, I thought the worst was over. But the next morning, waking to a silence where I usually heard my father's noises, hearing a vacancy before I even knew it for sure, I understood that the worst was yet to come. My playing had woken something in him. That was the reason he left. But I don't know why he had to take the violin. When I saw that it was missing, all breath left me, all thought, all feeling. For a while after that I was the same as my mother. In our loss, we were cut off from the true, bright, normal routines of living. I might have stayed that way, joined my mother in the darkness from which she could not return. I might have lived on in that diminished form, if I had not had a dream.

The dream was simple. A voice. *Go to the lake and sit by the southern rock. Wait there. I will come to you.*

I decided to follow these instructions. I took my bedroll, a scrap of   35 jerky, and a loaf of bannock, and sat myself down on the crackling lichen of the southern rock. That plate of stone jutted out into the water, which dropped off from its edges into a green-black depth. From that rock, I could see all that happened on the water. I put tobacco down for the spirits. All day, I sat there waiting. Flies bit me. The wind boomed in my ears. Nothing happened. I curled up when the light left and I slept. Stayed on the next morning. The next day, too. It was the first time that I had ever slept out on the shores, and I began to understand why people said of the lake that there was no end to it, even though it was bounded by rocks. There were rivers flowing in and flowing out, secret currents, six kinds of weather working on its surface and a hidden terrain beneath. Each wave washed in from somewhere unseen and washed out again to somewhere unknown. I saw birds, strange-feathered and unfamiliar, passing through on their way to somewhere else. Listening to the water, I was for the first time comforted by sounds other than my fiddle-playing. I let go. I thought I might just stay there forever, staring at the blue thread of the horizon. Nothing mattered. When a small bit of the horizon's thread detached, darkened, proceeded forward slowly, I observed it with only mild interest. The speck seemed to both advance and retreat. It wavered back and forth. I lost sight of it for long stretches, then it popped closer, over a wave.

It was a canoe. But either the paddler was asleep in the bottom or the canoe was drifting. As it came nearer, I decided for sure that it must be adrift, it rode so lightly in the waves, nosing this way, then the other. But always, no matter how hesitantly, it ended up advancing straight toward the southern rock, straight toward me. I watched until I could clearly see there was nobody in it. Then the words of my dream returned. *I will come to you.* I dove in eagerly, swam for the canoe — I had learned, as boys do, to compensate for my arm, and although my stroke was peculiar, I was strong. I thought perhaps the canoe had been badly tied and slipped its mooring, but no rope trailed. Perhaps high waves had coaxed it off a beach where its owner had dragged it up, thinking it safe. I pushed the canoe in to shore, then pulled it up behind me, wedged it in a cleft between two rocks. Only then did I look inside. There, lashed to a crosspiece in the bow, was a black case of womanly shape that fastened on the side with two brass locks.

That is how my fiddle came to me, Shamengwa said, raising his head to look steadily at me. He smiled, shook his fine head, and spoke softly. And that is why no other fiddle will I play.

III

Corwin shut the door to his room. It wasn't really his room, but some people were letting him stay in their basement in return for several favors. Standing on a board propped on sawhorses, he pushed his outspread fingers against the panel of the false ceiling. He placed the panel to one side and groped up behind it among wires and underneath a pad of yellow fiberglass insulation, until he located the handle of the case. He bore it down to the piece of foam rubber that served as his mattress and through which, every night, he felt the hard cold of the concrete floor seep into his legs. He had taken the old man's fiddle because he needed money, but he hadn't thought much about where he would sell it or who would buy it. Then he had an inspiration. One of the women in the house went to Spirit Lake every weekend to stay with her boyfriend's family. He'd put the fiddle in the trunk and hitch along. They'd let him out at Miracle Village Mall, and he'd take the violin there and sell it to a music lover.

Corwin got out of the car and carried the violin into the mall. There are two kinds of people, he thought, the givers and the takers. I'm a taker. Render unto Corwin what is due him. His favorite movie of recent times was about a cop with such a twisted way of looking at the world that you couldn't tell if he was evil or good—you only knew that he could seize your mind with language. Corwin had a thing for language. He inhaled it from movies, rap and rock music, television. It rubbed around inside him, word against word. He thought he was writing poems sometimes in his thoughts, but the poems would not come out. The words stuck in odd configurations and made patterns that raced across the screen of his shut eyes and off the edge, down his temples and into the darkness of his neck. So when he walked through the air-lock doors into the warm cathedral-like space of the central food court, his brain was a mumble.

Taking a seat, peering at the distracted-looking shoppers, he quickly 40 understood that none of them was likely to buy the fiddle. He walked into a music store and tried to show the instrument to the manager, who said only, "Nah, we don't take used." Corwin walked out again. He tried a few people. They shied away or turned him down flat.

"Gotta regroup," Corwin told himself, and went back to sit on the length of bench he had decided to call his own. That was where he got the idea that became a gold mine. He remembered a scene from a TV show, a clip of a musician in a city street. He was playing a saxophone or something of that sort, and at his feet there was an open instrument case. A woman stopped and smiled and threw a dollar in the case. Corwin took the violin out and laid the open case invitingly at his feet. He took the fiddle in one hand and drew the bow across the strings with the other. It made a terrible, strange sound. The screech echoed in the food court and several people raised their lips from the waxed-paper food wrappers to look at Corwin. He looked back at them, poised and frozen. It was a moment of drama—he had them. An audience. He had to act instantly or lose them. Instinctively, he gave a flowery, low bow, as though he were accepting an ovation. There were a few murmurs of amusement. Someone even applauded. These sounds acted on Corwin Peace at once, more powerfully than any drug he had tried. A surge of unfamiliar zeal filled him, and he took up the instrument again, threw back his hair, and began to play a swift, silent passage of music.

His mimicry was impeccable. Where had he learned it? He didn't know. He didn't touch the bow to the strings, but he played music all the same. Music ricocheted around between his ears. He could hardly keep up with what he heard. His body spilled over with drama. When the music in his head stopped, he dipped low and did the splits, which he'd learned from Prince videos. He held the violin and the bow overhead. Applause broke over him. A skein of dazzling sound.

They picked up Corwin Peace pretending to play the fiddle in a Fargo mall, and brought him to me. I have a great deal of latitude in sentencing. In spite of myself, I was intrigued by Corwin's unusual treatment of the instrument, and I decided to set a precedent. First, I cleared my decision with Shamengwa. Then I sentenced Corwin to apprentice himself with the old master. Six days a week, two hours each morning. Three hours of practice after work. He would either learn to play the violin or he would do time. In truth, I didn't know who was being punished, the boy or the old man. But at least now, from Shamengwa's house, we began to hear the violin again.

It was the middle of September on the reservation, the mornings chill, the afternoons warm, the leaves still green and thick in their final sweetness. All the hay was mowed. The wild rice was beaten flat. The radiators in the tribal offices went on at night, but by noon we had to open the windows to cool off. The woodsmoke of parching fires and the spent breeze of diesel entered then, and sometimes the squall of Corwin's music from down the hill. The first weeks were not promising. Then the days turned uniformly cold, we kept the windows shut, and until spring the only news of Corwin's progress came through his probation officer. I didn't expect much. It was not until the first hot afternoon in early May that I opened my window and actually heard Corwin playing.

45   "Not half bad," I said that night when I visited Shamengwa. "I listened to your student."

"He's clumsy as hell, but he's got the fire," Shamengwa said, touching his chest. I could tell that he was proud of Corwin, and I allowed myself to consider the possibility that something as idealistic as putting an old man and a hard-core juvenile delinquent together had worked, or hadn't, anyway, ended up a disaster.

The lessons and the relationship outlasted, in fact, the sentence. Fall came, and we closed the windows again. In spring, we opened them, and once or twice heard Corwin playing. Then Shamengwa died.

His was a peaceful death, the sort of death we used to pray to St. Joseph to give us all. He was asleep, his violin next to the bed, covers pulled to his chin. Found in the morning by Geraldine.

There was a large funeral with the usual viewing, at which people filed up to his body and tucked flowers and pipe tobacco and small tokens into Shamengwa's coffin to accompany him into the earth. Geraldine placed a monarch butterfly upon his shoulder. She said that she had found it that morning on the grille of her car. Halfway through the service, she stood up and took the violin from the coffin, where it had been tucked up close to her father.

"A few months ago, Dad told me that when he died I was to give this violin to Corwin Peace," she told everyone. "And so I'm offering it to him now. And I've already asked him to play us one of Dad's favorites today."

Corwin had been sitting in the back and now he walked up to the front, his shoulders hunched, hands shoved in his pockets. The sorrow in his face surprised me. It made me uneasy to see such a direct show of emotion in one who had been so volatile. But Corwin's feelings seemed directed once he took up the fiddle and began to play. He played a chanson everyone knew, a song typical of our people because it began tender and slow, then broke into a wild strangeness that pricked our pulses and strained our breath. Corwin played with passion, if not precision, and there was enough of the old man's energy in his music that by the time he'd finished everybody was in tears.

Then came the shock. Amid the dabbing of eyes and discreet nose-blowing, Corwin stood gazing into the coffin at his teacher, the violin dangling from one hand. Beside the coffin there was an ornate Communion rail. Corwin raised the violin high and smashed it on the rail, once, twice, three times, to do the job right. I was in the front pew, and I jumped from my seat as though I'd been prepared for something like this. I grasped Corwin's arm as he laid the violin carefully back beside Shamengwa, but then I let him go, for I recognized that his gesture was spent. My focus moved from Corwin to the violin itself, because I saw, sticking from its smashed wood, a roll of paper. I drew the paper out. It was old and covered with a stiff, antique flow of writing. The priest, somewhat shaken, began the service again. I put the roll of paper into my jacket pocket and returned to my seat. I didn't exactly forget to read it. There was just so much happening after the funeral, what with the windy burial and then the six-kinds-of-fry-bread supper in the Knights of Columbus Hall, that I didn't get the chance to sit still and concentrate. It was evening and I was at home, comfortable in my chair with a bright lamp turned on behind me, so the radiance fell over my shoulder, before I finally read what had been hidden in the violin for so many years.

IV

I, Baptiste Parentheau, also known as Billy Peace, leave to my brother Edwin this message, being a history of the violin which on this day of Our Lord August 20, 1897, I send out onto the waters to find him.

A recapitulation to begin with: Having read of LaFountaine's mission to the Iroquois, during which that priest avoided having his liver plucked out before his eyes by nimbly playing the flute, our own Father Jasprine thought it wise to learn to play a musical instrument before he ventured forth into the wastelands past the Lake of the Woods. Therefore, he set off with music as his protection. He studied and brought along his violin, a noble instrument, which he played less than adequately. If the truth were told, he'd have done better not to impose his slight talents on the Ojibwa. Yet, as he died young and left the violin to his altar boy, my father, I should say nothing against good Jasprine. I should, instead, be grateful for the joys his violin afforded my family. I should be happy in the hours that my father spent tuning and then playing the thing, and in the devotion that my brother and I eagerly gave to it. Yet, as things ended so hard between my brother and myself because of the instrument, I find myself imagining that we never knew the violin, that I'd never played its music or understood its voice. For when my father died he left the fiddle to both my brother Edwin and myself, with the stipulation that were we unable to decide who should have it, then we were to race for it as true sons of the great waters, by paddling our canoes.

55   When my brother and I heard this declaration read, we said nothing. There was nothing to say, for as much as it was true that we loved each other, we both wanted that violin. Each of us had given it years of practice, each of us had whispered into its hollow our sorrows and taken hold of its joys. That violin had soothed our wild hours, courted our wives. But now we were done with the passing of it back and forth. And if it had to belong to one of us two brothers I determined that it would be me.

Two nights before we took our canoes out, I conceived of a sure plan. When the moon slipped behind clouds and the world was dark, I went out to the shore with a pannikin of heated pitch. I had decided to interfere with Edwin's balance. Our canoes were so carefully constructed that each side matched ounce for ounce. By thickening the seams on one side with a heavy application of pitch, I'd throw off Edwin's paddle stroke enough, I was sure, to give me a telling advantage.

Ours is a wide lake and full of islands. It is haunted by birds who utter sarcastic or sad cries. One loses sight of others easily, and sound travels skewed, bouncing off the rock cliffs. There are flying skeletons, floating bogs, caves containing the spirits of little children, and black moods of weather. We love it well, and we know its secrets — in some part, at least. Not all. And not the secret that I put in motion.

We were to set off on the far northern end of the lake and arrive at the south, where our uncles had lit fires and brought the violin, wrapped in red cloth, in its fancy case. We started out together, joking. Edwin, you remember how we paddled through the first two narrows, laughing as we exaggerated our efforts, and how I said, as what I'd done with the soft pitch weighed on me, "Maybe we should share the damn thing after all."

You laughed and said that our uncles would be disappointed, waiting there, and that when you won the contest things would be as they were before, except all would know that Edwin was the faster paddler. I promised you the same. Then you swerved behind a skim of rock and took your secret shortcut. As I paddled, I had to stop occasionally and bail. At first I thought that I had sprung a slow leak, but in time I understood. While I was painting on extra pitch, you were piercing the bottom of my canoe. I was not, in fact, in any danger, and when the wind shifted all of a sudden and it began to storm — no thunder or lightning, just a buffet of cold rain — I laughed and thanked you. For the water I took on actually helped to steady me. I rode lower, and stayed on course. But you foundered. It was worse to be set off balance. You must have overturned.

The bonfires die to coals on the south shore. I curl in blankets but I do not sleep. I am keeping watch. At first when you are waiting for someone, every shadow is an arrival. Then the shadows become the very substance of dread. We hunt for you, call your name until our voices are worn to whispers. No answer. In one old man's dream everything goes around the other way, the not-sun-way, counterclockwise, which means that the dream is of the spirit world. And then he sees you there in his dream, going the wrong way, too.

60

The uncles have returned to their houses, pastures, children, wives. I am alone on the shore. As the night goes black, I sing for you. As the sun comes up, I call across the water. White gulls answer. As the time goes on, I begin to accept what I have done. I begin to know the truth of things.

They have left the violin here with me. Each night I play for you, brother, and when I can play no more I'll lash our fiddle into the canoe and send it out to you, to find you wherever you are. I won't have to pierce the bottom so it will travel the bed of the lake. Your holes will do the trick, brother, as my trick did for you.

V

Of course, the canoe did not sink to the bottom of the lake. Nor did it stray. The canoe and its violin eventually found a different Peace, through the person of Shamengwa. The fiddle had searched long, I had no doubt of that. For what stuck in my mind, what woke me in the middle of the night, was the date on the letter: 1897. The violin had spoken to Shamengwa and called him out onto the lake more than twenty years later.

"How about that?" I said to Geraldine. "Can you explain such a thing?"

65   She looked at me steadily.

"We know nothing" is what she said.

I was to marry her. We took in Corwin. The violin lies buried in the arms of the man it saved, while the boy it also saved plays for money now and prospers here on the surface of the earth. I do my work. I do my best to make the small decisions well, and I try not to hunger for the greater things, for the deeper explanations. For I am sentenced to keep watch over this little patch of earth, to judge its miseries and tell its stories. That's who I am. *Mii'sago iw.*

"We Should Grow Too Fond of It": Why We Love the Civil War

DREW GILPIN FAUST began her academic career in 1975 when, after completing degrees at Bryn Mawr and the University of Pennsylvania, she joined the faculty at the University of Pennsylvania. A professor of history, she remained at Penn for twenty-five years until she was recruited to guide the transformation of Radcliffe College, historically Harvard's "female annex," into the Radcliffe Institute for Advanced Study. In 2007, Faust became the twenty-eighth president of Harvard University.

Born into a well-to-do family, Faust grew up in Clarke County, Virginia, a community where whites and blacks occupied separate spheres. Her intellectual interests and social commitments emerged early: in 1957, she wrote a letter to President Eisenhower that began, "I am nine years old and I am white, but I have many feelings about segregation," going on to urge the president to "please try and have schools and other things accept colored people." As a young woman, Faust participated in civil rights demonstrations. These experiences shaped her choices as a scholar: "I have always known," she wrote, "that I became a Southern historian because I grew up in that particular time and place. My sense of self, my story about how I became who I am, has always been situated" in the events of the 1960s as Southerners confronted the legal and moral imperative of integration.

Faust is the author of six books. The first, *Mothers of Invention: Women of the Slaveholding South in the American Civil War*, won the Francis Parkman Prize in 1997. Her most recent book, *This Republic of Suffering: Death and the American Civil War* (2008), appeals equally to professional historians and a popular audience; it was named by the *New York Times* as one of the ten best books of 2008 and was a finalist for both a National Book Award and the Pulitzer Prize for History.

"We Should Grow Too Fond of It" appeared in *Civil War History* in 2004. In this article, Faust returns to the relationship between narrative and identity. Just as an individual sense of self depends upon "the story about how I became who I am," a nation's identity depends upon the story we tell each other about our collective past. In this view, historians have a profound responsibility to tell a story that neither misrepresents nor romanticizes events of the past.

Drew Gilpin Faust lives in Cambridge, Massachusetts, with her husband, Charles Rosenberg, a historian of science and medicine. They have two grown daughters.

If war were not so terrible, Robert E. Lee observed as he watched the slaughter at Fredericksburg, "we should grow too fond of it." Lee's remark, uttered in the very midst of battle's horror and chaos, may be his most quoted — and misquoted — statement. His exact words are in some dispute, and it seems unlikely we shall ever be able to be certain of precisely what he said to James Longstreet on December 13, 1862. But in every rendition of the quotation, the contradiction between war's attraction and its horror remains at the heart. War is terrible and yet we love it; we need to witness the worst of its destruction in order not to love it even more. And both because and in spite of its terror, we must calibrate our feelings to ensure enough, but not too much, fondness. It is Lee's succinct, surprising, and almost poetic expression of a too often unacknowledged truth about war that has made this statement so quotable. Lee, the romantic hero of his own time and the marble man of ages that followed, displays here a complexity, an ambivalence, a capacity for irony that suggest cracks in the marble. His observation seems to reach beyond his era and its sensibilities into our own.[1]

---

[1] The most-often-quoted version of this remark — "It is well that war is so terrible — we should grow too fond of it" — is from Douglas Southall Freeman, *R.E. Lee: A Biography*, 4 vols. (New York: Charles Scribner's Sons, 1934–35), 2:462. But Freeman seems to have altered an earlier rendition of the statement: either "It is well this is so terrible! We should grow too fond of it!" from John Esten Cooke, *A Life of Gen. Robert E. Lee* (New York: D. Appleton, 1871), 184, or "It is well that war is so terrible, or we would grow too

Lee was not alone among his contemporaries in articulating a fondness for war, though few had his sense of irony. Many Americans
North and South looked forward to battle in 1861, anticipating a stage
on which to perform deeds appropriate to a Romantic age but believ-
ing, too, that war would be salutary for both the nation and its citizens.
Judah P. Benjamin, attorney general of the new Confederacy, reassured
a New Orleans crowd in the winter of 1861 that war was far from an
"unmixed evil," for it would "stimulate into active development the no-
bler impulses and more elevated sentiments which else had remained
torpid in our souls." *DeBow's Review* anticipated from war "a sublime
and awful beauty — a fearful and terrible loveliness — that atones in
deeds of high enterprise and acts of heroic valor for the carnage, the
desolation, the slaughter." Others were not so rash in their estimates of
the likely balance between glory and horror yet nevertheless found in
the coming of war welcome opportunity for self-definition and fulfill-
ment. In the North, Henry Lee Higginson later looked back on his
hopes for the conflict: "I always did long for some such war, and it came
in the nick of time for me."[2]

Northerners and Southerners alike saw in imminent war the possibility for a cleansing corrective to the greed and corruption into which
Americans had fallen. Historian Francis Parkman wrote to the *Boston
Advertiser* that American society had been "cramped and vitiated" by
"too exclusive a pursuit of material success," but he was certain that
through war the nation would be "clarified and pure in a renewed and
strengthened life." In a June 1861 editorial, the *Richmond Enquirer*

---

fond of it," from Edward Porter Alexander, *Military Memoirs of a Confederate: A Critical
Narrative* (New York: Charles Scribner's Sons, 1907), 302. Gary Gallagher carefully traces
this history and notes that Longstreet, to whom the remark was made, never mentioned it
in his own writings. See his *The Fredericksburg Campaign: Decision on the Rappahannock*
(Chapel Hill: Univ. of North Carolina Press, 1995) xii n1. Thomas L. Connelly, *The Marble
Man: Robert E. Lee and His Image in American Society* (New York: Alfred Knopf, 1977).
I am grateful to comments from many friends and colleagues who helped me think about
why we love the Civil War: Lynn Hunt, Charles Rosenberg, Tony Horwitz, Edward Ayers,
James McPherson, Yonatan Eyal, Michael Bernath, Peter Kolchin, Bertram Wyatt-Brown,
Gabor Boritt, Homi Bhabha, Jeremy Knowles, and all the participants in the Huntington
Library's Civil War conference in October 2003 and in the AHA Presidential Session in
January 2004, where I delivered versions of this paper.
   [2] Benjamin quoted in *Richmond Enquirer*, Mar. 8, 1861; *DeBow's Review* 30 (Jan.
1861); 52; Higginson quoted in George M. Fredrickson, *The Inner Civil War: Northern
Intellectuals and The Crisis of the Union* (New York: Harper & Row, 1965), 73. Because my
focus in this essay is on the love of war, I have not discussed the voices opposing it.

rhapsodized that "a season of war . . . calls out new ideas and kindles new and more elevated emotions and sentiments. It appeals to all that is noble in the soul . . . it revives the slumbering emotions of patriotism, with all their generous joys. It restores the general brotherhood. It destroys selfishness. It begets the spirit of self sacrifice. It gives to sufferers a portion of that ecstasy which martyrs feel." The paper assured its readers that "many virtues will glow and brighten in . . . [war's] path, like fragrant flowers in the wilderness." But it would not be fragrant flowers that Virginians would soon be finding in the wilderness.[3]

Often war's expected transformations were framed in religious terms — as processes of divine purification resulting from the sacrifices required by war. Sermons in the North and the South hailed war's chastening rod. More secular observers welcomed war's imposition of discipline and even subordination into a society disrupted by undue egalitarianism, selfishness, and disorder.[4]

5   The realities of battlefield slaughter and enormous death tolls did not destroy this enthusiasm for war's purposes. Paeans to war did not cease as the conflict grew more intense and more terrible. Fought in April 1862, Shiloh marked a new departure in warfare, a level of death and destruction previously unknown and unimagined. Yet Charles Eliot Norton responded to the carnage by writing, "I can hardly help wishing that the war might go on and on till it has brought suffering and sorrow enough to quicken our consciences and cleanse our hearts." Great battles were believed to be occasions and sites for profound reflection and insight, and Northerners and Southerners alike were eager to learn, to borrow the title of a *Richmond Enquirer* editorial, "What War Should Teach Us."[5] . . .

Historians have shared this intoxication with war. War has been perhaps history's most popular subject, and recent years have only seen

---

[3] Fredrickson, *Inner Civil War*, 75; *Richmond Enquirer*, June 29, 1861.

[4] See, for example, Stephen Elliott, *God's Presence with Our Army at Manassas* (Savannah, Ga.: W. Thorne Williams, 1861); Elliott, *How to Renew Our National Strength* (Richmond, Va.: MacFarlane and Fergusson, 1862); Alexander Gregg, *The Duties Growing Out of It and The Benefits to be Expected From the Present War* (Austin, Tex.: The State Gazette, 1861); T. L. De Veaux, *Fast-Day Sermon* (Wytheville, Va.: D. A. St. Clair, 1864); John William Draper, *Thoughts on the Future Civil Policy of America* (New York: Harper, 1865), 251. One can find very similar statements on both sides at the outset of World War I. See Eric Leed, *No Man's Land: Combat and Identity in World War I* (Cambridge: Cambridge Univ. Press., 1979).

[5] Fredrickson, 80; *Richmond Enquirer*, June 29, 1861.

that interest intensify. Within the American field this fondness for war has manifested itself most dramatically in the dedication of so many historians to Civil War subjects. Many of us have chosen to devote our professional lives to exploring the Civil War, identifying it as a topic that interests us above all others. Certainly a desire to study war is different from a passion to fight it, but both acknowledge its attraction, its fascination, its power, and its importance.

Why do historians love the Civil War? Why has the Civil War come to be one of the liveliest fields in American history? We are part of a long tradition of writing about the war. More than 60,000 volumes of Civil War history had appeared by the end of the twentieth century, more than a book a day since Appomattox. But we represent a more recent phenomenon as well—one that has been characterized as an explosion of Civil War scholarship—what has been called a Civil War "industry" and a "new Civil War history."[6]

How can we more precisely describe this explosion, this new and sizeable "wave" of Civil War studies? What are the factors that have produced this recent volume of writing? And what are the new directions and perspectives that have made the Civil War so attractive a subject to the current generation of scholars? How should we understand this growing fondness for the Civil War?[7]

Many commentators have dated the beginning of the recent dramatic expansion of interest in Civil War history to the 1988 publication and astonishing popular success of James M. McPherson's *Battle Cry of Freedom*. Oxford University Press planned a very respectable initial print run for *Battle Cry* of 20,000 books. In what was,

---

[6] William Blair, "The Quest for Understanding the Civil War," *Reviews in American History* 27 (Sept. 1999): 421; Susan-Mary Grant, "Introduction," in Grant and Peter Parish, eds., *Legacy of Disunion: The Enduring Significance of the American Civil War* (Baton Rouge: Louisiana State Univ. Press, 2003), 4. See also James M. McPherson, "The War That Never Goes Away," in *Drawn with the Sword: Reflections on the American Civil War* (New York: Oxford Univ. Press, 1996), 55–66.

[7] Prior to the recent wave of scholarship, the Civil War was all but ignored by academic historians. As Edward Ayers has observed, "The war itself became something of a scholarly backwater, neglected by the leading historians of nineteenth century America. The distaste for the war in Vietnam manifested itself in an aversion to any kind of military history, while the fascination with social history made generals and their maneuvers seem irrelevant and boring at best." Edward Ayers, "Worrying About the Civil War," in *Moral Problems in American Life: New Perspectives on Cultural History*, eds. Karen Halttunen and Lewis Perry (Ithaca: Cornell Univ. Press, 1998), 155.

McPherson says, a "BIG (though of course pleasant) surprise" to both author and publisher, it became a *New York Times* hard-cover best-seller for sixteen weeks, won the Pulitzer Prize, and has ultimately sold more than 600,000 copies. Successfully appealing both to professional historians and to a wider popular audience of Civil War enthusiasts, *Battle Cry* demonstrated that scholarship produced in the academy could indeed reach beyond its walls. The inspiring—as well as venal—hope for such a wide readership riveted historians' attention on *Battle Cry* as a publishing event and on the Civil War as a subject that might bring attention, acclaim, and even riches. But in fact, McPherson's book was the beneficiary rather than the cause of an already increasing interest in the Civil War.[8]

10   In an effort better to understand the dimensions of the much noted recent growth in Civil War history, I undertook a survey of Civil War books reviewed since 1976 in the *Journal of Southern History*, which, despite its title, considers studies on both Northern and Southern aspects of the conflict. The *JSH* includes a broader representation of general-interest Civil War books than are reviewed by either the *Journal of American History* or the *American Historical Review*, yet it draws the line at works of such specialized focus as to address no significant interpretive or intellectual questions.

In 1976 the *JSH* reviewed 13 Civil War books. In 2002 it reviewed 66. That is a fivefold increase. How did we get from there to here? From 1976 through 1987 the numbers average 13 a year, varying between a low of 7 in 1980 to a high of 21 in 1982. We should remember the idiosyncrasies of academic reviewing, especially the lag of about a year between publication date and published review. But through these twelve years, the numbers are quite consistent. Then in 1989 there is a dramatic rise—to 27 books. This is, in fact, the year that *Battle Cry* was reviewed, suggesting, intriguingly, that McPherson's book was part of an already emerging phenomenon. For four years the number of books hovers at this level, and then we see a second significant increase, in 1993, to 45 books. Over the next decade the average number per year is 48, though the two most recent years, with totals of 64 and 66, may represent the beginning of a third, still higher, phase.

---

[8] E-mail from James M. McPherson to Drew Faust, Oct. 7, 2003.

The jump in 1993 from an average in the preceding four years of 28 books to an average of 45 books over the next ten years (an increase of more than 60 percent) may well be attributable to the extraordinary reception and impact of Ken Burns's *The Civil War*. This eleven-hour series broke television records in the fall of 1990 when it attracted an audience of 14 million. By the end of the decade more than 40 million Americans had watched one or more episodes. Burns has himself offered an explanation of why Americans loved his *Civil War*. The conflict, he explained, "continues to speak to central questions of our present time." He noted "an imperial presidency, a growing feminist movement . . . an ever present civil rights question . . . greedy Wall Street speculators who stole millions trading on inside information . . . unscrupulous military contractors . . . new weapons capable of mass destruction" as Civil War–era issues with particular resonance for contemporary Americans.[9]

Writers before Burns had found evidence in the Civil War era of what historians Peter Parish and Adam I. P. Smith have called the "increasingly recognizable shape of modern America." We see ourselves and our concerns reflected in this history. Yet the war intrigues us not simply because we identify with its central issues, not just because it seems curiously modern. We have found in it, as David Montgomery has explained, "so critical a moment in the formation of the world in which we live that it compels us to contemplate the most basic features and values of modern society." The war, he suggests, has in fact made us, has set the agenda for the world we now inhabit. We look to the war for our origins.[10]

But this sense of the war, embraced and represented by Burns, was also far from new with him, even if he was the first to offer it so compellingly in the magical medium of television. Historians and writers had long been captivated by the war as the site and reason for the emergence of modern America, even though they might have disagreed about

---

[9] Toplin, "Introduction," in *Ken Burns's The Civil War*, xv; Burns, "Four O'Clock in the Morning Courage," *ibid.*, 164.

[10] Adam I. P. Smith and Peter J. Parish, "A Contested Legacy: The Civil War and Party Politics in the North," in Grant and Parish, *Legacy of Disunion*, 81; David Montgomery, *The American Civil War and the Meanings of Freedom* (New York: Oxford Univ. Press, 1987), 1. See also Robert Penn Warren, *The Legacy of the Civil War: Meditations on the Centennial* (New York: Random House, 1961).

which attributes of this modernity to stress: the establishment of a centralized nation-state, the creation of a vigorous industrial economy, the forging of new meanings for freedom and citizenship of and by and for the people.

15   Was there a reason in the late 1980s and early 1990s that what we might call a chronic interest in the Civil War became acute? The Gulf War of 1991 was, of course, a significant factor, for Burns's series aired during a fall of anticipations and anxieties about the outbreak of war. The contemporary relevance of Civil War questions was forcefully underscored by the coincidence of the release of Burns's documentary with a real-life military drama. President George H. W. Bush, Colin Powell, and even General Norman Schwarzkopf at his post in Saudi Arabia watched the series as they contemplated their own decisions about the conflict they inaugurated in January 1991. Burns's depiction of the Civil War's terrible casualties reportedly reinforced their commitment to minimize American deaths as they developed their strategic plans.[11]

Operation Desert Storm, with its quick, seemingly easy, and, in U.S. terms, almost bloodless victory, brought war back into fashion in America. The bitterness that had followed Vietnam and the rejection of war as an effective instrument of national policy had been challenged throughout the Reagan years. But the slow rehabilitation of war in the course of the 1980s culminated in 1991's dramatic victory. Growing interest in the Civil War in the late 1980s reflected gradually changing American attitudes about military action, attitudes further and decisively affected by the conjunction in the fall of 1990 and the winter of 1991 of Ken Burns's compelling visual rendition of the conflict with George H. W. Bush's splendid little war.

Historians who recognized war as back in fashion in Reagan-Bush America did not necessarily celebrate its return, just as many scholars vehemently criticized the overwhelming military focus of the Burns's documentary. A considerable proportion of the scholars who began to direct their attention to the Civil War were children of the Viet-

---

[11] Gabor Boritt, "Lincoln and Gettysburg," in Toplin, ed., *Ken Burns's The Civil War*, 84. Boritt cites his own phone discussions with Powell in 1992 as well as newspaper reports. Boritt has also pointed out to me that the creation of the Lincoln Prize in 1991, with its $50,000 award for a work of Civil War scholarship, may have helped attract historians' attention to the war.

nam era, individuals struck by the changed political atmosphere in the 1980s, individuals who had lived through a period when war was at the heart of American public life and discourse in the late 1960s and 1970s, individuals who wanted to understand the historic roots of America's relationship with war as they now witnessed its late-century return to respectability. And although their critical perspective sharply differentiated them from a wider public that gloried in the success of Desert Storm and relished the elegiac seriousness of Ken Burns's soldier-patriots, these scholars saw in Civil War history the possibility of reaching across this divide not only to sell books but also to add important considerations to wider American public discourse. Loving the Civil War, we must not forget, has created some strange bedfellows.

The Civil War created strange bedfellows within the historical profession as well. Many academics who discovered an awakening interest in the Civil War in the late 1980s and early 1990s came to the subject with historical training and experience quite different from that of the military and political historians who had overwhelmingly dominated the literature. "Never before," wrote James McPherson and William Cooper looking back in 1998, "have so many scholars of the war ranged so widely over so many fields." If Maris Vinovskis worried in 1989 that social historians had lost the Civil War, they had by the end of the next decade certainly found it, connecting home and battle fronts and situating the Civil War battlefield decisively in the larger context of nineteenth-century American life. Three developments seem to me of particular note: the introduction of social history, with particular emphasis on the life and importance of the common soldier, into study of the Civil War military; the use of the community study as a window into the interplay of war's myriad effects and actors; and the growing interest in the experience of women and of African Americans.[12]

Significantly, this new social history—this invasion into Civil War territory by social historians, women's historians, African American historians—has done little to diminish the proportional strength of military history. As the number of social histories of the war has increased, so too has the number of military studies. Military history

[12] James M. McPherson and William J. Cooper Jr., eds., *Writing the Civil War: The Quest to Understand* (Columbia: Univ. of South Carolina Press, 1998), 3; Maris A. Vinovskis, ed., *Toward a Social History of the American Civil War: Exploratory Essays* (New York; Cambridge University Press, 1990). See also McPherson, *Drawn with the Sword*.

made up 57 percent of titles in 1988 and 69 percent of titles in 2002. On average over that fifteen-year period, 65 percent of titles were in military history. To some degree the military history of 2002 represented a changed and broadened approach, as it considered civilians in collections of essays on particular battles or explored the life of the common soldier as well as that of the general or, in the words of the editors of one series on Great Campaigns, looked "beyond the battlefield and headquarters tent." But the rapprochement of Civil War military history with social and cultural concerns is far from complete; audiences remain largely separate and segmented. The "crossover" success of *Battle Cry* remains the exception rather than the rule.[13]

20   Yet social historians have been attracted to the war by some of the same elements that engage military scholars. The Civil War offers an authenticity and intensity of experience that can rivet both researcher and reader; the war serves as a moment of truth, a moment when individuals — be they soldiers or civilians — have to define their deeply held priorities and act on them. War is a crucible that produces unsurpassed revelations about the essence of historical actors and their worlds. James McPherson has described his work with the papers of more than a thousand soldiers: "From such writings I have come to know these men better than I know most of my living acquaintances, for in their personal letters written in a time of crisis that might end their lives at any moment they revealed more of themselves than we do in our normal everyday lives." War can exact from individuals just what historians hope to find: expressions of their truest selves. We follow as historians in the footsteps of many of our century's — and our civilization's — greatest writers. As Ernest Hemingway once explained to F. Scott Fitzgerald, who enlisted too late for any significant World War I experience, "The reason you are so sore you missed the war is because war is the best subject of all. It groups the maximum of material and speeds up the action and brings out all sorts of stuff that normally you have to wait a lifetime to get." No wonder we love to study war.[14]

---

[13] This is from the mission statement for the Great Campaigns of the Civil War Series at the University of Nebraska Press, Brooks Simpson and Anne Bailey, series editors.

[14] James M. McPherson, *For Cause and Comrades: Why Men Fought in the Civil War* (New York: Oxford Univ. Press, 1997), x; Hemingway quoted by David Lipsky in "Left Behind," *New York Times Book Review*, Dec. 14, 2003, 9. See also Emory Thomas, "Rebellion and Conventional Warfare," in *Writing the Civil War*, 59.

The new Civil War historians have found in the war years an extraordinarily rich field for exploration of many of the approaches and issues that had become central to professional historical practice since the 1970s. Because the war had been almost exclusively the domain of military historians, it represented an almost untapped resource for social and cultural historians. The war was, in addition, a historical moment that was extraordinarily well documented, for mid-nineteenth-century Americans were highly literate; soldiers' letters were uncensored; and expanding government and military bureaucracies North and South accumulated vast records of both public and private lives. Historians confronted a combination of unstudied questions and vast documentation as they recognized the opportunity to pursue previously neglected issues central to the revolution the 1970s and 1980s had brought to the historical enterprise.

Historians' work in uncovering and documenting the lives of groups once labeled "inarticulate" — workers, slaves, women — had embodied a fundamental commitment to giving these new subjects of historical inquiry both voice and agency. We learned in the 1970s and 1980s how workers' actions shaped economic growth, how slaves manipulated and resisted their masters, how women used voluntary associations to control men in domains of life from sexuality to party politics. The Civil War, with its decisive events in the realms both of battle and of national policy, with its clearly defined moments of truth, offered unparalleled opportunity to explore, document, and highlight these examples of human agency. Military and political historians have long loved war because they could demonstrate the critically important actions of generals and politicians. As Mark Grimsley has observed, "Battles alter history. They decide things." Now social historians would seize the same opportunity to demonstrate far more dramatically than had been possible in their studies of lengthy social movements and processes that the actions of the so-called inarticulate mattered. . . .[15]

But to describe the movement by social historians into the Civil War as just a calculated strategy to extend domain and audience is to miss a critical component of the phenomenon. The new Civil War historians have been caught up, like their predecessors, in the drama of the conflict, in the powerful human stories that stand apart from the analytic

[15] Mark Grimsley, reviews of *This Terrible Sword*, by Peter Cozzens, and *Pea Ridge* by William Shea and Earl J. Hess, *Journal of Southern History* 60 (May 1994): 405.

and interpretive goals of the historian as social scientist. Ken Burns has described himself as above all "a historian of emotions." Emotion, he has said, "is the great glue of history." Certainly it was the glue and the appeal of his television narrative. The American public loved *The Civil War* not primarily because it dealt with constitutional or political or racial or social questions that matter today, but because it was about individual human beings whose faces we could see, whose words we could hear, as they confronted war's challenges. The presence, the threat, even the likelihood of death imposes a narrative structure and thrust on Civil War stories. The exercise of agency is always inflected by this unavoidable question; decisions are quite literally matters of life and death. The presence of such risks places the lives that interest us on a plane of enhanced meaning and value, for life itself has become the issue and cannot be taken for granted. Death offers every chronicler of war a natural narrative shape, an implicit climax for every story, a structured struggle for every tale.[16]

And the accumulations of these many narratives, these thousands and thousands of deaths into the Civil War's massive death toll, have given the conflict, as James McPherson has written, a "horrifying but hypnotic fascination," a fascination I would suggest is almost pornographic in its combination of thrill and terror. We are in some sense not so different from those New Yorkers who in 1862 crowded in to see Mathew Brady's photographs of the Antietam dead, photographs fresh from the front offering the Northern public — as they still offer us — a vicarious taste of war. We are not, as Lee reminds us, the first Americans to grow fond of the Civil War. We are both moved by the details of war's suffering and terror and captivated by the unsurpassed insight war offers into the fundamental assumptions and values of historical actors. Despite our dispassionate, professional, analytic stance, we have not remained untouched by war's elemental attractions and its emotional and sentimental fascinations. We count on these allures to build a sizeable audience for our books. In both the reality and irony of our fondness for war, we are not so unlike the Civil War generation we study.[17]

---

[16] Toplin, quoting Burns in "Introduction," Toplin, ed., *Ken Burns's The Civil War*, xxii.

[17] McPherson, *Drawn with the Sword*, 57; "Brady's Photographs of the War," *New York Times*, Sept. 26, 1862, and "Pictures of the Dead at Antietam," *New York Times*, Oct 20, 1862. See Geoffrey Gorer, "The Pornography of Death," *Encounter* 5 (1955): 49–52.

As America stood on the brink of our most recent war with Iraq, 25
journalist Chris Hedges published a best-selling book warning of war's
seductive power, its addictiveness. War, he explained, simplifies and focuses life; it offers purpose and thus exhilarates and intoxicates; it is, in
the words of Hedges's title, a "force that gives us meaning." And humans
crave meaning as much as life itself. Caught in war's allure, we ignore its
destructiveness — not just of others but of ourselves.[18]

The love affair with war Hedges describes has deep roots in history.
He invokes examples from classical Greece, from Shakespeare, as well
as from wars of our own time, just as I have been exploring the seduc-
tions of America's Civil War. Hedges offers no real solution to the problem he describes. He simply ends his book with calls for love, for Eros
in face of Thanatos. And indeed, as his book climbed the best-seller
list, the United States turned its love of war into the invasion of Iraq,
endeavoring to transform the uncertainty of fighting a terrorist enemy
without a face or location into a conflict with a purposeful, coherent,
and understandable structure — with a comprehensible narrative.

In the United States's need to respond to terrorism with war, we can
see a key element of war's appeal. War is not random, shapeless violence.
It is a human, a cultural *construction*, an "invention," as Margaret Mead
once described it, that imposes an order, a purpose, and indeed a control on violence. Through its implicit and explicit conventions, through
its rules, war limits and structures its violence; it imbues violence with
a justification, a trajectory, and a purpose. The United States sought a
war through which to respond to terrorism — even a war against an
enemy who had no relationship to September 11's terrorist acts would
do — because the nation required the sense of meaning, intention, and
goal-directedness, the lure of efficacy that war promises; the control
that terrorism obliterates. The nation needed the sense of agency that
operates within the structure of narrative provided by war.

War is defined and framed as a story, with a plot that imbues its
actors with purpose and moves toward victory for one or another side.

---

[18] Chris Hedges, *War Is a Force That Gives Us Meaning* (New York: Public Affairs
Press, 2002). As novelist and literary critic Nancy Huston has written, "Specifically in
order that human violence not be reducible to animal violence, it is imperative for men
to establish a narrative sequence." By its very definition as war, violence gains a logic, a
structure, a goal, *a story*. Nancy Huston, "Tales of War and Tears of Women," *Women's
Studies International Forum* 5 (1982): 271. See also Margaret Mead, "Warfare Is Only an
Invention — Not a Biological Necessity," *Asia* 40 (1940): 402–5.

This is why it provides the satisfaction of meaning to its participants; this is why, too, it offers such a natural attraction to writers and historians. Yet just as we need war, because in Hemingway's words, it is "the best subject of all," so in some sense war needs us. Writers and historians are critical to defining and elaborating the narratives that differentiate war from purposeless violence, the stories that explain, contextualize, construct, order, and rationalize — eliding from one to the other meaning of that word — what we call war. Are we then simply another part of the dangerous phenomenon Hedges has described? In writing about war, even against war, do we nevertheless reinforce its attraction and affirm its meaning? "When we write about warfare," Hedges warns, "the prurient fascination usually rises up to defeat the message." What, indeed, is the message that our historiography conveys? "Is there," as Susan Sontag has asked, "an antidote to the perennial seductiveness of war?" Are we as historians part of the problem or part of the solution?[19] Attracted by the potential narrative coherence of war, we also create and reinforce it. Out of historians' war stories — from Thucydides onward — we have fashioned war's seeming rationality and helped to define its meaning. Have we in so doing contributed to its allure?

Historian George Mosse once warned, "We must never lose our horror, never try to integrate war and its consequences into our longing for the sacred.... If we confront mass death naked, stripped of all myth, we may have slightly more chance to avoid making the devil's pact" with war. But the effort to retain our horror is immensely aided by our recognition and acknowledgment of war's attractions. The complexity of irony disrupts myth, undermines unified narrative and unexamined purpose, questions meaning.[20]

30   When we recognize, like Robert E. Lee, that war is both terrible and alluring, we may move both ourselves and our history to a different place. We separate ourselves from war's myths through irony and open ourselves to its contradictions. Yet if we cannot understand why we love it, we cannot comprehend and explain why it has seduced so many others. In acknowledging its attraction we diminish its power. Perhaps

---

[19] Hedges, *War Is a Force*, 91; Susan Sontag, *Regarding the Pain of Others* (New York: Farrar, Straus, Giroux, 2003), 122. See also a powerful statement on the attractions of war: James Carroll "War's Power of Seduction," *Boston Globe*, Mar. 11, 2003.

[20] George Mosse, quoted in David Maraniss, *They Marched Into Sunlight* (New York: Simon and Schuster, 2003), 101.

we can free ourselves to construct a different sort of narrative about its meaning. But I am not sure. . . .

. . . I have written elsewhere about the role of war stories in mobilizing both men and women for war.[21] Seductive tales of glory, honor, sacrifice provide one means of making war possible.

But there is another more complex way as well, one that does not depend on an idealization or romanticization of war. War is, by its very definition, a story. War imposes an orderly narrative on what without its definition of purpose and structure would be simply violence. We as writers create that story; we remember that story; we provide the narrative that by its very existence defines war's purpose and meaning. We love war because of these stories. But we should ask ourselves how in the construction of war's stories we may be helping to construct war itself. "War is a force that gives *us* meaning." But what do we and our writings give to war?

---

[21] Faust, "Altars of Sacrifice."

Sin Boldly

HENRY LOUIS GATES JR. is a professor at Harvard University, where he chaired the Department of African and African American Studies from 1991 to 2006. He is currently director of the W. E. B. Du Bois Institute for African and African American Research.

In his 1994 memoir, *Colored People*, Gates describes his early life in Piedmont, West Virginia, the small mill town where he grew up. His father was a millworker, his mother a housecleaner; both were avid readers, with high expectations for their sons' academic success. Gates began elementary school in 1956, the year after the school was integrated in response to the Supreme Court's order in *Brown v. Board of Education*. Following in the footsteps of his brother Rocky, six years his senior, Gates was an excellent student, and he went on to Potomac State College of West Virginia.

In 1969, at the end of his freshman year, Gates transferred to Yale. He quickly distinguished himself: in his senior year, he was one of twelve students selected as "scholars of the house," which meant that he was freed from his classes and permitted to work independently on a single project. After graduating from Yale *summa cum laude* in history, he earned a Mellon Fellowship to support study at Cambridge. There, he earned his M.A. and Ph.D. in English literature and began his career as a literary critic specializing in early African American writing.

Gates has written in many genres. As a young man, he was a journalist, writing for the *Yale Daily News* and working briefly as a correspondent for *Time*. He has written a column for the *New York Times* and many articles for *The New Yorker*. As a scholar, Gates has written books of literary theory and criticism, biography, and cultural criticism. He has edited encyclopedias of African American history and culture, and he has assumed many roles—writer, narrator, host, co-producer—in the creation of documentary films and public television series.

Gates's writing often blends his scholarly interest in African American life and literature with reflections on his personal experiences—his childhood in Piedmont, his involvement in the politicized world of academia during the last decades of the twentieth century, his travels to Africa, his interactions with America's leading artists, entertainers, and intellectuals. You'll hear a sampling of his narrative voice in "Sin Boldly," a chapter from *Colored People* recounting his first year after high school.

———————

In 1968, three of the Fearsome Foursome graduated from high school. Soul Moe was called upon to serve his country in Vietnam, and Swano and I would head down to Potomac State. (Roland had been held back a couple of years.) I gave the valedictory address at graduation, defying tradition by writing my own speech—surreptitiously, because this was not allowed. All through the last six weeks of marking period I had practiced delivering the traditional prepared speech with Miss Twigg, our senior English teacher, then had gone home to rehearse my real speech with Mama. Mama had a refined sense of vocal presentation and a wonderful sense of irony and timing. My speech was about Vietnam, abortion, and civil rights, about the sense of community our class shared, since so many of us had been together for twelve years, about the individual's rights and responsibilities in his or her community, and about the necessity to defy norms out of love. I searched the audience for Miss Twigg's face, just to see her expression when I read the speech! She turned as red as a beet, but she liked the speech, and as good as told me so with a big wink at the end of the ceremony.

My one year at Potomac State College of West Virginia University, in Keyser, all of five miles away, was memorable for two reasons: because of my English classes with Duke Anthony Whitmore and my first real love affair, with Maura Gibson.

I came to Potomac State to begin that long, arduous trek toward medical school. I enrolled in August 1968, a week before Labor Day, and I was scared to death. While I had been a good student at Piedmont High, I had no idea how well I would fare in the big-time competition of a college class that included several of the best students from Keyser High, as well as bright kids from throughout the state. I had never questioned my decision to attend Potomac State; it was inevitable: you went there after Piedmont High, as sure as the night follows the day. My uncles Raymond and David had attended it in the fifties, my brother in the early sixties, and my cousin Greg had begun the year before. I would attend too, then go off to "the university" — in Morgantown — to become a doctor.

Greg had told me about life on campus, about the freedom of choice, about card parties in the Union, and, of course, about the women. But he had also told me one thing early in his freshman year that had stayed with me throughout my senior year in Piedmont. "There's an English teacher down there," he had said, "who's going to blow your mind."

5   "What's his name?" I responded.

"Duke Anthony Whitmore," he replied.

"Duke?" I said. "What kind of name is Duke? Is he an Englishman?"

"No, dummy," Greg replied. "He's a white guy from Baltimore."

So as I nervously slouched my way through registration a year later, I found myself standing before the ferocious Mr. Gallagher, who enjoyed the reputation of being tough. He gave me the name of my adviser.

10   I looked at the name; it was not Whitmore. "Can I be assigned to Mr. Whitmore?" I ventured. "Because I've heard quite a lot about him from my cousin."

"You'll have to ask him," Mr. Gallagher said. "He's over there."

I made my way to Mr. Whitmore's table, introduced myself tentatively, stated my case, telling him my cousin Greg had said that he was a great teacher, a wonderful inspiration, etc., etc. What Greg had really said was: "This guy Whitmore is crazy, just like you!" It was love at first sight, at least for me. And that, in retrospect, was the beginning of the end of my twelve-year-old dream of becoming a doctor.

Learning English and American literature from the Duke was a game to which I looked forward every day. I had always loved English and had been blessed with some dedicated and able teachers. But reading books was something I had always thought of as a pastime, certainly not as a vocation. The Duke made the study of literature an alluring prospect.

Duke Whitmore did not suffer fools gladly. He did not suffer fools at all. Our classes — I enrolled in everything he taught, despite his protests, which I have to say weren't very strenuous — soon came to be dominated by three or four voices. We would argue and debate just about everything from Emerson and Thoreau to the war in Vietnam and racial discrimination. He would recite a passage from a poem or play, then demand that we tell him, rapid-fire, its source.

"*King Lear,*" I responded one day. 15

"What act, what scene, Mr. Gates?" he demanded.

"Act Three, Scene Four," I shouted out blindly, not having the faintest clue as to whether the passage that he had recited was from *Hamlet* or the Book of Job.

"Exactly," he responded with a certain twinkle in his eye. "Sin boldly," he would tell me later, citing Martin Luther. My reckless citation was wrong, of course, but he wished to reward me for my audacity.

It was a glorious experience. Words and thoughts, ideas and visions, came alive for me in his classroom. It was he who showed me, by his example, that ideas had a life of their own and that there were other professions as stimulating and as rewarding as being a doctor.

After an academically successful year, Professor Whitmore encour- 20 aged me to transfer to the Ivy League. I wrote to Harvard, Yale, and Princeton. Since I had cousins who had gone to Harvard and Princeton, I decided to try for Yale. I sent off the application and took a summer job in the personnel office of the paper mill. I'd been hired for the express purpose of encouraging a few black people to transfer into the craft unions; I recruited them and administered the necessary tests. In three months, each union had been integrated, with barely an audible murmur from its members. Things were changing in Piedmont — a little.

Though we didn't become an item until our freshman year at Potomac State, Maura Gibson and I had known each other from a distance in high school. I used to run into her at the bowling alley and at Jimmy's Pizza next door. She was sharp on her feet and loved to argue. Once, she took me to task for talking about race so much. You can't talk about the weather without bringing up race, she charged. I was embarrassed about that at first, then pleased.

Once we were at college, Maura and I started having long talks on the phone, first about nothing at all and then about everything. The next thing I remember happening between us was parking in her green Dodge up in the colored cemetery on Radical Hill, near where just about all the Keyser colored, and much of the white trash, lived. "Radical" is a synonym in the valley for tacky or ramshackle. I'm not sure which came first, the name or what it came to mean. That's where we were when Horse Lowe (the coach of the college's football team and the owner of the property that abuts the colored cemetery) put his big red face into Maura's window, beat on the windshield with his fist, then told me to get the hell off his property.

Horse Lowe would wait until a couple had begun to pet heavily, then he'd sneak up on the car. He liked to catch you exposed. Even so, we used to park up there all the time. I figured that he'd get tired of throwing us out before I got tired of parking.

On weekends during the summer of 1969, I'd drive over to Rehoboth Beach, in Delaware, to see Maura, who was working as a waitress at a place called the Crab Pot. I'd leave work on Friday at about four o'clock, then drive all the way to Delaware, through Washington and the Beltway, past Baltimore and Annapolis, over the Chesapeake Bridge, past Ocean City, arriving at Rehoboth before midnight, with as much energy as if I had just awakened. We'd get a motel room after her shift ended, and she'd bring a bushel of crabs, steamed in the hot spice called Old Bay. We'd get lots of ice-cold Budweiser and we'd have a feast, listening to Junior Walker play his saxophone, play "What Does It Take" over and over and over again. "What does it take to win your love for me? . . ."

25   Since Maura was white, I felt that I was making some sort of vague political statement, especially in the wake of Sammy Davis Jr. and *Guess Who's Coming to Dinner*. Others concurred. We were hassled at the beach. Somehow, for reasons having to do with nudity and sensuality, blacks were not allowed to walk along most beachfronts or attend resorts. I personally integrated many places at Rehoboth Beach that summer.

I was used to being stared at and somewhat used to being the only black person on the beach, or in a restaurant, or at a motel. But I hadn't quite realized how upset people could be until the day that some white guy sicced his Saint Bernard on me as Maura and I walked by. Certainly Maura and I had been no strangers to controversy, but we usually took pains not to invite it. Back home, we had sneaked around at first, hiding in cemeteries and in a crowd of friends, almost never being seen together in public alone. Until we were found out — by her father, of all people. A man called "'Bama," of all things.

It was the evening we had agreed to meet at the big oak tree on Spring Street in Keyser, near one of her friends' houses. I picked her up in my '57 Chevrolet, and we went up to harass the Horse. Afterward,

I dropped her off, then drove the five miles back to Piedmont. By the time I got home, Maura had called a dozen times. It turned out that her father had followed her down the street and hidden behind a tree while she waited, had watched her climb into my car. He knew the whole thing.

And he, no progressive on race matters, was sickened and outraged.

Soon, it seemed, all of the Valley knew the whole thing, and everybody had an opinion about it. We were apparently the first interracial couple in Mineral County, and there was hell to pay. People began making oblique threats, in the sort of whispers peculiar to small towns. When friends started warning my parents about them, they bought me a '69 Mustang so I could travel to and from school — and the colored graveyard — safely. (The Chevy had taken to conking out unpredictably.) Some kids at Potomac State started calling us names, anonymously, out of dormitory windows. And in the middle of all this chaos, 'Bama Gibson, Maura's father, decided he was going to run for mayor.

Lawd, Lawd, Lawd.

In his own redneck way, 'Bama Gibson was a perfectly nice man, but he was not exactly mayoral material. He had been a postman and became some sort of supervisor at the post office. He was very personable, everybody liked him, and he knew everybody's business, the way a postman in any small town does. With the whole town talking about how terrible it was that his daughter was dating a colored boy, and the men giving him their sympathy and declaring what they'd do to that nigger if that nigger ever touched their daughter, old 'Bama up and announced his candidacy.

Dr. Church, former president of the college, was the obvious frontrunner. People were saying he'd already started to measure the mayor's office for new curtains. Certainly no one would have given 'Bama any hope of beating Dr. Church, even before my nappy head came on the horizon. With you on these crackers' minds, Daddy told me, he's got two chances: slim and none. Boy, how do you *get* into all this trouble?

Meantime, at the height of the campaign, Roland, Jerry, Swano, and I decided to integrate the Swordfish, a weekend hangout where all the college kids went to listen to a live band — usually E. G. Taylor and the Sounds of Soul, a white band with a black, Eugene Taylor, as lead singer. Eugene could *sing*. He wasn't so great with learning the words, but that Negro could warble. He'd make up words as he went along, using sounds similar to those he could not remember but making no sense.

Still, we wanted the right to hear Eugene mess up James Brown's words, same as anybody else, so we started to plot our move. Late one Friday night, when the Swordfish was rocking and packed, we headed up New Creek in our Soul Mobile, which we had washed for the occasion, even replacing the old masking tape over the holes in the roof. The Fearsome Foursome made their date with destiny. We were silent as we drove into the parking lot. There was nothing left to say. We were scared to death but just had to get on with it.

35   We parked the car and strolled up the stairs to the Swordfish. Since there was no cover charge, we walked straight into the middle of the dance floor. That's when the slo-mo started, an effect exacerbated by the strobe lights. Everybody froze: the kids from Piedmont and Keyser who had grown up with us; the students from Potomac State; the rednecks and crackers from up the hollers, the ones who came to town once a week all dressed up in their Sears, Roebuck perma-pressed drawers, their Thom McAn semi-leather shoes, their ultimately *white* sox, and their hair slicked back and wet-looking. The kids of rednecks, who liked to drink gallons of 3.2 beer, threaten everybody within earshot, and puke all over themselves — they froze too, their worst nightmare staring them in the face.

After what seemed like hours but was probably less than a minute, a homely white boy with extra-greasy blond hair recovered and began to shout "Niggers" as his face assumed the ugly mask of hillbilly racism. I stared at this white boy's face, which turned redder and redder as *he* turned into the Devil, calling on his boys to kick our asses: calling us niggers and niggers and niggers to help them summon up their courage. White boys started moving around us, forming a circle around ours. Our good friends from Keyser and Potomac State were still frozen, embarrassed that we were *in* there, that we had violated their space, dared to cross the line. No help from them. (I lost lots of friends that night.) Then, breaking through the circle of rednecks, came the owner, who started screaming: Get out of here! Get out of here! and picked up Fisher and slammed his head against the wall. It wasn't easy to see because of all the smoke and because of the strobe effect of the flashing blue lights, but I remember being surprised at how Roland's Afro had kept its shape when his head sprang back off the wall, the way a basketball keeps its shape no matter how much or how hard you dribble it.

Moe and I hauled Fisher off the ground, with Swano's broad shoulders driving through the 'necks the way Bubba Smith used to do for the Baltimore Colts. I wondered if Roland's head would stop bleeding. Fuck you, motherfucker, I heard myself say. We're gonna shut your racist ass down. We're gonna shut your ass down, repeated Moe and Swano in chorus. Take a good look around you, you crackers, cuz this is your last time here.

We dragged Fisher to the car, ducking the bottles and cans as we sped away. Roland's head had stopped its bleeding by the time we passed Potomac Valley Hospital, which we called the meat factory because one of the doctors was reputed to be such a butcher, so we drove on past it and headed for my house. What'll y'all do now? Daddy asked as Mama bandaged Roland Fisher's head.

And yes, the place was shut down. We called the State Human Rights Commission on Monday, and the commissioner, Carl Glass, came up to Piedmont a few days later. He interviewed the four of us separately, and then he went out to the Swordfish and interviewed the proprietor, who by this time had told everybody white and colored in Keyser that he was going to get that troublemaker Gates. He swore to the commissioner that he would close down before he let niggers in. The commissioner took him at his word and sent an official edict telling him to integrate or shut down. As the man promised, he shut it down. And that is why the Swordfish nightclub is now Samson's Family Restaurant, run by a very nice Filipino family.

Well, all of this broke out in the middle of 'Bama Gibson's campaign 40 to be the first postman elected as Mayor of Keyser, West Virginia, The Friendliest City in the U.S.A., as the road sign boasted — to which we chorused "bullshit" whenever we passed it.

The whole town talked about this campaign, from sunup to sundown. And there were some curious developments. Our family doctor, Dr. Staggers (our high school principal, Mr. Staggers's son), went out of his way to tell me that lots of his friends, well-educated and liberal, had decided to suspend disbelief and vote for 'Bama, just to prove (as he put it) that Keyser is not Birmingham. Then the colored people, who never voted, decided to register and turn out for good ole 'Bama. The college kids at Potomac State, the ones not busy calling Maura "nigger-lover" from their dormitory windows, turned out in droves. And all the romantics who lived in Keyser, those who truly respected the idea of love and passion, voted for 'Bama. All both of them. Bizarrely enough, the election was turning into a plebiscite on interracial relationships.

I stayed out of Keyser on the day of the election, terrified that I'd already caused Maura's father to lose. If it's close, there's no sense aggravating the ones sitting on the fence, rubbing their nose in it, Daddy had said. And so I waited for Maura's phone call, which came around eleven-thirty and informed me that we had nothing more to worry about, her father had trampled Dr. Church. No longer would the police follow us, daring us to go even one mile over the speed limit. That's what she told me, and I could scarcely believe it. I started parking my car on red lines and in front of fire hydrants, just to test her assertion. She was right.

It was also because of 'Bama's new office that I learned that the West Virginia State Police had opened a file on me in Mineral County, which identified me for possible custodial detention if and when race riots started. Maura gave me the news late one night, whispering it over the phone. Old 'Bama, whom victory had made magnanimous, had wanted me to know and to be warned.

I remember feeling sick and scared . . . and then, when that passed, a little flattered. I was eighteen, had scarcely been outside Mineral County, and someone in authority decided I was dangerous? I mean, I liked to think so. But that an official establishment should collude with my fantasies of importance was quite another matter.

45   I took it as a sign that it was time for me to leave the Valley and go Elsewhere. I did leave it, that very fall, packing my bags for New Haven. But leaving it *behind* was never a possibility. It did not take me long to realize that.

The "Personal Statement" for my Yale application began: "My grandfather was colored, my father was Negro, and I am black." And it concluded: "As always, whitey now sits in judgment of me, preparing to cast my fate. It is your decision either to let me blow with the wind as a non-entity or to encourage the development of self. Allow me to prove myself."

I wince at the rhetoric today, but they let me in.

A More Perfect Union

BARACK OBAMA's story is well known. The son of "a black
man from Kenya and a white woman from Kansas," he was born
in 1961 in Honolulu, Hawaii, where he spent his first six years. In
1967, his mother married a man from Indonesia, and the family
moved to Jakarta. Because his mother believed that he would find
better educational opportunities in the United States, Obama returned to Honolulu in 1971, taking up residence with his grandpar-
ents. He attended Occidental College in Los Angeles, then moved to
New York to attend Columbia University, graduating in 1983.

From 1985 to 1988, Obama worked as a community organizer
on Chicago's South Side, helping the people of the Altgeld Gardens
housing project to advocate for safer housing and more effective
social services. "It was in these neighborhoods," he later said, "that
I received the best education I ever had"; specifically, he learned
to listen well and to seek common ground upon which alliances
could be formed. His pursuit of a more formal education took him
to Harvard Law School, where he became president of the *Harvard
Law Review.*

Because he was the first African American to lead the *Law Review*, Obama became the subject of "a burst of publicity," which
created the opportunity to write his first book. "A few publishers
called," he wrote, "and I, imagining myself to have something original to say about the current state of race relations, agreed to take
a year off after graduation and put my thoughts to paper." *Dreams
from My Father* recounts Obama's youth, his schooling, and his experiences as a community organizer. The memoir is carefully crafted,
its narrative line often curving to accommodate vivid descriptions of
places Obama lived or people he met, or to offer reflections about
his search for identity as a mixed-race African American.

Returning to Chicago in 1992, Obama took a position at the
University of Chicago Law School teaching constitutional law. His
career as a legislator began in 1996 with his election to the Illinois

state senate; in 2004 he was elected to the U.S. Senate, and four years later, he won the Democratic nomination for the presidency.

In the spring of 2008, Obama's campaign was threatened by the disclosure of remarks by Reverend Jeremiah Wright that were widely perceived as anti-white or anti-American. Wright was the pastor of Trinity Baptist Church, which the Obama family had attended for years. When tapes of Reverend Wright's comments went viral on the Internet, Obama was called upon to condemn them. He criticized the most inflammatory remarks, but he also used the occasion to set forth his vision of an America in which divisions between black and white, or between liberal and conservative, could be overcome. Reading "A More Perfect Union" in Philadelphia on March 18 of that year, Obama effected a turning point in the campaign. In November, he defeated Republican John McCain to become the forty-fourth president of the United States.

"We the people, in order to form a more perfect union."

Two hundred and twenty-one years ago, in a hall that still stands across the street, a group of men gathered and, with these simple words, launched America's improbable experiment in democracy. Farmers and scholars, statesmen and patriots who had traveled across an ocean to escape tyranny and persecution finally made real their declaration of independence at a Philadelphia convention that lasted through the spring of 1787.

The document they produced was eventually signed but ultimately unfinished. It was stained by this nation's original sin of slavery, a question that divided the colonies and brought the convention to a stalemate until the founders chose to allow the slave trade to continue for at least twenty more years, and to leave any final resolution to future generations.

Of course, the answer to the slavery question was already embedded within our Constitution — a Constitution that had at its very core the ideal of equal citizenship under the law; a Constitution that promised its people liberty, and justice, and a union that could be and should be perfected over time.

5   And yet words on a parchment would not be enough to deliver slaves from bondage, or provide men and women of every color and creed their full rights and obligations as citizens of the United States.

What would be needed were Americans in successive generations who were willing to do their part — through protests and struggle, on the streets and in the courts, through a civil war and civil disobedience and always at great risk — to narrow that gap between the promise of our ideals and the reality of their time.

This was one of the tasks we set forth at the beginning of this campaign — to continue the long march of those who came before us, a march for a more just, more equal, more free, more caring, and more prosperous America. I chose to run for the presidency at this moment in history because I believe deeply that we cannot solve the challenges of our time unless we solve them together — unless we perfect our union by understanding that we may have different stories, but we hold common hopes; that we may not look the same and we may not have come from the same place, but we all want to move in the same direction — towards a better future for our children and our grandchildren.

This belief comes from my unyielding faith in the decency and generosity of the American people. But it also comes from my own American story.

I am the son of a black man from Kenya and a white woman from Kansas. I was raised with the help of a white grandfather who survived a Depression to serve in Patton's Army during World War II and a white grandmother who worked on a bomber assembly line at Fort Leavenworth while he was overseas. I've gone to some of the best schools in America and lived in one of the world's poorest nations. I am married to a black American who carries within her the blood of slaves and slaveowners — an inheritance we pass on to our two precious daughters. I have brothers, sisters, nieces, nephews, uncles, and cousins, of every race and every hue, scattered across three continents, and for as long as I live, I will never forget that in no other country on Earth is my story even possible.

It's a story that hasn't made me the most conventional candidate. But it is a story that has seared into my genetic makeup the idea that this nation is more than the sum of its parts — that out of many, we are truly one.

Throughout the first year of this campaign, against all predictions   10
to the contrary, we saw how hungry the American people were for this message of unity. Despite the temptation to view my candidacy through a purely racial lens, we won commanding victories in states with some of the whitest populations in the country. In South Carolina, where

the Confederate Flag still flies, we built a powerful coalition of African Americans and white Americans.

This is not to say that race has not been an issue in the campaign. At various stages in the campaign, some commentators have deemed me either "too black" or "not black enough." We saw racial tensions bubble to the surface during the week before the South Carolina primary. The press has scoured every exit poll for the latest evidence of racial polarization, not just in terms of white and black, but black and brown as well.

And yet, it has only been in the last couple of weeks that the discussion of race in this campaign has taken a particularly divisive turn.

On one end of the spectrum, we've heard the implication that my candidacy is somehow an exercise in affirmative action; that it's based solely on the desire of wide-eyed liberals to purchase racial reconciliation on the cheap. On the other end, we've heard my former pastor, Reverend Jeremiah Wright, use incendiary language to express views that have the potential not only to widen the racial divide, but views that denigrate both the greatness and the goodness of our nation; that rightly offend white and black alike.

I have already condemned, in unequivocal terms, the statements of Reverend Wright that have caused such controversy. For some, nagging questions remain. Did I know him to be an occasionally fierce critic of American domestic and foreign policy? Of course. Did I ever hear him make remarks that could be considered controversial while I sat in church? Yes. Did I strongly disagree with many of his political views? Absolutely—just as I'm sure many of you have heard remarks from your pastors, priests, or rabbis with which you strongly disagreed.

15   But the remarks that have caused this recent firestorm weren't simply controversial. They weren't simply a religious leader's effort to speak out against perceived injustice. Instead, they expressed a profoundly distorted view of this country—a view that sees white racism as endemic, and that elevates what is wrong with America above all that we know is right with America; a view that sees the conflicts in the Middle East as rooted primarily in the actions of stalwart allies like Israel, instead of emanating from the perverse and hateful ideologies of radical Islam.

As such, Reverend Wright's comments were not only wrong but divisive, divisive at a time when we need unity; racially charged at a time when we need to come together to solve a set of monumental problems—two wars, a terrorist threat, a falling economy, a chronic health care crisis, and potentially devastating climate change; problems that are neither black or white or Latino or Asian, but rather problems that confront us all.

Given my background, my politics, and my professed values and ideals, there will no doubt be those for whom my statements of condemnation are not enough. Why associate myself with Reverend Wright in the first place, they may ask? Why not join another church? And I confess that if all that I knew of Reverend Wright were the snippets of those sermons that have run in an endless loop on the television and YouTube, or if Trinity United Church of Christ conformed to the caricatures being peddled by some commentators, there is no doubt that I would react in much the same way.

But the truth is, that isn't all that I know of the man. The man I met more than twenty years ago is a man who helped introduce me to my Christian faith, a man who spoke to me about our obligations to love one another; to care for the sick and lift up the poor. He is a man who served his country as a U.S. Marine; who has studied and lectured at some of the finest universities and seminaries in the country, and who for over thirty years led a church that serves the community by doing God's work here on Earth — by housing the homeless, ministering to the needy, providing day care services and scholarships and prison ministries, and reaching out to those suffering from HIV/AIDS. . . .

. . . Like other predominantly black churches across the country, Trinity embodies the black community in its entirety — the doctor and the welfare mom, the model student and the former gang-banger. Like other black churches, Trinity's services are full of raucous laughter and sometimes bawdy humor. They are full of dancing, clapping, screaming, and shouting that may seem jarring to the untrained ear. The church contains in full the kindness and cruelty, the fierce intelligence and the shocking ignorance, the struggles and successes, the love and yes, the bitterness and bias that make up the black experience in America.

And this helps explain, perhaps, my relationship with Reverend 20 Wright. As imperfect as he may be, he has been like family to me. He strengthened my faith, officiated my wedding, and baptized my children. Not once in my conversations with him have I heard him talk about any ethnic group in derogatory terms, or treat whites with whom he interacted with anything but courtesy and respect. He contains within him the contradictions — the good and the bad — of the community that he has served diligently for so many years.

I can no more disown him than I can disown the black community. I can no more disown him than I can my white grandmother — a woman who helped raise me, a woman who sacrificed again and again for me, a woman who loves me as much as she loves anything in this world, but a woman who once confessed her fear of black men who passed by her on the street, and who on more than one occasion has uttered racial or ethnic stereotypes that made me cringe.

These people are a part of me. And they are a part of America, this country that I love.

Some will see this as an attempt to justify or excuse comments that are simply inexcusable. I can assure you it is not. I suppose the politically safe thing would be to move on from this episode and just hope that it fades into the woodwork. We can dismiss Reverend Wright as a crank or a demagogue, just as some have dismissed Geraldine Ferraro, in the aftermath of her recent statements, as harboring some deep-seated racial bias.

But race is an issue that I believe this nation cannot afford to ignore right now. We would be making the same mistake that Reverend Wright made in his offending sermons about America — to simplify and stereotype and amplify the negative to the point that it distorts reality.

25   The fact is that the comments that have been made and the issues that have surfaced over the last few weeks reflect the complexities of race in this country that we've never really worked through — a part of our union that we have yet to perfect. And if we walk away now, if we simply retreat into our respective corners, we will never be able to come together and solve challenges like health care, or education, or the need to find good jobs for every American.

Understanding this reality requires a reminder of how we arrived at this point. As William Faulkner once wrote, "The past isn't dead and buried. In fact, it isn't even past." We do not need to recite here the history of racial injustice in this country. But we do need to remind ourselves that so many of the disparities that exist in the African American community today can be directly traced to inequalities passed on from an earlier generation that suffered under the brutal legacy of slavery and Jim Crow.

Segregated schools were, and are, inferior schools; we still haven't fixed them, fifty years after *Brown v. Board of Education*, and the inferior education they provided, then and now, helps explain the pervasive achievement gap between today's black and white students.

Legalized discrimination — where blacks were prevented, often through violence, from owning property, or loans were not granted to African American business owners, or black homeowners could not access FHA mortgages, or blacks were excluded from unions, or the police force, or fire departments — meant that black families could not amass any meaningful wealth to bequeath to future generations. That history helps explain the wealth and income gap between black and white, and the concentrated pockets of poverty that persist in so many of today's urban and rural communities.

A lack of economic opportunity among black men, and the shame and frustration that came from not being able to provide for one's family, contributed to the erosion of black families — a problem that welfare policies for many years may have worsened. And the lack of basic services in so many urban black neighborhoods — parks for kids to play in, police walking the beat, regular garbage pick-up and building code enforcement — all helped create a cycle of violence, blight, and neglect that continue to haunt us.

This is the reality in which Reverend Wright and other African Americans of his generation grew up. They came of age in the late fifties and early sixties, a time when segregation was still the law of the land and opportunity was systematically constricted. What's remarkable is not how many failed in the face of discrimination, but rather how many men and women overcame the odds; how many were able to make a way out of no way for those like me who would come after them.

But for all those who scratched and clawed their way to get a piece of the American Dream, there were many who didn't make it — those who were ultimately defeated, in one way or another, by discrimination. That legacy of defeat was passed on to future generations — those young men and increasingly young women who we see standing on street corners or languishing in our prisons, without hope or prospects for the future. Even for those blacks who did make it, questions of race, and racism, continue to define their worldview in fundamental ways. For the men and women of Reverend Wright's generation, the memories of humiliation and doubt and fear have not gone away; nor has the anger and the bitterness of those years. That anger may not get expressed in public, in front of white coworkers or white friends. But it does find voice in the barbershop or around the kitchen table. At times, that anger is exploited by politicians, to gin up votes along racial lines, or to make up for a politician's own failings.

And occasionally it finds voice in the church on Sunday morning, in the pulpit and in the pews. The fact that so many people are surprised to hear that anger in some of Reverend Wright's sermons simply reminds us of the old truism that the most segregated hour in American life occurs on Sunday morning. That anger is not always productive; indeed, all too often it distracts attention from solving real problems; it keeps us from squarely facing our own complicity in our condition, and prevents the African American community from forging the alliances it needs to bring about real change. But the anger is real; it is powerful; and to simply wish it away, to condemn it without understanding its roots, only serves to widen the chasm of misunderstanding that exists between the races.

In fact, a similar anger exists within segments of the white community. Most working- and middle-class white Americans don't feel that they have been particularly privileged by their race. Their experience is the immigrant experience — as far as they're concerned, no one's handed them anything, they've built it from scratch. They've worked hard all their lives, many times only to see their jobs shipped overseas or their pension dumped after a lifetime of labor. They are anxious about their futures, and feel their dreams slipping away; in an era of stagnant wages and global competition, opportunity comes to be seen as a zero sum game, in which your dreams come at my expense. So when they are told to bus their children to a school across town; when they hear that an African American is getting an advantage in landing a good job or a spot in a good college because of an injustice that they themselves never committed; when they're told that their fears about crime in urban neighborhoods are somehow prejudiced, resentment builds over time.

Like the anger within the black community, these resentments aren't always expressed in polite company. But they have helped shape the political landscape for at least a generation. Anger over welfare and affirmative action helped forge the Reagan Coalition. Politicians routinely exploited fears of crime for their own electoral ends. Talk show hosts and conservative commentators built entire careers unmasking bogus claims of racism while dismissing legitimate discussions of racial injustice and inequality as mere political correctness or reverse racism.

35   Just as black anger often proved counterproductive, so have these white resentments distracted attention from the real culprits of the middle class squeeze — a corporate culture rife with inside dealing,

questionable accounting practices, and short-term greed; a Washington dominated by lobbyists and special interests; economic policies that favor the few over the many. And yet, to wish away the resentments of white Americans, to label them as misguided or even racist, without recognizing they are grounded in legitimate concerns — this too widens the racial divide, and blocks the path to understanding.

This is where we are right now. It's a racial stalemate we've been stuck in for years. Contrary to the claims of some of my critics, black and white, I have never been so naïve as to believe that we can get beyond our racial divisions in a single election cycle, or with a single candidacy — particularly a candidacy as imperfect as my own.

But I have asserted a firm conviction — a conviction rooted in my faith in God and my faith in the American people — that working together we can move beyond some of our old racial wounds, and that in fact we have no choice if we are to continue on the path of a more perfect union.

For the African American community, that path means embracing the burdens of our past without becoming victims of our past. It means continuing to insist on a full measure of justice in every aspect of American life. But it also means binding our particular grievances — for better health care, and better schools, and better jobs — to the larger aspirations of all Americans — the white woman struggling to break the glass ceiling, the white man who's been laid off, the immigrant trying to feed his family. And it means taking full responsibility for our own lives — by demanding more from our fathers, and spending more time with our children, and reading to them, and teaching them that while they may face challenges and discrimination in their own lives, they must never succumb to despair or cynicism; they must always believe that they can write their own destiny.

Ironically, this quintessentially American — and yes, conservative — notion of self-help found frequent expression in Reverend Wright's sermons. But what my former pastor too often failed to understand is that embarking on a program of self-help also requires a belief that society can change.

The profound mistake of Reverend Wright's sermons is not that he   40
spoke about racism in our society. It's that he spoke as if our society was static; as if no progress has been made; as if this country — a country that has made it possible for one of his own members to run for the highest office in the land and build a coalition of white and black,

Latino and Asian, rich and poor, young and old — is still irrevocably bound to a tragic past. But what we know — what we have seen — is that America can change. That is the true genius of this nation. What we have already achieved gives us hope — the audacity to hope — for what we can and must achieve tomorrow.

In the white community, the path to a more perfect union means acknowledging that what ails the African American community does not just exist in the minds of black people; that the legacy of discrimination — and current incidents of discrimination, while less overt than in the past — are real and must be addressed. Not just with words, but with deeds — by investing in our schools and our communities; by enforcing our civil rights laws and ensuring fairness in our criminal justice system; by providing this generation with ladders of opportunity that were unavailable for previous generations. It requires all Americans to realize that your dreams do not have to come at the expense of my dreams; that investing in the health, welfare, and education of black and brown and white children will ultimately help all of America prosper.

In the end, then, what is called for is nothing more, and nothing less, than what all the world's great religions demand: that we do unto others as we would have them do unto us. Let us be our brother's keeper, Scripture tells us. Let us be our sister's keeper. Let us find that common stake we all have in one another, and let our politics reflect that spirit as well.

For we have a choice in this country. We can accept a politics that breeds division, and conflict, and cynicism. We can tackle race only as spectacle — as we did in the O. J. trial — or in the wake of tragedy, as we did in the aftermath of Katrina — or as fodder for the nightly news. We can play Reverend Wright's sermons on every channel, every day and talk about them from now until the election, and make the only question in this campaign whether or not the American people think that I somehow believe or sympathize with his most offensive words. We can pounce on some gaffe by a Hillary supporter as evidence that she's playing the race card, or we can speculate on whether white men will all flock to John McCain in the general election regardless of his policies.

We can do that.

45   But if we do, I can tell you that in the next election, we'll be talking about some other distraction. And then another one. And then another one. And nothing will change.

That is one option. Or, at this moment, in this election, we can come together and say, "Not this time." . . .

I would not be running for president if I didn't believe with all my heart that this is what the vast majority of Americans want for this country. This union may never be perfect, but generation after generation has shown that it can always be perfected. And today, whenever I find myself feeling doubtful or cynical about this possibility, what gives me the most hope is the next generation — the young people whose attitudes and beliefs and openness to change have already made history in this election.

There is one story in particular that I'd like to leave you with today — a story I told when I had the great honor of speaking on Dr. King's birthday at his home church, Ebenezer Baptist, in Atlanta.

There is a young, 23-year-old white woman named Ashley Baia who organized for our campaign in Florence, South Carolina. She had been working to organize a mostly African American community since the beginning of this campaign, and one day she was at a roundtable discussion where everyone went around telling their story and why they were there.

And Ashley said that when she was nine years old, her mother got 50
cancer. And because she had to miss days of work, she was let go and lost her health care. They had to file for bankruptcy, and that's when Ashley decided that she had to do something to help her mom.

She knew that food was one of their most expensive costs, and so Ashley convinced her mother that what she really liked and really wanted to eat more than anything else was mustard and relish sandwiches. Because that was the cheapest way to eat.

She did this for a year until her mom got better, and she told everyone at the roundtable that the reason she joined our campaign was so that she could help the millions of other children in the country who want and need to help their parents too.

Now Ashley might have made a different choice. Perhaps somebody told her along the way that the source of her mother's problems were blacks who were on welfare and too lazy to work, or Hispanics who were coming into the country illegally. But she didn't. She sought out allies in her fight against injustice.

Anyway, Ashley finishes her story and then goes around the room and asks everyone else why they're supporting the campaign. They all have different stories and reasons. Many bring up a specific issue. And finally they come to this elderly black man who's been sitting there quietly the entire time. And Ashley asks him why he's there. And he does not bring up a specific issue. He does not say health care or the economy. He does not say education or the war. He does not say that he was there because of Barack Obama. He simply says to everyone in the room, "I am here because of Ashley."

55   "I'm here because of Ashley." By itself, that single moment of recognition between that young white girl and that old black man is not enough. It is not enough to give health care to the sick, or jobs to the jobless, or education to our children.

But it is where we start. It is where our union grows stronger. And as so many generations have come to realize over the course of the two hundred and twenty-one years since a band of patriots signed that document in Philadelphia, that is where the perfection begins.

TIM O'BRIEN

On the Rainy River

TIM O'BRIEN was born in 1946 in Austin, Minnesota, to an insurance salesman and an elementary school teacher. Both of his parents were veterans: his father had been in the Navy in Iwo Jima and Okinawa during World War II, and his mother had served with the WAVES (Women Accepted for Volunteer Emergency Service). As a child, O'Brien spent time reading in the county library, learning to perform magic tricks, and playing baseball (his first piece of fiction was called "Timmy of the Little League").

O'Brien attended Macalester College in Saint Paul, Minnesota, majoring in political science. When he graduated in 1968, he hoped to join the State Department as a diplomat—but instead, just weeks after graduation, he was drafted into the Army. O'Brien nearly fled to Canada: during his training in Fort Lewis, Washington, he planned to desert, but he went only as far as Seattle before turning back. In 1969, at the age of twenty-two, he went to Quang Ngai, Vietnam, first as a rifleman and later as a Radio Telephone Operator and clerk. He completed a thirteen-month tour of duty, earning a Purple Heart and a Bronze Star.

After his return to the United States in 1970, O'Brien enrolled in Harvard's doctoral program in government and spent his summers working as an intern for the *Washington Post*. He became a full-time national affairs reporter, covering Senate hearings and political events. Several years later, O'Brien left both his graduate work and his job at the *Post* to pursue a career as a writer.

"On the Rainy River" describes a young man who has to choose between going to Vietnam and fleeing to Canada to evade the draft. He blames the war on everyone—the president, the joint chiefs of staff, the knee-jerk patriots in his hometown—but ultimately takes his place among them, choosing to go to war. His decision precipitates the events of the book, *The Things They Carried*, just as O'Brien's own conflicted decision to go to war set the course of his life, first as a soldier and then as a writer.

211

The Things They Carried (1990) was a finalist for both the Pulitzer Prize and the National Book Critics Circle Award. O'Brien's other significant books include *If I Die in a Combat Zone, Box Me Up and Ship Me Home* (1973); *Going after Cacciato* (1978); *The Nuclear Age* (1985); and *In the Lake of the Woods* (1994). O'Brien lives in Texas with his wife and sons. He teaches creative writing at Texas State University—where, he says, he teaches sentence craftsmanship: "I try to talk about grace and rhythm of sentences and pacing, and the kind of music that underlies prose . . . All the things like plot and character, they all ride on sentences, on language."

This is one story I've never told before. Not to anyone. Not to my parents, not to my brother or sister, not even to my wife. To go into it, I've always thought, would only cause embarrassment for all of us, a sudden need to be elsewhere, which is the natural response to a confession. Even now, I'll admit, the story makes me squirm. For more than twenty years I've had to live with it, feeling the shame, trying to push it away, and so by this act of remembrance, by putting the facts down on paper, I'm hoping to relieve at least some of the pressure on my dreams. Still, it's a hard story to tell. All of us, I suppose, like to believe that in a moral emergency we will behave like the heroes of our youth, bravely and forthrightly, without thought of personal loss or discredit. Certainly that was my conviction back in the summer of 1968. Tim O'Brien: a secret hero. The Lone Ranger. If the stakes ever became high enough — if the evil were evil enough, if the good were good enough — I would simply tap a secret reservoir of courage that had been accumulating inside me over the years. Courage, I seemed to think, comes to us in finite quantities, like an inheritance, and by being frugal and stashing it away and letting it earn interest, we steadily increase our moral capital in preparation for that day when the account must be drawn down. It was a comforting theory. It dispensed with all those bothersome little acts of daily courage; it offered hope and grace to the repetitive coward; it justified the past while amortizing the future.

In June of 1968, a month after graduating from Macalester College, I was drafted to fight a war I hated. I was twenty-one years old. Young, yes, and politically naïve, but even so the American war in Vietnam seemed to me wrong. Certain blood was being shed for uncertain reasons. I saw no unity of purpose, no consensus on matters of philosophy or history or law. The very facts were shrouded in uncertainty: Was it a civil war? A war of national liberation or simple aggression? Who started it, and when, and why? What really happened to the USS Maddox on that dark night in the Gulf of Tonkin? Was Ho Chi Minh a Communist stooge, or a nationalist savior, or both, or neither? What about the Geneva Accords? What about SEATO and the Cold War? What about dominoes? America was divided on these and a thousand other issues, and the debate had spilled out across the floor of the United States Senate and into the streets, and smart men in pinstripes could not agree on even the most fundamental matters of public policy. The only certainty that summer was moral confusion. It was my view then, and still is, that you don't make war without knowing why. Knowledge, of course, is always imperfect, but it seemed to me that when a nation goes to war it must have reasonable confidence in the justice and imperative of its cause. You can't fix your mistakes. Once people are dead, you can't make them undead.

In any case those were my convictions, and back in college I had taken a modest stand against the war. Nothing radical, no hothead stuff, just ringing a few doorbells for Gene McCarthy, composing a few tedious, uninspired editorials for the campus newspaper. Oddly, though, it was almost entirely an intellectual activity. I brought some energy to it, of course, but it was the energy that accompanies almost any abstract endeavor; I felt no personal danger, I felt no sense of an impending crisis in my life. Stupidly, with a kind of smug removal that I can't begin to fathom, I assumed that the problems of killing and dying did not fall within my special province.

The draft notice arrived on June 17, 1968. It was a humid afternoon, I remember, cloudy and very quiet, and I'd just come in from a round of golf. My mother and father were having lunch out in the kitchen. I remember opening up the letter, scanning the first few lines, feeling the blood go thick behind my eyes. I remember a sound in my head. It wasn't thinking, just a silent howl. A million things all at once — I was too good for this war. Too smart, too compassionate, too everything. It couldn't happen. I was above it. I had the world dicked — Phi Beta Kappa and summa cum laude and president of the student body and a full-ride scholarship for grad studies at Harvard. A mistake, maybe — a foul-up in the paperwork. I was no soldier. I hated Boy Scouts. I hated camping out. I hated dirt and tents and mosquitoes. The sight of blood made me queasy, and I couldn't tolerate authority, and I didn't know a rifle from a slingshot. I was a *liberal*, for Christ sake: If they needed fresh bodies, why not draft some back-to-the-stone-age hawk? Or some dumb jingo in his hard hat and Bomb Hanoi button, or one of LBJ's pretty daughters, or Westmoreland's whole handsome family — nephews and nieces and baby grandson. There should be a law, I thought. If you support a war, if you think it's worth the price, that's fine, but you have to put your own precious fluids on the line. You have to head for the front and hook up with an infantry unit and help spill the blood. And you have to bring along your wife, or your kids, or your lover. A *law*, I thought.

5   I remember the rage in my stomach. Later it burned down to a smoldering self-pity, then to numbness. At dinner that night my father asked what my plans were.

"Nothing," I said. "Wait."

I spent the summer of 1968 working in an Armour meat-packing plant in my hometown of Worthington, Minnesota. The plant specialized in pork products, and for eight hours a day I stood on a quarter-mile assembly line — more properly, a disassembly line — removing blood clots from the necks of dead pigs. My job title, I believe, was Declotter. After slaughter, the hogs were decapitated, split down the length of the belly, pried open, eviscerated, and strung up by the hind hocks on a high conveyer belt. Then gravity took over. By the time a carcass reached my spot on the line, the fluids had mostly drained out, everything except for thick clots of blood in the neck and upper chest cavity. To remove the stuff, I used a kind of water gun. The machine was heavy, maybe eighty pounds, and was suspended from the ceiling by a heavy rubber cord. There was some bounce to it, an elastic up-and-down give, and the trick was to maneuver the gun with your whole body, not lifting with the arms, just letting the rubber cord do the work for you. At one end was a trigger; at the muzzle end was a small nozzle and a steel roller brush. As a carcass passed by, you'd lean forward and swing the gun up against the clots and squeeze the trigger, all in one motion, and the brush would whirl and water would come shooting out and you'd hear a quick splattering sound as the clots dissolved into a fine red mist. It was not pleasant work. Goggles were a necessity, and a rubber apron, but even so it was like standing for eight hours a day under a lukewarm blood-shower. At night I'd go home smelling of pig. It wouldn't go away.

Even after a hot bath, scrubbing hard, the stink was always there — like old bacon, or sausage, a dense greasy pig-stink that soaked deep into my skin and hair. Among other things, I remember, it was tough getting dates that summer. I felt isolated; I spent a lot of time alone. And there was also that draft notice tucked away in my wallet.

In the evenings I'd sometimes borrow my father's car and drive aimlessly around town, feeling sorry for myself, thinking about the war and the pig factory and how my life seemed to be collapsing toward slaughter. I felt paralyzed. All around me the options seemed to be narrowing, as if I were hurtling down a huge black funnel, the whole world squeezing in tight. There was no happy way out. The government had ended most graduate school deferments; the waiting lists for the National Guard and Reserves were impossibly long; my health was solid; I didn't qualify for CO status — no religious grounds, no history as a pacifist. Moreover, I could not claim to be opposed to war as a matter of general principle. There were occasions, I believed, when a nation was justified in using military force to achieve its ends, to stop a Hitler or some comparable evil, and I told myself that in such circumstances I would've willingly marched off to the battle. The problem, though, was that a draft board did not let you choose your war.

Beyond all this, or at the very center, was the raw fact of terror. I did not want to die. Not ever. But certainly not then, not there, not in a wrong war. Driving up Main Street, past the courthouse and the Ben Franklin store, I sometimes felt the fear spreading inside me like weeds. I imagined myself dead. I imagined myself doing things I could not do — charging an enemy position, taking aim at another human being.

At some point in mid-July I began thinking seriously about Canada.   10
The border lay a few hundred miles north, an eight-hour drive. Both my conscience and my instincts were telling me to make a break for it, just take off and run like hell and never stop. In the beginning the idea seemed purely abstract, the word Canada printing itself out in my head; but after a time I could see particular shapes and images, the sorry details of my own future — a hotel room in Winnipeg, a battered old suitcase, my father's eyes as I tried to explain myself over the telephone. I could almost hear his voice, and my mother's. Run, I'd think. Then I'd think, Impossible. Then a second later I'd think, *Run*.

It was a kind of schizophrenia. A moral split. I couldn't make up my mind. I feared the war, yes, but I also feared exile. I was afraid of walking away from my own life, my friends and my family, my whole history, everything that mattered to me. I feared losing the respect of my parents. I feared the law. I feared ridicule and censure. My hometown was a conservative little spot on the prairie, a place where tradition counted, and it was easy to imagine people sitting around a table down at the old Gobbler Café on Main Street, coffee cups poised, the conversation slowly zeroing in on the young O'Brien kid, how the damned sissy had taken off for Canada. At night, when I couldn't sleep, I'd sometimes carry on fierce arguments with those people. I'd be screaming at them, telling them how much I detested their blind, thoughtless, automatic acquiescence to it all, their simpleminded patriotism, their prideful ignorance, their love-it-or-leave-it platitudes, how they were sending me off to fight a war they didn't understand and didn't want to understand. I held them responsible. By God, yes, I *did*. All of them — I held them personally and individually responsible — the polyestered Kiwanis boys, the merchants and farmers, the pious churchgoers, the chatty housewives, the PTA and the Lions club and the Veterans of Foreign Wars and the fine upstanding gentry out at the country club. They didn't know Bao Dai from the man in the moon. They didn't know history. They didn't know the first thing about Diem's tyranny, or the nature of Vietnamese nationalism, or the long colonialism of the French — this was all too damned complicated, it required some reading — but no matter, it was a war to stop the Communists, plain and simple, which was how they liked things, and you were a treasonous pussy if you had second thoughts about killing or dying for plain and simple reasons.

I was bitter, sure. But it was so much more than that. The emotions went from outrage to terror to bewilderment to guilt to sorrow and then back again to outrage. I felt a sickness inside me. Real disease.

Most of this I've told before, or at least hinted at, but what I have never told is the full truth. How I cracked. How at work one morning, standing on the pig line, I felt something break open in my chest. I don't know what it was. I'll never know. But it was real, I know that much, it was a physical rupture — a cracking-leaking-popping feeling. I remember dropping my water gun. Quickly, almost without thought, I took off my apron and walked out of the plant and drove home. It was midmorning, I remember, and the house was empty. Down in my chest there was still that leaking sensation, something very warm and precious spilling out, and I was covered with blood and hog-stink, and for a long while I just concentrated on holding myself together. I remember taking a hot shower. I remember packing a suitcase and carrying it out to the kitchen, standing very still for a few minutes, looking carefully at the familiar objects all around me. The old chrome toaster, the telephone, the pink and white Formica on the kitchen counters. The room was full of bright sunshine. Everything sparkled. My house, I thought. My life. I'm not sure how long I stood there, but later I scribbled out a short note to my parents.

What it said, exactly, I don't recall now. Something vague. Taking off, will call, love Tim.

I drove north.   15

It's a blur now, as it was then, and all I remember is a sense of high velocity and the feel of the steering wheel in my hands. I was riding on adrenaline. A giddy feeling, in a way, except there was the dreamy edge of impossibility to it — like running a dead-end maze — no way out — it couldn't come to a happy conclusion and yet I was doing it anyway because it was all I could think of to do. It was pure flight, fast and mindless. I had no plan. Just hit the border at high speed and crash through and keep on running. Near dusk I passed through Bemidji, then turned northeast toward International Falls. I spent the night in the car behind a closed-down gas station a half mile from the border. In the morning, after gassing up, I headed straight west along the Rainy River, which separates Minnesota from Canada, and which for me separated one life from another. The land was mostly wilderness. Here and there I passed a motel or bait shop, but otherwise the country unfolded in great sweeps of pine and birch and sumac. Though it was still August, the air already had the smell of October, football season, piles of yellow-red leaves, everything crisp and clean. I remember a huge blue sky. Off to my right was the Rainy River, wide as a lake in places, and beyond the Rainy River was Canada.

For a while I just drove, not aiming at anything, then in the late morning I began looking for a place to lie low for a day or two. I was exhausted, and scared sick, and around noon I pulled into an old fishing resort called the Tip Top Lodge. Actually it was not a lodge at all, just eight or nine tiny yellow cabins clustered on a peninsula that jutted northward into the Rainy River. The place was in sorry shape. There was a dangerous wooden dock, an old minnow tank, a flimsy tar paper boathouse along the shore. The main building, which stood in a cluster of pines on high ground, seemed to lean heavily to one side, like a cripple, the roof sagging toward Canada. Briefly, I thought about turn-ing around, just giving up, but then I got out of the car and walked up to the front porch.

The man who opened the door that day is the hero of my life. How do I say this without sounding sappy? Blurt it out — the man saved me. He offered exactly what I needed, without questions, without any words at all. He took me in. He was there at the critical time — a silent, watchful presence. Six days later, when it ended, I was unable to find a proper way to thank him, and I never have, and so, if nothing else, this story represents a small gesture of gratitude twenty years overdue.

Even after two decades I can close my eyes and return to that porch at the Tip Top Lodge. I can see the old guy staring at me. Elroy Ber-dahl: eighty-one years old, skinny and shrunken and mostly bald. He wore a flannel shirt and brown work pants. In one hand, I remember, he carried a green apple, a small paring knife in the other. His eyes had the bluish gray color of a razor blade, the same polished shine, and as he peered up at me I felt a strange sharpness, almost painful, a cutting sensation, as if his gaze were somehow slicing me open. In part, no doubt, it was my own sense of guilt, but even so I'm absolutely certain that the old man took one look and went right to the heart of things — a kid in trouble. When I asked for a room, Elroy made a little clicking sound with his tongue. He nodded, led me out to one of the cabins, and dropped a key in my hand. I remember smiling at him. I also remember wishing I hadn't. The old man shook his head as if to tell me it wasn't worth the bother.

20   "Dinner at five-thirty," he said. "You eat fish?"

"Anything," I said.

Elroy grunted and said, "I'll bet."

We spent six days together at the Tip Top Lodge. Just the two of us. Tourist season was over, and there were no boats on the river, and the wilderness seemed to withdraw into a great permanent stillness. Over those six days Elroy Berdahl and I took most of our meals together. In the mornings we sometimes went out on long hikes into the woods, and at night we played Scrabble or listened to records or sat reading in front of his big stone fireplace. At times I felt the awkwardness of an intruder, but Elroy accepted me into his quiet routine without fuss or ceremony. He took my presence for granted, the same way he might've sheltered a stray cat — no wasted sighs or pity — and there was never any talk about it. Just the opposite. What I remember more than anything is the man's willful, almost ferocious silence. In all that time together, all those hours, he never asked the obvious questions: Why was I there? Why alone? Why so preoccupied? If Elroy was curious about any of this, he was careful never to put it into words.

My hunch, though, is that he already knew. At least the basics. After all, it was 1968, and guys were burning draft cards, and Canada was just a boat ride away. Elroy Berdahl was no hick. His bedroom, I remember, was cluttered with books and newspapers. He killed me at the Scrabble board, barely concentrating, and on those occasions when speech was necessary he had a way of compressing large thoughts into small, cryptic packets of language. One evening, just at sunset, he pointed up at an owl circling over the violet-lighted forest to the west.

"Hey, O'Brien," he said. "There's Jesus."   25

The man was sharp — he didn't miss much. Those razor eyes. Now and then he'd catch me staring out at the river, at the far shore, and I could almost hear the tumblers clicking in his head. Maybe I'm wrong, but I doubt it.

One thing for certain, he knew I was in desperate trouble. And he knew I couldn't talk about it. The wrong word — or even the right word — and I would've disappeared. I was wired and jittery. My skin felt too tight. After supper one evening I vomited and went back to my cabin and lay down for a few moments and then vomited again; another time, in the middle of the afternoon, I began sweating and couldn't shut it off. I went through whole days feeling dizzy with sorrow. I couldn't sleep; I couldn't lie still. At night I'd toss around in bed, half awake, half dreaming, imagining how I'd sneak down to the beach and quietly push one of the old man's boats out into the river and start paddling my way toward Canada. There were times when I thought I'd gone off the psychic edge. I couldn't tell up from down, I was just falling, and late in the night I'd lie there watching weird pictures spin through my head. Getting chased by the Border Patrol — helicopters and searchlights and barking dogs — I'd be crashing through the woods, I'd be down on my hands and knees — people shouting out my name — the law closing in on all sides — my hometown draft board and the FBI and the Royal Canadian Mounted Police. It all seemed crazy and impossible. Twenty-one years old, an ordinary kid with all the ordinary dreams and ambitions, and all I wanted was to live the life I was born to — a mainstream life — I loved baseball and hamburgers and cherry Cokes — and now

I was off on the margins of exile, leaving my country forever, and it seemed so impossible and terrible and sad.

I'm not sure how I made it through those six days. Most of it I can't remember. On two or three afternoons, to pass some time, I helped Elroy get the place ready for winter, sweeping down the cabins and hauling in the boats, little chores that kept my body moving. The days were cool and bright. The nights were very dark. One morning the old man showed me how to split and stack firewood, and for several hours we just worked in silence out behind his house. At one point, I remember, Elroy put down his maul and looked at me for a long time, his lips drawn as if framing a difficult question, but then he shook his head and went back to work. The man's self-control was amazing. He never pried. He never put me in a position that required lies or denials. To an extent, I suppose, his reticence was typical of that part of Minnesota, where privacy still held value, and even if I'd been walking around with some horrible deformity — four arms and three heads — I'm sure the old man would've talked about everything except those extra arms and heads. Simple politeness was part of it. But even more than that, I think, the man understood that words were insufficient. The problem had gone beyond discussion. During that long summer I'd been over and over the various arguments, all the pros and cons, and it was no longer a question that could be decided by an act of pure reason. Intellect had come up against emotion. My conscience told me to run, but some irrational and powerful force was resisting, like a weight pushing me toward the war. What it came down to, stupidly, was a sense of shame. Hot, stupid shame. I did not want people to think badly of me. Not my parents, not my brother and sister, not even the folks down at the Gobbler Café. I was ashamed to be there at the Tip Top Lodge. I was ashamed of my conscience, ashamed to be doing the right thing.

Some of this Elroy must've understood. Not the details, of course, but the plain fact of crisis.

30   Although the old man never confronted me about it, there was one occasion when he came close to forcing the whole thing out into the open. It was early evening, and we'd just finished supper, and over coffee and dessert I asked him about my bill, how much I owed so far. For a long while the old man squinted down at the tablecloth.

"Well, the basic rate," he said, "is fifty bucks a night. Not counting meals. This makes four nights, right?"

I nodded. I had three hundred and twelve dollars in my wallet.

Elroy kept his eyes on the tablecloth. "Now that's an on-season price. To be fair, I suppose we should knock it down a peg or two." He leaned back in his chair. "What's a reasonable number, you figure?"

"I don't know," I said. "Forty?"

"Forty's good. Forty a night. Then we tack on food — say another   35 hundred? Two hundred sixty total?"

"I guess."

He raised his eyebrows. "Too much?"

"No, that's fair. It's fine. Tomorrow, though . . . I think I'd better take off tomorrow."

Elroy shrugged and began clearing the table. For a time he fussed with the dishes, whistling to himself as if the subject had been settled. After a second he slapped his hands together.

"You know what we forgot?" he said. "We forgot wages. Those odd   40 jobs you done. What we have to do, we have to figure out what your time's worth. Your last job — how much did you pull in an hour?"

"Not enough," I said.

"A bad one?"

"Yes. Pretty bad."

Slowly then, without intending any long sermon, I told him about my days at the pig plant. It began as a straight recitation of the facts, but before I could stop myself I was talking about the blood clots and the water gun and how the smell had soaked into my skin and how I couldn't wash it away. I went on for a long time. I told him about wild hogs squealing in my dreams, the sounds of butchery, slaughterhouse sounds, and how I'd sometimes wake up with that greasy pig-stink in my throat.

When I was finished, Elroy nodded at me.   45

"Well, to be honest," he said, "when you first showed up here, I wondered about all that. The aroma, I mean. Smelled like you was awful damned fond of pork chops." The old man almost smiled. He made a snuffling sound, then sat down with a pencil and a piece of paper. "So what'd this crud job pay? Ten bucks an hour? Fifteen?"

"Less."

Elroy shook his head. "Let's make it fifteen. You put in twenty-five hours here, easy. That's three hundred seventy-five bucks total wages. We subtract the two hundred sixty for food and lodging, I still owe you a hundred and fifteen."

He took four fifties out of his shirt pocket and laid them on the table.

50   "Call it even," he said.

"No."

"Pick it up. Get yourself a haircut."

The money lay on the table for the rest of the evening. It was still there when I went back to my cabin. In the morning, though, I found an envelope tacked to my door. Inside were the four fifties and a two-word note that said EMERGENCY FUND.

The man knew.

55   Looking back after twenty years, I sometimes wonder if the events of that summer didn't happen in some other dimension, a place where your life exists before you've lived it, and where it goes afterward. None of it ever seemed real. During my time at the Tip Top Lodge I had the feeling that I'd slipped out of my own skin, hovering a few feet away while some poor yo-yo with my name and face tried to make his way toward a future he didn't understand and didn't want. Even now I can see myself as I was then. It's like watching an old home movie: I'm young and tan and fit. I've got hair — lots of it. I don't smoke or drink. I'm wearing faded blue jeans and a white polo shirt. I can see myself sitting on Elroy Berdahl's dock near dusk one evening, the sky a bright shimmering pink, and I'm finishing up a letter to my parents that tells what I'm about to do and why I'm doing it and how sorry I am that I'd never found the courage to talk to them about it. I ask them not to be angry. I try to explain some of my feelings, but there aren't enough words, and so I just say that it's a thing that has to be done. At the end of the letter I talk about the vacations we used to take up in this north country, at a place called Whitefish Lake, and how the scenery here reminds me of those good times. I tell them I'm fine. I tell them I'll write again from Winnipeg or Montreal or wherever I end up.

On my last full day, the sixth day, the old man took me out fishing on the Rainy River. The afternoon was sunny and cold. A stiff breeze came in from the north, and I remember how the little fourteen-foot boat made sharp rocking motions as we pushed off from the dock. The current was fast. All around us, I remember, there was a vastness to the world, an unpeopled rawness, just the trees and the sky and the water reaching out toward nowhere. The air had the brittle scent of October.

For ten or fifteen minutes Elroy held a course upstream, the river choppy and silver-gray, then he turned straight north and put the engine on full throttle. I felt the bow lift beneath me. I remember the wind in my ears, the sound of the old outboard Evinrude. For a time I didn't pay attention to anything, just feeling the cold spray against my face, but then it occurred to me that at some point we must've passed into Canadian waters, across that dotted line between two different worlds, and I remember a sudden tightness in my chest as I looked up and watched the far shore come at me. This wasn't a daydream. It was tangible and real. As we came in toward land, Elroy cut the engine, letting the boat fishtail lightly about twenty yards off shore. The old man didn't look at me or speak. Bending down, he opened up his tackle box and busied himself with a bobber and a piece of wire leader, humming to himself, his eyes down.

It struck me then that he must've planned it. I'll never be certain, of course, but I think he meant to bring me up against the realities, to guide me across the river and to take me to the edge and to stand a kind of vigil as I chose a life for myself.

I remember staring at the old man, then at my hands, then at Canada. The shoreline was dense with brush and timber. I could see tiny red berries on the bushes. I could see a squirrel up in one of the birch trees, a big crow looking at me from a boulder along the river. That close — twenty yards — and I could see the delicate latticework of the leaves, the texture of the soil, the browned needles beneath the pines, the configurations of geology and human history. Twenty yards. I could've done it. I could've jumped and started swimming for my life. Inside me, in my chest, I felt a terrible squeezing pressure. Even now, as I write this, I can still feel that tightness. And I want you to feel it — the wind coming off the river, the waves, the silence, the wooded frontier. You're at the bow of a boat on the Rainy River. You're twenty-one years old, you're scared, and there's a hard squeezing pressure in your chest.

What would you do?   60

Would you jump? Would you feel pity for yourself? Would you think about your family and your childhood and your dreams and all you're leaving behind? Would it hurt? Would it feel like dying? Would you cry, as I did?

I tried to swallow it back. I tried to smile, except I was crying.

Now, perhaps, you can understand why I've never told this story before. It's not just the embarrassment of tears. That's part of it, no doubt, but what embarrasses me much more, and always will, is the paralysis that took my heart. A moral freeze: I couldn't decide, I couldn't act, I couldn't comport myself with even a pretense of modest human dignity. All I could do was cry. Quietly, not bawling, just the chest-chokes.

65   At the rear of the boat Elroy Berdahl pretended not to notice. He held a fishing rod in his hands, his head bowed to hide his eyes. He kept humming a soft, monotonous little tune. Everywhere, it seemed, in the trees and water and sky, a great worldwide sadness came pressing down on me, a crushing sorrow, sorrow like I had never known it before. And what was so sad, I realized, was that Canada had become a pitiful fantasy. Silly and hopeless. It was no longer a possibility. Right then, with the shore so close, I understood that I would not do what I should do. I would not swim away from my hometown and my country and my life. I would not be brave. That old image of myself as a hero, as a man of conscience and courage, all that was just a threadbare pipe dream. Bobbing there on the Rainy River, looking back at the Minnesota shore, I felt a sudden swell of helplessness come over me, a drowning sensation, as if I had toppled overboard and was being swept away by the silver waves. Chunks of my own history flashed by. I saw a seven-year-old boy in a white cowboy hat and a Lone Ranger mask and a pair of holstered six-shooters; I saw a twelve-year-old Little League shortstop pivoting to turn a double play; I saw a sixteen-year-old kid decked out for his first prom, looking spiffy in a white tux and a black bow tie, his hair cut short and flat, his shoes freshly polished. My whole life seemed to spill out into the river, swirling away from me, everything I had ever been or ever wanted to be. I couldn't get my breath; I couldn't stay afloat; I couldn't tell which way to swim. A hallucination, I suppose, but it was as real as anything I would ever feel. I saw my parents calling to me from the far shoreline. I saw my brother and sister, all the townsfolk, the mayor and the entire Chamber of Commerce and all my old teachers and girlfriends and high school buddies. Like some weird sporting event: everybody screaming from the sidelines, rooting me on — a loud stadium roar. Hotdogs and popcorn — stadium smells, stadium heat. A squad of cheerleaders did cartwheels along the banks of the Rainy River; they had megaphones and pompoms and smooth brown thighs. The crowd swayed left and right. A marching band played fight songs. All my aunts and uncles were there, and Abraham Lincoln, and Saint George, and a nine-year-old girl named Linda who had died of a brain tumor back in fifth grade, and several members of the United States

Senate, and a blind poet scribbling notes, and LBJ, and Huck Finn, and Abbie Hoffman, and all the dead soldiers back from the grave, and the many thousands who were later to die — villagers with terrible burns, little kids without arms or legs — yes, and the Joint Chiefs of Staff were there, and a couple of popes, and a first lieutenant named Jimmy Cross, and the last surviving veteran of the American Civil War, and Jane Fonda dressed up as Barbarella, and an old man sprawled beside a pig-pen, and my grandfather, and Gary Cooper, and a kind-faced woman carrying an umbrella and a copy of Plato's Republic, and a million ferocious citizens waving flags of all shapes and colors — people in hard hats, people in headbands — they were all whooping and chanting and urging me toward one shore or the other. I saw faces from my distant past and distant future. My wife was there. My unborn daughter waved at me, and my two sons hopped up and down, and a drill sergeant named Blyton sneered and shot up a finger and shook his head. There was a choir in bright purple robes. There was a cabbie from the Bronx. There was a slim young man I would one day kill with a hand grenade along a red clay trail outside the village of My Khe.

The little aluminum boat rocked softly beneath me. There was the wind and the sky.

I tried to will myself overboard.

I gripped the edge of the boat and leaned forward and thought, Now.

I did try. It just wasn't possible.

All those eyes on me — the town, the whole universe — and I 70 couldn't risk the embarrassment. It was as if there were an audience to my life, that swirl of faces along the river, and in my head I could hear people screaming at me. Traitor! they yelled. Turncoat! Pussy! I felt myself blush. I couldn't tolerate it. I couldn't endure the mockery, or the disgrace, or the patriotic ridicule. Even in my imagination, the shore just twenty yards away, I couldn't make myself be brave. It had nothing to do with morality. Embarrassment, that's all it was.

And right then I submitted.

I would go to the war — I would kill and maybe die — because I was embarrassed not to.

That was the sad thing. And so I sat in the bow of the boat and cried. It was loud now. Loud, hard crying.

Elroy Berdahl remained quiet. He kept fishing. He worked his line 75 with the tips of his fingers, patiently, squinting out at his red and white bobber on the Rainy River. His eyes were flat and impassive. He didn't speak. He was simply there, like the river and the late-summer sun. And yet by his presence, his mute watchfulness, he made it real. He was the true audience. He was a witness, like God, or like the gods, who look on in absolute silence as we live our lives, as we make our choices or fail to make them.

"Ain't biting," he said.

Then after a time the old man pulled in his line and turned the boat back toward Minnesota.

I don't remember saying goodbye. That last night we had dinner together, and I went to bed early, and in the morning Elroy fixed breakfast for me. When I told him I'd be leaving, the old man nodded as if he already knew. He looked down at the table and smiled.

At some point later in the morning it's possible that we shook hands — I just don't remember — but I do know that by the time I'd finished packing the old man had disappeared. Around noon, when I took my suitcase out to the car, I noticed that his old black pickup truck was no longer parked in front of the house. I went inside and waited for a while, but I felt a bone certainty that he wouldn't be back. In a way, I thought, it was appropriate. I washed up the breakfast dishes, left his two hundred dollars on the kitchen counter, got into the car, and drove south toward home.

80   The day was cloudy. I passed through towns with familiar names, through the pine forests and down to the prairie, and then to Vietnam, where I was a soldier, and then home again. I survived, but it's not a happy ending. I was a coward. I went to the war.

The Conservative Case
for Gay Marriage

THEODORE OLSON was born on September 11, 1940, in Chicago and raised in Mountain View, California, just south of San Francisco. After completing his undergraduate degree in forensics and journalism from the University of the Pacific in 1962, he received his law degree in 1965 from the University of California at Berkeley, where he was a member of the *California Law Review*.

A conservative Republican, Olson has argued many highly controversial cases in the interest of Republican politicians. In 1981, he took a position in the Reagan administration, where, in one case, he defended Reagan's role in the notorious Iran-Contra scandal. He has argued more than fifty cases before the Supreme Court, winning more than forty. In 2000, he represented George W. Bush in *Bush v. Gore*. The court voted to end the recount of ballots in Florida, effectively handing the presidency to Bush. The next year, President Bush named Olson the solicitor general of the United States, a position he held until 2004.

Given Olson's conservative credentials, many were surprised when, in 2009, he partnered with David Boies (his opponent in *Bush v. Gore*) to challenge the constitutionality of Proposition 8, a California proposition banning gay marriage. In legal briefs, television interviews, speeches, and articles, Olson has explained that the right to marry is not a liberal or conservative issue but a matter of equal rights; he frequently argues by analogy, comparing the right to marry a same-sex partner to other rights, such as the right to marry across racial lines, that were once unpopular with voters but are nevertheless protected by law.

Most of Theodore Olson's writing is produced in the course of his legal work, consisting of briefs and, in recent years, "Supreme Court Round-Ups" summarizing cases before the Supreme Court. These are written in a formal style, with a singular focus on relevant laws and precedents and few traces of the individual writer's opinions or personality. But Olson also contributes to newspapers and magazines such as the *Wall Street Journal* and *The American Spectator*, venues where his carefully reasoned arguments are expressed in a warm, human voice. "The Conservative Case for Gay Marriage" was published in *Newsweek* in January 2010.

In 2010, Theodore Olson was listed in the "Time 100," *Time*'s annual list of the 100 most influential people, and he regularly appears on lists of Washington, D.C.'s superstar lawyers. Olson lives in Great Falls, Virginia, with his wife, Lady Booth Olson.

Together with my good friend and occasional courtroom adversary David Boies, I am attempting to persuade a federal court to invalidate California's Proposition 8 — the voter-approved measure that overturned California's constitutional right to marry a person of the same sex.

My involvement in this case has generated a certain degree of consternation among conservatives. How could a politically active, lifelong Republican, a veteran of the Ronald Reagan and George W. Bush administrations, challenge the "traditional" definition of marriage and press for an "activist" interpretation of the Constitution to create another "new" constitutional right?

My answer to this seeming conundrum rests on a lifetime of exposure to persons of different backgrounds, histories, viewpoints, and intrinsic characteristics, and on my rejection of what I see as superficially appealing but ultimately false perceptions about our Constitution and its protection of equality and fundamental rights.

Many of my fellow conservatives have an almost knee-jerk hostility toward gay marriage. This does not make sense, because same-sex unions promote the values conservatives prize. Marriage is one of the basic building blocks of our neighborhoods and our nation. At its best, it is a stable bond between two individuals who work to create a loving household and a social and economic partnership. We encourage couples to marry because the commitments they make to one another provide benefits not only to themselves but also to their families and communities. Marriage requires thinking beyond one's own needs. It transforms two individuals into a union based on shared aspirations, and in doing so establishes a formal investment in the well-being of society. The fact that individuals who happen to be gay want to share in this vital social institution is evidence that conservative ideals enjoy widespread acceptance. Conservatives should celebrate this, rather than lament it.

Legalizing same-sex marriage would also be a recognition of basic   5 American principles, and would represent the culmination of our nation's commitment to equal rights. It is, some have said, the last major civil-rights milestone yet to be surpassed in our two-century struggle to attain the goals we set for this nation at its formation.

This bedrock American principle of equality is central to the political and legal convictions of Republicans, Democrats, liberals, and conservatives alike. The dream that became America began with the revolutionary concept expressed in the Declaration of Independence in words that are among the most noble and elegant ever written: "We hold these truths to be self-evident, that all men are created equal, that they are endowed by their Creator with certain unalienable Rights, that among these are Life, Liberty and the pursuit of Happiness."

Sadly, our nation has taken a long time to live up to the promise of equality. In 1857, the Supreme Court held that an African American could not be a citizen. During the ensuing Civil War, Abraham Lincoln eloquently reminded the nation of its founding principle: "our fathers brought forth on this continent, a new nation, conceived in liberty and dedicated to the proposition that all men are created equal."

At the end of the Civil War, to make the elusive promise of equality a reality, the Fourteenth Amendment to the Constitution added the command that "no State shall deprive any person of life, liberty, or property, without due process of law; nor deny to any person the equal protection of the laws."

Subsequent laws and court decisions have made clear that equality under the law extends to persons of all races, religions, and places of origin. What better way to make this national aspiration complete than to apply the same protection to men and women who differ from others only on the basis of their sexual orientation? I cannot think of a single reason — and have not heard one since I undertook this venture — for continued discrimination against decent, hardworking members of our society on that basis.

Various federal and state laws have accorded certain rights and privi-   10 leges to gay and lesbian couples, but these protections vary dramatically at the state level, and nearly universally deny true equality to gays and lesbians who wish to marry. The very idea of marriage is basic to recognition as equals in our society; any status short of that is inferior, unjust, and unconstitutional.

The United States Supreme Court has repeatedly held that marriage is one of the most fundamental rights that we have as Americans under our Constitution. It is an expression of our desire to create a social partnership, to live and share life's joys and burdens with the person we love, and to form a lasting bond and a social identity. The Supreme Court has said that marriage is a part of the Constitution's protections of liberty, privacy, freedom of association, and spiritual identification. In short, the right to marry helps us to define ourselves and our place in a community. Without it, there can be no true equality under the law.

It is true that marriage in this nation traditionally has been regarded as a relationship exclusively between a man and a woman, and many of our nation's multiple religions define marriage in precisely those terms. But while the Supreme Court has always previously considered marriage in that context, the underlying rights and liberties that marriage embodies are not in any way confined to heterosexuals.

Marriage is a civil bond in this country as well as, in some (but hardly all) cases, a religious sacrament. It is a relationship recognized by governments as providing a privileged and respected status, entitled to the state's support and benefits. The California Supreme Court described marriage as a "union unreservedly approved and favored by the community." Where the state has accorded official sanction to a relationship and provided special benefits to those who enter into that relationship, our courts have insisted that withholding that status requires powerful justifications and may not be arbitrarily denied.

What, then, are the justifications for California's decision in Proposition 8 to withdraw access to the institution of marriage for some of its citizens on the basis of their sexual orientation? The reasons I have heard are not very persuasive.

15   The explanation mentioned most often is tradition. But simply because something has always been done a certain way does not mean that it must always remain that way. Otherwise we would still have segregated schools and debtors' prisons. Gays and lesbians have always been among us, forming a part of our society, and they have lived as couples in our neighborhoods and communities. For a long time, they have experienced discrimination and even persecution; but we, as a society, are starting to become more tolerant, accepting, and understanding. California and many other states have allowed gays and lesbians to

form domestic partnerships (or civil unions) with most of the rights of married heterosexuals. Thus, gay and lesbian individuals are now permitted to live together in state-sanctioned relationships. It therefore seems anomalous to cite "tradition" as a justification for withholding the status of marriage and thus to continue to label those relationships as less worthy, less sanctioned, or less legitimate.

The second argument I often hear is that traditional marriage furthers the state's interest in procreation—and that opening marriage to same-sex couples would dilute, diminish, and devalue this goal. But that is plainly not the case. Preventing lesbians and gays from marrying does not cause more heterosexuals to marry and conceive more children. Likewise, allowing gays and lesbians to marry someone of the same sex will not discourage heterosexuals from marrying a person of the opposite sex. How, then, would allowing same-sex marriages reduce the number of children that heterosexual couples conceive?

This procreation argument cannot be taken seriously. We do not inquire whether heterosexual couples intend to bear children, or have the capacity to have children, before we allow them to marry. We permit marriage by the elderly, by prison inmates, and by persons who have no intention of having children. What's more, it is pernicious to think marriage should be limited to heterosexuals because of the state's desire to promote procreation. We would surely not accept as constitutional a ban on marriage if a state were to decide, as China has done, to discourage procreation.

Another argument, vaguer and even less persuasive, is that gay marriage somehow does harm to heterosexual marriage. I have yet to meet anyone who can explain to me what this means. In what way would allowing same-sex partners to marry diminish the marriages of heterosexual couples? Tellingly, when the judge in our case asked our opponent to identify the ways in which same-sex marriage would harm heterosexual marriage, to his credit he answered honestly: he could not think of any.

The simple fact is that there is no good reason why we should deny marriage to same-sex partners. On the other hand, there are many reasons why we should formally recognize these relationships and embrace the rights of gays and lesbians to marry and become full and equal members of our society.

No matter what you think of homosexuality, it is a fact that gays and lesbians are members of our families, clubs, and workplaces. They are our doctors, our teachers, our soldiers (whether we admit it or not), and our friends. They yearn for acceptance, stable relationships, and success in their lives, just like the rest of us.

Conservatives and liberals alike need to come together on principles that surely unite us. Certainly, we can agree on the value of strong families, lasting domestic relationships, and communities populated by persons with recognized and sanctioned bonds to one another. Confining some of our neighbors and friends who share these same values to an outlaw or second-class status undermines their sense of belonging and weakens their ties with the rest of us and what should be our common aspirations. Even those whose religious convictions preclude endorsement of what they may perceive as an unacceptable "lifestyle" should recognize that disapproval should not warrant stigmatization and unequal treatment.

When we refuse to accord this status to gays and lesbians, we discourage them from forming the same relationships we encourage for others. And we are also telling them, those who love them, and society as a whole that their relationships are less worthy, less legitimate, less permanent, and less valued. We demean their relationships and we demean them as individuals. I cannot imagine how we benefit as a society by doing so.

I understand, but reject, certain religious teachings that denounce homosexuality as morally wrong, illegitimate, or unnatural; and I take strong exception to those who argue that same-sex relationships should be discouraged by society and law. Science has taught us, even if history has not, that gays and lesbians do not choose to be homosexual any more than the rest of us choose to be heterosexual. To a very large extent, these characteristics are immutable, like being left-handed. And, while our Constitution guarantees the freedom to exercise our individual religious convictions, it equally prohibits us from forcing our beliefs on others. I do not believe that our society can ever live up to the promise of equality, and the fundamental rights to life, liberty, and the pursuit of happiness, until we stop invidious discrimination on the basis of sexual orientation.

If we are born heterosexual, it is not unusual for us to perceive those who are born homosexual as aberrational and threatening. Many religions and much of our social culture have reinforced those impulses. Too often, that has led to prejudice, hostility, and discrimination. The antidote is understanding, and reason. We once tolerated laws throughout this nation that prohibited marriage between persons of different races. California's Supreme Court was the first to find that discrimination unconstitutional. The U.S. Supreme Court unanimously agreed twenty years later, in 1967, in a case called *Loving v. Virginia*. It seems inconceivable today that only forty years ago there were places in this country where a black woman could not legally marry a white man. And it was only fifty years ago that seventeen states mandated segregated public education — until the Supreme Court unanimously struck down that practice in *Brown v. Board of Education*. Most Americans are proud of these decisions and the fact that the discriminatory state laws that spawned them have been discredited. I am convinced that Americans will be equally proud when we no longer discriminate against gays and lesbians and welcome them into our society.

Reactions to our lawsuit have reinforced for me these essential truths. 25 I have certainly heard anger, resentment, and hostility, and words like "betrayal" and other pointedly graphic criticism. But mostly I have been overwhelmed by expressions of gratitude and good will from persons in all walks of life, including, I might add, from many conservatives and libertarians whose names might surprise. I have been particularly moved by many personal renditions of how lonely and personally destructive it is to be treated as an outcast and how meaningful it will be to be respected by our laws and civil institutions as an American, entitled to equality and dignity. I have no doubt that we are on the right side of this battle, the right side of the law, and the right side of history.

Some have suggested that we have brought this case too soon, and that neither the country nor the courts are "ready" to tackle this issue and remove this stigma. We disagree. We represent real clients — two wonderful couples in California who have longtime relationships. Our lesbian clients are raising four fine children who could not ask for better parents. Our clients wish to be married. They believe that they have that constitutional right. They wish to be represented in court to seek vindication of that right by mounting a challenge under the United States Constitution to the validity of Proposition 8 under the equal-protection and due-process clauses of the Fourteenth Amendment. In fact, the California attorney general has conceded the unconstitutionality of Proposition 8, and the city of San Francisco has joined our case to defend the rights of gays and lesbians to be married. We do not tell persons who have a legitimate claim to wait until the time is "right" and the populace is "ready" to recognize their equality and equal dignity under the law.

Citizens who have been denied equality are invariably told to "wait their turn" and to "be patient." Yet veterans of past civil-rights battles found that it was the act of insisting on equal rights that ultimately sped acceptance of those rights. As to whether the courts are "ready" for this case, just a few years ago, in *Romer v. Evans*, the United States Supreme Court struck down a popularly adopted Colorado constitutional amendment that withdrew the rights of gays and lesbians in that state to the protection of anti-discrimination laws. And seven years ago, in *Lawrence v. Texas*, the Supreme Court struck down, as lacking any rational basis, Texas laws prohibiting private, intimate sexual practices between persons of the same sex, overruling a contrary decision just twenty years earlier.

These decisions have generated controversy, of course, but they are decisions of the nation's highest court on which our clients are entitled to rely. If all citizens have a constitutional right to marry, if state laws that withdraw legal protections of gays and lesbians as a class are unconstitutional, and if private, intimate sexual conduct between persons of the same sex is protected by the Constitution, there is very little left on which opponents of same-sex marriage can rely. As Justice Antonin Scalia, who dissented in the *Lawrence* case, pointed out, "What [remaining] justification could there possibly be for denying the benefits of marriage to homosexual couples exercising 'the liberty protected by the Constitution'?" He is right, of course. One might agree or not with these decisions, but even Justice Scalia has acknowledged that they lead in only one direction.

California's Proposition 8 is particularly vulnerable to constitutional challenge, because that state has now enacted a crazy-quilt of marriage regulation that makes no sense to anyone. California recognizes marriage between men and women, including persons on death row, child abusers, and wife beaters. At the same time, California prohibits marriage by loving, caring, stable partners of the same sex, but tries to make up for it by giving them the alternative of "domestic partnerships" with virtually all of the rights of married persons except the official, state-approved status of marriage. Finally, California recognizes 18,000 same-sex marriages that took place in the months between the state

Supreme Court's ruling that upheld gay-marriage rights and the decision of California's citizens to withdraw those rights by enacting Proposition 8.

So there are now three classes of Californians: heterosexual couples   30
who can get married, divorced, and remarried, if they wish; same-sex couples who cannot get married but can live together in domestic partnerships; and same-sex couples who are now married but who, if they divorce, cannot remarry. This is an irrational system, it is discriminatory, and it cannot stand.

Americans who believe in the words of the Declaration of Independence, in Lincoln's Gettysburg Address, in the Fourteenth Amendment, and in the Constitution's guarantees of equal protection and equal dignity before the law cannot sit by while this wrong continues. This is not a conservative or liberal issue; it is an American one, and it is time that we, as Americans, embraced it.

Papa Blows His Nose in G: Absolute Pitch

When **OLIVER SACKS** was born in 1933, he was already on the path toward a life in science. His father was a physician in general practice, his mother a surgeon, and they lived in London near a large extended family that included mathematicians, chemists, and other physical scientists. As a boy, he spent many hours with his Uncle Dave, a chemist who encouraged his fascination with metals and helped him build his own laboratory.

As he grew older, Sacks's interest shifted from chemistry to medicine; he studied at Oxford University, graduating in 1958 with a medical degree from Queen's College. Three years later, he relocated to the United States, serving as an intern at Mount Zion Hospital in San Francisco and as a resident in neurology at UCLA. In 1965, he settled in New York. He is a professor of neurology and psychiatry at Columbia University.

As a neurologist, Sacks has written dozens of articles for medical journals. But his most influential writing appears in narrative case studies of patients with neurological disorders such as Tourette's syndrome or autism. These essays, written for a general audience, are frequently published in *The New Yorker* or *The New York Review of Books* and then included in "best of" anthologies such as *The Best American Essays* and *The Best American Science Writing*. Sacks's eleven books include *The Man who Mistook His Wife for a Hat* (1985), *An Anthropologist on Mars* (1995), *The Island of the Colorblind* (1996), and *The Mind's Eye* (2010). A memoir, *Uncle Tungsten: Memories of a Chemical Boyhood*, was published in 2001.

As the editor of *The Best American Science Writing of 2003*, Sacks wrote an introductory essay explaining what he values in writing:

The best science writing, it seems to me, has a swiftness and naturalness, a transparency and clarity, not clogged with pretentiousness or literary artifice. The science writer gives himself or herself to the subject completely, does not intrude on it in an annoying or impertinent way, and yet gives a personal warmth and perspective to every word. . . . It is, at best, a wonderful fusion, as factual as a news report, as imaginative as a novel.

"Papa Blows His Nose in G" appears in *Musicophilia: Tales of Music and the Brain* (2007).

People with absolute pitch can immediately, unthinkingly tell the pitch of any note, without either reflection or comparison with an external standard. They can do this not only with any note they hear, but with any note they imagine or hear in their heads. Indeed, Gordon B., a professional violinist who wrote to me about tinnitus, or ringing in his ears, remarked matter-of-factly that his tinnitus was "a high F-natural." He did not realize, I think, that saying this was in any way unusual; but of the millions of people with tinnitus, probably not one in ten thousand could say what pitch their tinnitus has.

The precision of absolute pitch varies, but it is estimated that most people with it can identify upwards of seventy tones in the middle region of the auditory range, and each of these seventy tones has, for them, a unique and characteristic quality that distinguishes it absolutely from any other note.

The Oxford Companion to Music was a sort of *Arabian Nights* for me as a boy, an inexhaustible source of musical stories, and it gives many charming examples of absolute pitch. Sir Frederick Ouseley, a former professor of music at Oxford, for example, "was all his life remarkable for his sense of absolute pitch. At five he was able to remark, 'Only think, Papa blows his nose in G.' He would say that it thundered in G or that the wind was whistling in D, or that the clock (with a two-note chime) struck in B minor, and when the assertion was tested it would invariably be found correct." For most of us, such an ability to recognize an exact pitch seems uncanny, almost like another sense, a sense we can never hope to possess, such as infrared or X-ray vision; but for those who are born with absolute pitch, it seems perfectly normal.

The Finnish entomologist Olavi Sotavalta, an expert on the sounds of insects in flight, was greatly assisted in his studies by having absolute pitch — for the sound pitch of an insect in flight is produced by the frequency of its wingbeats. Not content with musical notation, Sotavalta was able to estimate very exact frequencies by ear. The sound pitch made by the moth *Plusia gamma* approximates a low F-sharp, but Sotavalta could estimate it more precisely as having a frequency of 46 cycles per second. Such an ability, of course, requires not only a remarkable ear, but a knowledge of the scales and frequencies with which pitch can be correlated.

5   Yet such a correlation, though immensely impressive, deflects attention from the real wonder of absolute pitch: to those with absolute pitch, every tone, every key seems qualitatively different, each possessing its own "flavor" or "feel," its own character. Those who have absolute pitch often compare it to color — they "hear" G-sharpness as instantly and automatically as we "see" blue. (Indeed, the word "chroma" is sometimes used in musical theory.)

While absolute pitch may sound like a delicious extra sense, allowing one to instantly sing or notate any music at its correct pitch, it may cause problems too. One such problem occurs with the inconstant tuning of musical instruments. Thus the seven-year-old Mozart, comparing his own little violin to that of his friend Schactner, said, "If you have not altered the tuning of your violin since I last played on it, it is half a quarter of a tone flatter than mine here." (So it is related in *The Oxford Companion to Music*; there are many tales about Mozart's ear, some no doubt apocryphal.) When the composer Michael Torke encountered my own ancient piano, which — still having its original nineteenth-century strings — is not tuned up to the 440 cycles per second standard of modern pianos, he instantly remarked that it was a third of a tone flat. Such an overall sharpness or flatness would not be noticed by someone without absolute pitch, but it can be distressing and even disabling to those who do have it. *The Oxford Companion to Music* again gives many examples, including one of an eminent pianist who, playing the *Moonlight* Sonata (a piece which "every schoolgirl plays"), got through it only "with the greatest difficulty" because the piano was tuned to a pitch he was not accustomed to, and he "experienced the distress of playing the piece in one key and hearing it in another."

When people with absolute pitch "hear a familiar piece of music played in the wrong key," Daniel Levitin and Susan Rogers write, "they often become agitated or disturbed. . . . To get a sense of what it is like, imagine going to the produce market and finding that, because of a temporary disorder of visual processing, the bananas all appear orange, the lettuce yellow, and the apples purple."

Transposing music from one key to another is something which any competent musician can do easily and almost automatically. But for someone with absolute pitch, each key has its own unique character, and the key in which one has always heard a piece is likely to be felt as the only right one. Transposing a piece of music, for someone with absolute pitch, can be analogous to painting a picture with all the wrong colors.

Another difficulty was mentioned to me by the neurologist and musician Steven Frucht, who himself has absolute pitch. He sometimes experiences a certain difficulty in hearing intervals or harmonies because he is so conscious of the chroma of the notes that compose them. If, for example, one plays a C on the piano and the F-sharp above this, he might be so conscious of the C-ness of the C and the F-sharpness of the F-sharp that he fails to notice that they form a tritone, a dissonance which makes most people wince.[1]

Absolute pitch is not necessarily of much importance even to musicians — Mozart had it, but Wagner and Schumann lacked it. But for anyone who has it, the loss of absolute pitch may be felt as a severe privation. This sense of loss was clearly brought out by one of my patients, Frank V., a composer who suffered brain damage from the rupture of an aneurysm of the anterior communicating artery. Frank was highly gifted musically, and had been musically trained since the age of four. He had had absolute pitch as long as he could recall, but now, he said, "it is gone, or it has certainly been eroded." Since absolute pitch was of advantage to him as a musician, he felt its "erosion" keenly.

10

---

[1] The tritone — an augmented fourth (or, in jazz parlance, a flatted fifth — is a difficult interval to sing and has often been regarded as having an ugly, uncanny, or even diabolical quality. Its use was forbidden in early ecclesiastical music, and early theorists called it *diabolus in musica* ("the devil in music"). But Tartini used it, for this very reason, in his *Devil's Trill* Sonata for violin.

Though the raw tritone sounds so harsh, it is easily filled out with another tritone to form a diminished seventh. And this, the *Oxford Companion to Music* notes, "has a luscious effect. . . . The chord is indeed the most Protean in all harmony. In England the nickname has been given it of "The Clapham Junction of Harmony'— from a railway station in London where so many lines join that once arrived there one can take a train for almost anywhere else."

Originally, he said, he perceived pitches instantly, absolutely, as he perceived colors — no "mental process" was involved, no inference, no reference to other pitches or intervals or scales. This form of absolute pitch
had vanished completely; it was, he said, as if he had become "colorblind" in this regard. But as he convalesced from his brain injury, he
found that he still possessed reliable pitch memories of certain pieces
and certain instruments, and he could use these reference points to in-
fer other pitches — though this, in comparison to his "instant" absolute
pitch, was a slower process.

It was also, subjectively, entirely different, for previously every note
and every key had had a distinctive flavor for him, a character uniquely
its own. Now all of this was gone, and there was no longer any real difference, for him, between one key and another.[2]

It seems curious, in a way, that absolute pitch is so rare (it is estimated
as occurring in less than one person in ten thousand). Why don't all of
us hear "G-sharpness" as automatically as we see blue or smell a rose?
"The real question concerning absolute pitch," wrote Diana Deutsch et
al. in 2004, ". . . is not why some people possess it, but rather why it is
not universal. It is as though most people have a syndrome with respect
to the labeling of pitches which is like color anomia, in which the pa-

---

[2] Absolute pitch can shift with age, and this has often been a problem for older musicians. Marc Damashek, a piano tuner, wrote to me about such a problem:

> When I was four, my older sister discovered that I had perfect pitch — could instantly
> identify any note across the keyboard without looking. . . . I've been surprised (and dis-
> turbed) to find that my perceived piano pitch has shifted upwards by perhaps 150 cents
> [a semitone and a half]. . . . Now when I hear a recorded piece or a live performance, my
> best guess at what note is being played is consistently, absurdly high.

Damashek relates that he cannot easily compensate for this because "I'm always so
firmly convinced that the note I'm hearing is the one that I've always called by its correct
name: it still sounds like an F, damn it, but it's an E-flat!"

In general, as Patrick Baron, a musician and piano tuner, has written to me, "older piano
tuners tend to tune the highest treble octaves quite sharp, and the last three or four notes
incredibly sharp (sometimes more than a semitone). . . . Perhaps there is some sort of
atrophy of the basilar membrane or a stiffening of the hair cells which causes this, rather
than a template shift."

Other conditions may cause a temporary or permanent shift of absolute pitch,
including strokes, head injuries, and brain infections. One correspondent told me that
his absolute pitch shifted a semitone during an attack of multiple sclerosis and remained
slightly off thereafter.

tient can recognize colors, and discriminate between them, but cannot associate them with verbal labels."

Deutsch speaks here from personal experience as well. As she wrote to me in a recent letter:

> My realization that I had absolute pitch — and that this was unusual — came in the form of a great surprise when I discovered, at age four, that other people had difficulty naming notes out of context. I still remember vividly my shock at discovering that when I played a note on the piano, others had to see what key was being struck in order to name it. . . .
>
> To give you a sense of how strange a lack of absolute pitch appears to those of us who have it, take color naming as an analogy. Suppose you showed someone a red object and asked him to name the color. And suppose he answered, "I can recognize the color, and I can discriminate it from other colors, but I just can't name it." Then you juxtaposed a blue object and named its color, and he responded, "OK, since the second color is blue, the first one must be red." I believe that most people would find this process rather bizarre. Yet from the perspective of someone with absolute pitch this is precisely how most people name pitches — they evaluate the relationship between the pitch to be named and another pitch whose name they already know. . . . When I hear a musical note and identify its pitch, much more happens than simply placing its pitch on a point (or in a region) along a continuum. Suppose I hear an F-sharp sounded on the piano. I obtain a strong sense of familiarity for "F-sharpness" — like the sense one gets when one recognizes a familiar face. The pitch is bundled in with other attributes of the note — its timbre (very importantly), its loudness, and so on. I believe that, at least for some people with absolute pitch, notes are perceived and remembered in a way that is far more concrete than for those who do not possess this faculty.

Absolute pitch is of special interest because it exemplifies a whole other realm of perception, of qualia, something which most of us cannot even begin to imagine; because it is an isolated ability with little inherent connection to musicality or anything else; and because it shows how genes and experience can interact in its production.

It has long been clear anecdotally that absolute pitch is commoner   15
in musicians than in the general public, and this has been confirmed by large-scale studies. Among musicians, absolute pitch is commoner in those who have had musical training from an early age. But the correlation does not always hold: many gifted musicians fail to develop

absolute pitch, despite intensive early training. It is commoner in certain families — but is this because of a genetic component or because some families provide a richer musical environment? There is a striking association of absolute pitch with early blindness (some studies estimate that about 50 percent of children born blind or blinded in infancy have absolute pitch).

One of the most intriguing correlations occurs between absolute pitch and linguistic background. For the past few years, Diana Deutsch and her colleagues have studied such correlations in greater detail, and they observed in a 2006 paper that "native speakers of Vietnamese and Mandarin show very precise absolute pitch in reading lists of words"; most of these subjects showed variation of a quarter tone or less. Deutsch et al. have also showed very dramatic differences in the incidence of absolute pitch in two populations of first-year music students: one at the Eastman School of Music in Rochester, New York, and the other at the Central Conservatory of Music in Beijing. "For students who had begun musical training between ages four and five," they wrote, "approximately 60 percent of the Chinese students met the criterion for absolute pitch, while only about 14 percent of the U.S. nontone language speakers met the criterion." For those who had begun musical training at age six or seven, the numbers in both groups were correspondingly lower, about 55 percent and 6 percent. And for students who had begun musical training later still, at age eight or nine, "roughly 42 percent of the Chinese students met the criterion while none of the U.S. nontone language speakers did so." There were no differences between genders in either group.

This striking discrepancy led Deutsch et al. to conjecture that "if given the opportunity, infants can acquire AP as a feature of speech, which can then carry over to music." For speakers of a nontonal language such as English, they felt, "the acquisition of AP during music training is analogous to learning the tones of a second language." They observed that there was a critical period for the development of absolute pitch, before the age of eight or so — roughly the same age at which children find it much more difficult to learn the phonemes of another language (and thus to speak a second language with a native accent). Deutsch et al. suggested, therefore, that all infants might have the potential for acquiring absolute pitch, which could perhaps be "realized by enabling infants to associate pitches with verbal labels during the critical period" for language acquisition. (They did not exclude the possibility, nonetheless, that genetic differences might be important, too.)

The neural correlates of absolute pitch have been illuminated by comparing the brains of musicians with and without absolute pitch using a refined form of structural brain imaging (MRI morphometry), and by functional imaging of the brain as subjects identify musical tones and intervals. A 1995 paper by Gottfried Schlaug and his colleagues showed that in musicians with absolute pitch (but not musicians without), there was an exaggerated asymmetry between the volumes of the right and left planum temporale, structures in the brain that are important for the perception of speech and music. Similar asymmetries in the size and activity of the planum temporale have been shown in other people with absolute pitch.[3]

Absolute pitch is not just a matter of pitch perception. People with absolute pitch must be able not only to perceive precise pitch differences, but to label them, to line them up with the notes or names of a musical scale. It is this ability which Frank V. lost with the frontal lobe damage caused by the rupture of his cerebral aneurysm. The additional cerebral mechanisms required to correlate pitch and label are in the frontal lobes, and this, too, can be seen in functional MRI studies; thus, if someone with absolute pitch is asked to name tones or intervals, MRIs will show focal activation in certain associative areas of the frontal cortex. In those with relative pitch, this region is activated only when naming intervals.

While such categorical labeling is learned by all people with absolute   20
pitch, it is not clear that this excludes a prior *categorical* perception of pitch that is not dependent on association and learning. And the insistence of many with absolute pitch on the unique perceptual qualities of every pitch — its "color" or "chroma" — suggests that before the learning of categorical labels, there may be a purely perceptual categorization.

Jenny Saffran and Gregory Griepentrog at the University of Wisconsin compared eight-month-old infants to adults with and without musical training in a learning test of tone sequences. The infants, they found, relied much more heavily on absolute pitch cues; the adults, on relative pitch cues. This suggested to them that absolute pitch may be universal and highly adaptive in infancy but becomes maladaptive later

---

[3] Such asymmetries are not seen, interestingly, in blind subjects with absolute pitch, where there may be radical reorganizations of the brain, with parts of the visual cortex being recruited for the detection of pitch, as well as a variety of other auditory and tactile perceptions.

and is therefore lost. "Infants limited to grouping melodies by perfect pitches," they pointed out, "would never discover that the songs they hear are the same when sung in different keys or that words spoken at different fundamental frequencies are the same." In particular, they argued, the development of language necessitates the inhibition of absolute pitch, and only unusual conditions enable it to be retained. (The acquisition of a tonal language may be one of the "unusual conditions" that lead to the retention and perhaps heightening of absolute pitch.)

Deutsch and her colleagues, in their 2006 paper, suggested that their work not only has "implications for the issues of modularity in the processing of speech and music ... [but] of the evolutionary origin" of both. In particular, they see absolute pitch, whatever its subsequent vicissitudes, as having been crucial to the origins of both speech and music. In his book *The Singing Neanderthals: The Origins of Music, Language, Mind and Body*, Steven Mithen takes this idea further, suggesting that music and language have a common origin, and that a sort of combined protomusic-cum-protolanguage was characteristic of the Neanderthal mind.[4] This sort of singing language of meanings, without individual words as we understand them, he calls Hmmm (for holistic-mimetic-musical-multimodal) — and it depended, he speculates, on a conglomeration of isolated skills, including mimetic abilities and absolute pitch.

With the development of "a compositional language and syntactic rules," Mithen writes, "allowing an infinite number of things to be said, in contrast to the limited number of phrases that Hmmm allowed ... the brains of infants and children would have developed in a new fashion, one consequence of which would have been the loss of perfect pitch in the majority of individuals, and a diminution of musical abilities." We have little evidence as yet for this audacious hypothesis, but it is a tantalizing one.

---

[4] Though intriguingly elaborated by Mithen, this idea is not new. Jean-Jacques Rousseau (who was a composer as well as a philosopher) suggested in his "Essai sur l'Origine des Langues" that in primitive society, speech and song were not distinct from each other. For Rousseau, primitive languages were "melodic and poetic rather than practical or prosaic," as Maurice Cranston wrote, and were not so much uttered as chanted or sung. One sees this in many present-day religious and bardic traditions, from the cantillation of litanies and prayers to the singsong recital of epic poems.

I was once told of an isolated valley somewhere in the Pacific where all the inhabitants have absolute pitch. I like to imagine that such a place is populated by an ancient tribe that has remained in the state of Mithen's Neanderthals, with a host of exquisite mimetic abilities and communicating in a protolanguage as musical as it is lexical. But I suspect that the Valley of Absolute Pitch does not exist, except as a lovely, Edenic metaphor, or perhaps some sort of collective memory of a more musical past.

Genetic Engineering

DAVID SEDARIS was born in Johnson City, New York, in 1956 and grew up in Raleigh, North Carolina. He attended Kent State University but dropped out in 1977. Sedaris characterizes his early adult years as aimless: he hitchhiked around the country, then settled in Chicago, making a living (and supporting a drug habit) by doing odd jobs. He also read voraciously and kept a diary, which became a rich source of material for his later writing. In 1987, Sedaris graduated from the School of the Art Institute of Chicago.

Sedaris transformed his diary entries into humorous sketches. It was while reading such a sketch at a Chicago nightclub that he was "discovered" by Ira Glass, who invited him to appear on his local radio program. Sedaris first read for a national radio audience in December of 1992, reading a story about his experience as a Christmas elf at Macy's in New York. He quickly became a regular contributor to the National Public Radio series "This American Life." His stories—about his family, his work, the odd characters he met— were enormously popular, and he soon contracted with Little, Brown to publish a collection.

His first book, *Barrel Fever: Stories and Essays,* was published in 1994. In the years since, Sedaris has written stories for magazines, published six more book-length collections, collaborated with his sister Amy Sedaris on plays, and traveled across the United States and Europe on lecture tours. He likes the opportunity to do public readings, not only because it's important to hear the sound of the prose but because the responses of the audience guide his work; after a reading, he sometimes returns to his hotel room to make revisions.

Sedaris's writing is autobiographical, often featuring the eccentricities of his family. "Genetic Engineering" focuses on his father, who worked for IBM as an engineer, and mentions his brother, four sisters, and his mother, all of whom play key roles in other stories.

Given the broad exaggeration of Sedaris's humor, it is difficult to know where autobiography ends and fiction begins. Asked about the accuracy of events in his stories, Sedaris has said, "I think autobiography is the last place you would look for truth." "Genetic Engineering," first published in *The New Yorker* in 1998, appears in *Me Talk Pretty One Day* (2000).

My father always struck me as the sort of man who, under the right circumstances, might have invented the microwave oven or the transistor radio. You wouldn't seek him out for advice on a personal problem, but he'd be the first one you'd call when the dishwasher broke or someone flushed a hairpiece down your toilet. As children, we placed a great deal of faith in his ability but learned to steer clear while he was working. The experience of watching was ruined, time and time again, by an interminable explanation of how things were put together. Faced with an exciting question, science tended to provide the dullest possible answer. Ions might charge the air, but they fell flat when it came to charging the imagination — my imagination, anyway. To this day I prefer to believe that inside every television there lives a community of versatile, thumb-size actors trained to portray everything from a thoughtful newscaster to the wife of a millionaire stranded on a desert island. Fickle gnomes control the weather, and an air conditioner is powered by a team of squirrels, their cheeks packed with ice cubes.

Once, while rifling through the tool shed, I came across a poster advertising an IBM computer the size of a refrigerator. Sitting at the control board was my dad the engineer, years younger, examining a printout no larger than a grocery receipt. When I asked about it, he explained that he had worked with a team devising a memory chip capable of storing up to fifteen pages' worth of information. Out came the notepad and pencil, and I was trapped for hours as he answered every question except the one I had asked: "Were you allowed to wear makeup and run through a variety of different poses, or did they get the picture on the first take?"

To me, the greatest mystery of science continues to be that a man could father six children who shared absolutely none of his interests. We certainly expressed enthusiasm for our mother's hobbies, from smoking and napping to the writings of Sidney Sheldon. (Ask my mother how the radio worked and her answer was simple: "Turn it on and pull out the goddamn antenna.") I once visited my father's office, and walked away comforted to find that at least there he had a few people he could talk to. We'd gone, my sister Amy and I, to settle a bet. She thought that my father's secretary had a sharp, protruding chin and long blond hair, while I imagined that the woman might more closely resemble a tortoise — chinless, with a beaky nose and a loose, sagging neck. The correct answer was somewhere in between. I was right about the nose and the neck, but Amy won on the chin and the hair color. The bet had been the sole reason for our visit, and the resulting insufferable tour of Buildings A through D taught us never again to express an interest in our father's workplace.

My own scientific curiosity eventually blossomed, but I knew enough to keep my freakish experiments to myself. When my father discovered my colony of frozen slugs in the basement freezer, I chose not to explain my complex theories of suspended animation. Why was I filling the hamster's water beaker with vodka? "Oh, no reason." If my experiment failed, and the drunken hamster passed out, I'd just put her in the deep freeze, alongside the slugs. She'd rest on ice for a few months and, once thawed and fully revived, would remember nothing of her previous life as an alcoholic. I also took to repairing my own record-player and was astonished by my ingenuity for up to ten minutes at a time — until the rubber band snapped or the handful of change came unglued from the arm, and the damned thing broke all over again.

5   During the first week of September, it was my family's habit to rent a beach house on Ocean Isle, a thin strip of land off the coast of North Carolina. As youngsters, we participated in all the usual seaside activities — which were fun, until my father got involved and systematically chipped away at our pleasure. Miniature golf was ruined with a lengthy dissertation on impact, trajectory, and wind velocity, and our sand castles were critiqued with stifling lectures on the dynamics of the vaulted ceiling. We enjoyed swimming, until the mystery of tides was explained in such a way that the ocean seemed nothing more than an enormous saltwater toilet, flushing itself on a sad and predictable basis.

By the time we reached our teens, we were exhausted. No longer interested in the water, we joined our mother on the beach blanket and dedicated ourselves to the higher art of tanning. Under her guidance, we learned which lotions to start off with, and what worked best for various weather conditions and times of day. She taught us that the combination of false confidence and Hawaiian Tropic could result in a painful and unsightly burn, certain to subtract valuable points when, on the final night of vacation, contestants gathered for the annual Miss Emollient Pageant. This was a contest judged by our mother, in which the holder of the darkest tan was awarded a crown, a sash, and a scepter.

Technically, the prize could go to either a male or a female, but the sash read MISS EMOLLIENT because it was always assumed that my sister Gretchen would once again sweep the title. For her, tanning had moved from an intense hobby to something more closely resembling a psychological dysfunction. She was what we called a tanorexic: someone who simply could not get enough. Year after year she arrived at the beach with a base coat that the rest of us could only dream of achieving as our final product. With a mixture of awe and envy, we watched her broiling away on her aluminum blanket. The spaces between her toes were tanned, as were her palms and even the backs of her ears. Her method involved baby oil and a series of poses that tended to draw crowds, the mothers shielding their children's eyes with sand-covered fingers.

It is difficult for me to sit still for more than twenty minutes at a stretch, so I used to interrupt my tanning sessions with walks to the pier. On one of those walks, I came across my father standing not far from a group of fishermen who were untangling knots in a net the size of a circus tent. A lifetime of work beneath the coastal sun had left them with what my sisters and I referred to as the Samsonite Syndrome, meaning that their enviable color was negated by a hard, leathery texture reminiscent of the suitcase my mother stored all our baby pictures in. The men drank from quart bottles of Mountain Dew as they paused from their work to regard my father, who stood at the water's edge, staring at the shoreline with a stick in his hand.

I tried to creep by unnoticed, but he stopped me, claiming that I was just the fellow he'd been looking for. "Do you have any idea how many grains of sand there are in the world?" he asked. It was a question that had never occurred to me. Unlike guessing the number of pickled eggs in a jar or the amount of human brains it might take to equal the weight of a portable television set, this equation was bound to involve the hateful word *googolplex*, a term I'd heard him use once or twice before. It was an idea of a number and was, therefore, of no use whatsoever.

10   I'd heard once in school that if a single bird were to transport all the sand, grain by grain, from the eastern seaboard to the west coast of Africa, it would take . . . I didn't catch the number of years, preferring to concentrate on the single bird chosen to perform this thankless task. It hardly seemed fair, because, unlike a horse or a Seeing Eye dog, the whole glory of being a bird is that nobody would ever put you to work. Birds search for grubs and build their nests, but their leisure time is theirs to spend as they see fit. I pictured this bird looking down from the branches to say, "You want me to do what?" before flying off, laughing at the foolish story he now had to tell his friends. How many grains of sand are there in the world? A lot. Case closed.

    My father took his stick and began writing an equation in the sand. Like all the rest of them, this one was busy with x's and y's resting on top of one another on dash-shaped bunks. Letters were multiplied by symbols, crowded into parentheses, and set upon by dwarfish numbers drawn at odd angles. The equation grew from six to twelve feet long before assuming a second line, at which point the fishermen took an interest. I watched them turn from their net, and admired the way they could smoke entire cigarettes without ever taking them from their mouths — a skill my mother had mastered and one that continues to elude me. It involves a symbiotic relationship with the wind: you have to know exactly how and when to turn your head in order to keep the smoke out of your eyes.

    One of the men asked my father if he was a tax accountant, and he answered, "No, an engineer." These were poor men, who could no longer afford to live by the ocean, who had long ago sold their one-story homes for the valuable sand beneath them. Their houses had been torn down to make room for high-priced hotels and the A-frame cottages that now rented in season for a thousand dollars a week.

    "Let me ask a little something," one of the men said, spitting his spent cigarette butt into the surf. "If I got paid twelve thousand dollars in 1962 for a half-acre beachfront lot, how much would that be worth per grain of sand by today's standard?"

    "That, my friend, is a very interesting question," my father said.

15   He moved several yards down the beach and began a new equation, captivating his audience with a lengthy explanation of each new and complex symbol. "When you say pie," one man asked, "do you mean a

real live pie, or one of those pie shapes they put on the news sometimes to show how much of your money goes to taxes?"

My father answered their questions in detail, and they listened intently — this group of men with nets, blowing their smoke into the wind. Stooped and toothless, they hung upon his every word while I stood in the lazy surf, thinking of the upcoming pageant and wondering if the light reflecting off the water might tan the underside of my nose and chin.

Mother Tongue

AMY TAN's first publication was a brief essay called "What the Library Means to Me." The essay, printed in the Santa Rosa *Press Democrat* in 1960, begins:

> My name is Amy Tan, 8 years old, a third grader in Matanzas School. It is a brand new school and everything is so nice and pretty. I love school because the many things I learn seem to turn on a light in the little room in my mind. . . . My father takes me to the library every two weeks, and I check five or six books each time. These books seem to open many windows in my little room.

Tan's father, John Tan, was a Baptist minister who nurtured his daughter's love of language not only through biweekly trips to the library but by reading bedtime stories, drafts of his sermons, even his homework for graduate courses in engineering. When Amy Tan was fifteen, she lost both her father and her older brother to brain tumors; they died within eight months of each other. Her mother moved with her surviving children to the Netherlands and then to Switzerland. After Tan's graduation from a high school in Switzerland, her family returned to California where she studied English and linguistics at San Jose State University.

Tan began a successful career as a business writer before turning, at the age of thirty-three, to fiction. Much of her fiction explores mother-daughter relationships in Chinese American families. Her first book, *The Joy Luck Club* (1989), was an extraordinary success. A finalist for the National Book Award and the National Book Critics Circle award, it was on the *New York Times* bestseller list for eight months. Tan's second novel, *The Kitchen God's Wife* (1991) is based on her mother's life. More recent novels include *The Hundred Secret Senses* (1995), *The Bonesetter's Daughter* (2001), and *Saving Fish from Drowning* (2005).

The intellectual curiosity evident in "What the Library Means to Me" motivates Tan's work as a writer. "I write for very much the same reason that I read: to startle my mind, to churn my heart, to tingle my spine, to knock the blinders off my eyes and allow me to see beyond the pale." Writers who have influenced Tan's work include Jamaica Kincaid, Vladimir Nabokov, and Louise Erdrich (she identifies Erdrich's *Love Medicine* as "the book that made me want to find my own voice").

"Mother Tongue" was written as a speech in 1989, then revised for publication in *The Threepenny Review.* It was selected for *The Best American Essays 1991,* and Tan included it in her 2003 collection, *The Opposite of Fate. A Book of Musings.*

I am not a scholar of English or literature. I cannot give you much more than personal opinions on the English language and its variations in this country or others.

I am a writer. And by that definition, I am someone who has always loved language. I am fascinated by language in daily life. I spend a great deal of my time thinking about the power of language — the way it can evoke an emotion, a visual image, a complex idea, or a simple truth. Language is the tool of my trade. And I use them all — all the Englishes I grew up with.

Recently, I was made keenly aware of the different Englishes I do use. I was giving a talk to a large group of people, the same talk I had already given to half a dozen other groups. The nature of the talk was about my writing, my life, and my book, *The Joy Luck Club.* The talk was going along well enough, until I remembered one major difference that made the whole talk sound wrong. My mother was in the room. And it was perhaps the first time she had heard me give a lengthy speech, using the kind of English I have never used with her. I was saying things like, "The intersection of memory upon imagination" and "There is an aspect of my fiction that relates to thus-and-thus" — a speech filled with carefully wrought grammatical phrases, burdened, it suddenly seemed to me, with nominalized forms, past perfect tenses, conditional phrases, all the forms of standard English that I had learned in school and through books, the forms of English I did not use at home with my mother.

Just last week, I was walking down the street with my mother, and I again found myself conscious of the English I was using, the English I do use with her. We were talking about the price of new and used furniture and I heard myself saying this: "Not waste money that way."

My husband was with us as well, and he didn't notice any switch in my English. And then I realized why. It's because over the twenty years we've been together I've often used that same kind of English with him, and sometimes he even uses it with me. It has become our language of intimacy, a different sort of English that relates to family talk, the language I grew up with.

5   So you'll have some idea of what this family talk I heard sounds like, I'll quote what my mother said during a recent conversation which I videotaped and then transcribed. During this conversation, my mother was talking about a political gangster in Shanghai who had the same last name as her family's, Du, and how the gangster in his early years wanted to be adopted by her family, which was rich by comparison. Later, the gangster became more powerful, far richer than my mother's family, and one day showed up at my mother's wedding to pay his respects. Here's what she said in part:

"Du Yusong having business like fruit stand. Like off the street kind. He is Du like Du Zong — but not Tsung-ming Island people. The local people call putong, the river east side, he belong to that side local people. That man want to ask Du Zong father take him in like become own family. Du Zong father wasn't look down on him, but didn't take seriously, until that man big like become a mafia. Now important person, very hard to inviting him. Chinese way, came only to show respect, don't stay for dinner. Respect for making big celebration, he shows up. Mean gives lots of respect. Chinese custom. Chinese social life that way. If too important won't have to stay too long. He come to my wedding. I didn't see, I heard it. I gone to boy's side, they have YMCA dinner. Chinese age I was nineteen."

You should know that my mother's expressive command of English belies how much she actually understands. She reads the *Forbes* report, listens to *Wall Street Week*, converses daily with her stockbroker, reads all of Shirley MacLaine's books with ease — all kinds of things I can't begin to understand. Yet some of my friends tell me they understand 50 percent of what my mother says. Some say they understand 80 to 90 percent. Some say they understand none of it, as if she were speaking pure Chinese. But to me, my mother's English is perfectly clear, perfectly natural. It's my mother tongue. Her language, as I hear it, is vivid, direct, full of observation and imagery. That was the language that helped shape the way I saw things, expressed things, made sense of the world.

Lately, I've been giving more thought to the kind of English my mother speaks. Like others, I have described it to people as "broken" or "fractured" English. But I wince when I say that. It has always bothered me that I can think of no way to describe it other than "broken," as if it were damaged and needed to be fixed, as if it lacked a certain wholeness and soundness. I've heard other terms used, "limited English," for example. But they seem just as bad, as if everything is limited, including people's perceptions of the limited English speaker.

I know this for a fact, because when I was growing up, my mother's "limited" English limited *my* perception of her. I was ashamed of her English. I believed that her English reflected the quality of what she had to say. That is, because she expressed them imperfectly her thoughts were imperfect. And I had plenty of empirical evidence to support me: the fact that people in department stores, at banks, and at restaurants did not take her seriously, did not give her good service, pretended not to understand her, or even acted as if they did not hear her.

My mother has long realized the limitations of her English as well. 10 When I was fifteen, she used to have me call people on the phone to pretend I was she. In this guise, I was forced to ask for information or even to complain and yell at people who had been rude to her. One time it was a call to her stockbroker in New York. She had cashed out her small portfolio and it just so happened we were going to go to New York the next week, our very first trip outside California. I had to get on the phone and say in an adolescent voice that was not very convincing, "This is Mrs. Tan."

And my mother was standing in the back whispering loudly, "Why he don't send me check, already two weeks late. So mad he lie to me, losing me money."

And then I said in perfect English, "Yes, I'm getting rather concerned. You had agreed to send the check two weeks ago, but it hasn't arrived."

Then she began to talk more loudly. "What he want, I come to New York tell him front of his boss, you cheating me?" And I was trying to calm her down, make her be quiet, while telling the stockbroker, "I can't tolerate any more excuses. If I don't receive the check immediately, I am going to have to speak to your manager when I'm in New York next week." And sure enough, the following week there we were in front of this astonished stockbroker, and I was sitting there red-faced and quiet, and my mother, the real Mrs. Tan, was shouting at his boss in her impeccable broken English.

We used a similar routine just five days ago, for a situation that was far less humorous. My mother had gone to the hospital for an appointment, to find out about a benign brain tumor a CAT scan had revealed a month ago. She said she had spoken very good English, her best English, no mistakes. Still, she said, the hospital did not apologize when they said they had lost the CAT scan and she had come for nothing. She said they did not seem to have any sympathy when she told them she was anxious to know the exact diagnosis, since her husband and son had both died of brain tumors. She said they would not give her any more information until the next time and she would have to make another appointment for that. So she said she would not leave until the doctor called her daughter. She wouldn't budge. And when the doctor finally called her daughter, me, who spoke in perfect English — lo and behold — we had assurances the CAT scan would be found, promises that a conference call on Monday would be held, and apologies for any suffering my mother had gone through for a most regrettable mistake.

15   I think my mother's English almost had an effect on limiting my possibilities in life as well. Sociologists and linguists probably will tell you that a person's developing language skills are more influenced by peers. But I do think that the language spoken in the family, especially in immigrant families which are more insular, plays a large role in shaping the language of the child. And I believe that it affected my results on achievement tests, IQ tests, and the SAT. While my English skills were never judged as poor, compared to math, English could not be considered my strong suit. In grade school I did moderately well, getting perhaps B's, sometimes B-pluses, in English and scoring perhaps in the sixtieth or seventieth percentile on achievement tests. But those scores were not good enough to override the opinion that my true abilities lay in math and science, because in those areas I achieved A's and scored in the ninetieth percentile or higher.

This was understandable. Math is precise; there is only one correct answer. Whereas, for me at least, the answers on English tests were always a judgment call, a matter of opinion and personal experience. Those tests were constructed around items like fill-in-the-blank sentence completion, such as "Even though Tom was _____, Mary thought he was _____." And the correct answer always seemed to be the most bland combinations of thoughts, for example, "Even though Tom was shy, Mary thought he was charming," with the grammatical structure "even though " limiting the correct answer to some sort of semantic opposites, so you wouldn't get answers like, "Even though Tom was foolish, Mary thought he was ridiculous." Well, according to my mother, there were very few limitations as to what Tom could have been and what Mary might have thought of him. So I never did well on tests like that.

The same was true with word analogies, pairs of words in which you were supposed to find some sort of logical, semantic relationship — for example, "*Sunset* is to *nightfall* as _____ is to _____." And here you would be presented with a list of four possible pairs, one of which showed the same kind of relationship: *red* is to *stoplight*, *bus* is to *arrival*, *chills* is to *fever*, *yawn* is to *boring*. Well, I could never think that way. I knew what the tests were asking, but I could not block out of my mind the images already created by the first pair, "*sunset* is to *nightfall*" — and I would see a burst of colors against a darkening sky, the moon rising, the lowering of a curtain of stars. And all the other pairs of words — red, bus, stoplight, boring — just threw up a mass of confusing images, making it impossible for me to sort out something as logical as saying: "A sunset precedes nightfall" is the same as "a chill precedes a fever." The only way I would have gotten that answer right would have been to imagine an associative situation, for example, my being disobedient and staying out past sunset, catching a chill at night, which turns into feverish pneumonia as punishment, which indeed did happen to me.

I have been thinking about all this lately, about my mother's English, about achievement tests. Because lately I've been asked, as a writer, why there are not more Asian Americans represented in American literature. Why are there few Asian Americans enrolled in creative writing programs? Why do so many Chinese students go into engineering? Well, these are broad sociological questions I can't begin to answer. But I have noticed in surveys — in fact, just last week — that Asian students, as a whole, always do significantly better on math achievement tests than in English. And this makes me think that there are other Asian American students whose English spoken in the home might also be described as "broken" or "limited." And perhaps they also have teachers who are steering them away from writing and into math and science, which is what happened to me.

Fortunately, I happen to be rebellious in nature and enjoy the challenge of disproving assumptions made about me. I became an English major my first year in college, after being enrolled as pre-med. I started writing nonfiction as a freelancer the week after I was told by my former boss that writing was my worst skill and I should hone my talents toward account management.

20   But it wasn't until 1985 that I finally began to write fiction. And at first I wrote using what I thought to be wittily crafted sentences, sentences that would finally prove I had mastery over the English language. Here's an example from the first draft of a story that later made its way into *The Joy Luck Club*, but without this line: "That was my mental quandary in its nascent state." A terrible line, which I can barely pronounce.

Fortunately, for reasons I won't get into today, I later decided I should envision a reader for the stories I would write. And the reader I decided upon was my mother, because these were stories about mothers. So with this reader in mind — and in fact she did read my early drafts — I began to write stories using all the Englishes I grew up with: the English I spoke to my mother, which for lack of a better term might be described as "simple"; the English she used with me, which for lack of a better term might be described as "broken"; my translation of her Chinese, which could certainly be described as "watered down"; and what I imagined to be her translation of her Chinese if she could speak in perfect English, her internal language, and for that I sought to preserve the essence, but neither an English nor a Chinese structure. I wanted to capture what language ability tests can never reveal: her intent, her passion, her imagery, the rhythms of her speech and the nature of her thoughts.

Apart from what any critic had to say about my writing, I knew I had succeeded where it counted when my mother finished reading my book and gave me her verdict: "So easy to read."

Loss of Family Languages: Should Educators Be Concerned?

The daughter of Chinese immigrants, **LILY WONG FILLMORE** grew up in Watsonville, a small city on California's central coast. She had firsthand experience of the value of linguistic and cultural diversity: at school, she was exposed to Cantonese, English, and Spanish, and waiting tables at her parents' restaurant, she met agricultural workers from Mexico, Japan, Eastern Europe, and the Philippines.

At the age of seventeen, Wong entered an arranged marriage and moved to nearby Gilroy, where she and her husband ran a laundry and dry cleaning firm. Twelve years later, with three children, the couple divorced, and she began taking classes at San Jose State University. She went on to study linguistics at Stanford University, completing her doctorate in 1976. Soon after taking a position in the Graduate School of Education at UC Berkeley, Wong met and married the linguist Charles Fillmore. Both scholars have retired after long careers at Berkeley.

Wong Fillmore's research investigates language acquisition in all its complexity, examining how children from immigrant families learn English in school, how they learn other subjects when the language of instruction is new to them, and how their exposure to English-dominant schooling affects their psychological and social development. Her research has taken her into schools and multilingual communities in California, New Mexico, and Alaska. An activist as well as a scholar, she has argued for bilingual education and for robust support for English language learners, including improved teacher education in language acquisition.

Wong Fillmore is primarily an academic writer, publishing her research findings in books and journal articles. Although she has observed that "bloated noun phrases" are the hallmark of academic writing, she values academic discourse as "the language that is capable of supporting complex thought and argumentation." In recent years, she has argued against using "dumbed down" materials for English language learners on the grounds that students can gain academic literacy only with exposure to genuine academic texts. Wong Fillmore's own prose is lean and energetic, often populated by the multilingual children she has met in the course of her research. She is also the author of a children's book, *Lady in the Moon*.

"Loss of Family Languages: Should Educators Be Concerned?" appeared in the autumn 2000 issue of *Theory into Practice*.

By conservative estimates, 3.5 million children in U.S. schools are identified as limited in English proficiency (LEP) (Macias, 1998). Their knowledge of English is so limited that without linguistic help they are excluded "from effective participation in the educational program offered" by the schools they attend (*Lau v. Nichols*, 1974). The Supreme Court's ruling in *Lau v. Nichols* held that these children must be provided instructional help to overcome the linguistic barrier to the school's instructional programs. The Court did not specify a particular programmatic remedy, but suggested that bilingual education was one possible approach, while instruction in English as a second language (ESL) was another. Since then, both bilingual and ESL programs have been established in many states to help children learn English and gain access to the curriculum.

The dilemma facing immigrant children, however, may be viewed as less a problem of learning English than of primary language loss. While virtually all children who attend American schools learn English, most of them are at risk of losing their primary languages as they do so.

In one sense, primary language loss as children acquire English is not a new problem. Few immigrant groups have successfully maintained their ethnic languages as they became assimilated into American life.[1] As they learned English, they used it more and more until English became their dominant language.

The outcome in earlier times was nonetheless bilingualism. The second generation could speak the ethnic language and English, although few people were equally proficient in both languages. The loss of the ethnic language occurred between the second and the third generations because second generation immigrants rarely used the ethnic language enough to impart it to their own children. Thus, the process of language loss used to take place over two generations (Fishman & Hofman, 1966; Portes & Rumbault, 1990).

The picture has changed dramatically in the case of present day immigrants. Few current second generation immigrants can be described as bilinguals (López, 1982). Ordinarily, we assume that when children acquire a second language, they add it to their primary language, and the result is bilingualism. But in the case of most present-day immigrant children, the learning of English is a subtractive process (Lambert, 1977), with English quickly displacing and replacing the primary language in young first generation immigrants. The result is that few immigrant children become bilinguals today by learning English. Over the past twenty-five years, this process of accelerated language loss in immigrant children and families has been documented repeatedly (Fillmore, 1991a, 1991b; Hinton, 1999; Kouritzin, 1999; Portes & Hao, 1998). The following is an account of the experiences of one such family. 5

A Case of Language Shift and Loss

The Chen[2] family is like many Chinese immigrants who have come to the United States over the past several decades. The family came from China's Canton province via Hong Kong, where they had spent nearly a decade waiting for a visa to immigrate to the United States.

---

[1] Some groups are more retentive of their ethnic languages than others, and have managed to maintain them even into the third generation (Fishman & Hofman, 1966; Portes & Hao, 1998).

[2] The family name Chen is a pseudonym, as are all the given names used here. Chen is about as common a surname among the Chinese as Smith or Jones is among Americans. I have tried to use both Chinese and American given names that are similar enough to the real names of family members since their names revealed how they were adjusting to the American experience.

The Chens arrived in the United States in 1989: Mother, Father, Uncle (Father's brother), Grandmother (Father's mother), and the children, Kai-Fong, age five at the time of arrival (now sixteen); and Chu-Mei, age four (now fifteen). Once settled, the family quickly added two more children — the "ABC" ("American born Chinese") members of the Chen family, both girls, Chu-wa (now ten); and Allison (now nine years old). A consideration of how the members of this family fared in their first decade in America is revealing. Sadly, it is a story that many immigrant families have experienced firsthand.

Contrasting Experiences   The Chens settled in a suburban town in the San Francisco Bay area where Father, Mother, and Uncle had jobs waiting for them in a restaurant owned by a relative. They went to work in the restaurant's kitchen, and because the kitchen workers were all Chinese, their lack of English was not a handicap. They worked long hours each day, leaving home early in the morning and returning close to midnight. Grandmother stayed at home with the children, and everything was fine at first. She got the children ready for school and was at home to care for them when they were out of school.

School was difficult for the children initially, but they did not complain much. The elementary school that Kai-fong and Chu-mei attended had many minority group students. Some, although not many, were LEP students like themselves. The school had no bilingual or ESL classes, so non-English speakers like Kai-fong and Chu-mei were simply placed in regular classes where it was assumed they would learn English. Both began kindergarten at the same time and were placed in the same classroom. The teacher spoke English only, but she gave the several non-English speakers in her class extra attention whenever she could.

Chu-mei soon made friends with classmates and learned some English from them and from the teacher. Her adjustment, after the first year in school, was excellent. She had learned enough English in kindergarten to make reading in the first grade more or less possible. She was neat, agreeable, and sociable. She fit into the social world of the classroom without difficulty.

10   Kai-fong had quite a different experience in school. He was not as outgoing as his sister, and from the start, had difficulty establishing himself socially with his classmates. Some of the boys in the class teased

him mercilessly. After Grandmother had cut his hair, it stuck straight out and would not lie flat. They called him "Chi, chi, chi, Chia-pet," after a then popular gift item that was advertised frequently on television — a pig-shaped vase that grew spikey grass hair when watered. Kai-fong probably did not know what a "Chia-pet" was, but he knew his classmates were making fun of his appearance. He wore homemade trousers that Grandmother had made from some polyester stretch yardage for him and for Chu-mei. The fabric worked well for Chu-mei, but not for Kai-fong. The boys in his class teased him about his "flower pants."

One day at school, there was a rock throwing incident involving Kai-fong and some other boys. It was unclear who started throwing rocks at whom, but they were all caught with rocks in their hands. The other children could tell their side of the story to the teacher on yard duty; Kai-fong could not. When the incident was reported to Father and Mother, they did not understand what had happened. They knew only that Kai-fong had gotten into trouble at school. Kai-fong was severely reprimanded by Father, Mother, and Grandmother, and he gradually began to withdraw.

In time, Kai-fong learned enough English to get by, and his wardrobe and hair became less distinctive. But he remained an outsider. In class, he was an indifferent student and rarely said anything spontaneously. He had a small group of friends with whom he played on the playground — other Asian immigrant boys who, like himself, were not finding it easy to fit into the social world of the school. Several boys were Vietnamese, one was Filipino, the others were Thai. The English they spoke had many dialect features that were picked up from the African American children in the school, although they had little interaction with them. Kai-fong and his friends seemed to admire the African American boys, and copied their dress, musical taste, and speech. The African American boys were also outsiders at school, but they were the "cool guys," and they operated within their own social sphere both in and out of school.

Increasing Separation   At home, Kai-fong became increasingly an outsider. Once he learned a little English, he stopped speaking Cantonese altogether. When Grandmother spoke to him, he either ignored her or would mutter a response in English that she did not understand. When pushed, he would simply stop speaking. Grandmother's complaints to Mother and Father resulted in frequent scoldings, and increasingly severe reprimands and sanctions. The more the adults scolded, the more sullen and angry Kai-fong became.

By the age of ten, Kai-fong, who was now known as Ken, was spending most of his time away from home, hanging out with his buddies, away from the scolding and haranguing. He and his friends spoke English only, and although some of them may have retained their primary languages, Kai-fong/Ken did not. He no longer understood Cantonese well and rarely said anything in that language.

15 Over time, Grandmother became withdrawn too. She had chronic headaches, which often immobilized her. Whether the headaches were caused by the tension in the home or not, it certainly did not help. The headaches made it hard for her to care for the younger children, and this was often left to Chu-mei. Each day, while her sisters were young, she hurried home from school and would play with them and teach them things she was learning. From her they learned English, the language she spoke at school and the language she could express herself in most easily.

Neither Chu-wa nor Allison (named after Chu-mei's best friend at school) speak Cantonese. They call Grandmother "Ah Yin-Yin" (the address term for paternal grandmother in Cantonese), but they do not know how to say much else in Cantonese to their grandmother or their parents. In fact, the only child in this family who can still communicate with the adults in Cantonese is Chu-mei, or Sondra, as she prefers to be called. She interprets for her family members when they need to communicate with one another.

But although Chu-mei/Sondra still speaks Cantonese, she is not as fluent as she should be. She is unable to express herself completely in Cantonese, and occasionally slips English words and phrases into her speech as she attempts to communicate with the adults in the family. This could be evidence of language loss or an indication that her primary language has not continued to develop as she has grown more mature. Either way, she is not as proficient in Cantonese as Chinese children her age ordinarily are.

Deteriorating Family Relations Accelerated language loss is a common occurrence these days among immigrant families, with the younger members losing the ethnic language after a short time in school. In the Chen family, the adult members have not learned much

English after a decade of residence in the United States. Mother, Father, and Uncle would like to study English, but their long work days do not allow them to take English as a second language classes at the adult education center in town. Father and Uncle have begun to pick up a little English from coworkers and from the Americans they see occasionally, but Mother and Grandmother have not learned much at all, although Grandmother spends most of her time at home with her English-speaking grandchildren.

Clearly, the Chen family was deeply affected by the ways in which the children adjusted to life in their new society. The shift from Cantonese to English in this family and the loss of the family language by the children have had a great impact on communication between the adults and the children and ultimately on family relations. There is tension in this home: the adults do not understand the children, and the children do not understand the adults. Father, Mother, and Grandmother do not feel they know the children, and they do not know what is happening in their lives.

This is most obvious in the case of Kai-fong/Ken, who spends   20
little time at home these days. He dropped out of school over a year ago and is out with his friends most of the time. His father says he does not know what Kai-fong is doing, but he does not think he has a job.

What Is Lost When a Language Is Lost?

From a strictly pragmatic perspective, what happened to this immigrant family appears unfortunate but hardly tragic. From the school's point of view, this could even be seen as a relative success story. Of the four children in the Chen family, three are doing well in school. Only one has gotten lost, but that can happen in any family. But is it an acceptable loss? The questions that must be asked are these: What does school success mean, and can we afford to lose one child in four in the process of educating them? The three Chen children who can be described as successful students are so because they have learned English quickly and have made progress at school. They are acquiring the skills and information they need for educational advancement and participation in the work world. But is that all that is important? Can school provide children with everything they need to learn through the formal educational process?

I contend that the school cannot provide children what is most fundamental to success in life. The family plays a crucial role in providing the basic elements for successful functioning. These include a sense of belonging; knowledge of who one is and where one comes from; an understanding of how one is connected to the important others and events in one's life; the ability to deal with adversity; and knowing one's responsibility to self, family, community. Other elements could be added to the list, but the point is that these are things the family must provide children at home while they are growing up. They cannot be taught at school. The content differs from family to family, but this is the curriculum of the home — what parents and other family members teach and inculcate in children in the socialization process.

The curriculum of the home is taught by word and example, by the way adults relate to the children of the family, beginning at birth and not ending until the children are mature and on their own. When parents send their children to school for formal education, they understand that their job of socializing their children is far from done. They continue to teach their children what they need to know as they mature. The school can take what the family has provided and augment or modify it even, but the foundation must be laid by the family.

What happens in families where parents cannot communicate easily with the children? What happens when the major means of socializing children into the beliefs, values, and knowledge base of the family and cultural group is lost? If the parents know any English, often they switch to that language and, while their capacity to socialize the children might be diminished, they are nonetheless able to teach their children some of what they need to learn. But it is not easy to socialize children in a language one does not know well. It takes thorough competence in a language to communicate the nuances of a culture to another.

25   In his autobiography, *Hunger of Memory* (1982), Rodriguez describes what happens in families when parents try to socialize their children in a language they do not know well. He recalls what happened as he and his siblings moved from Spanish to English after the parents were advised to stop using Spanish at home with the children:

> My mother and father, for their part, responded differently as their
> children spoke to them less. She grew restless, seemed anxious at
> the scarcity of words exchanged in the house. It was she who would

question me when I came home from school. She smiled at the small talk. She pried at the edges of my sentences to get me to say something more. (What?) She'd join conversations she overheard, but her intrusions often stopped her children's talking. By contrast, my father seemed reconciled to the new quiet. Though his English improved somewhat, he retired into silence. At dinner he spoke very little. One night his children and even his wife helplessly giggled at his garbled English pronunciation of the Catholic Grace before Meals. Thereafter he made his wife recite the prayer at the start of each meal, even on formal occasions, when guests were in the house. Hers became the public voice of the family. On official business, it was she, not my father, one would usually hear on the phone or in stores, talking to strangers. His children grew so accustomed to his silence that, years later, they would speak routinely of his shyness. But my father was not shy, I realized, when I'd watch him speaking Spanish with relatives. Using Spanish, he was quickly effusive. Especially when talking with other men, his voice would spark, flicker, flare alive with sounds. In Spanish, he expressed ideas and feelings he rarely revealed in English. With firm Spanish sounds, he conveyed confidence and authority English would never allow him. (pp. 24–25)

Can parents keep informed of what is happening to their children? Can they stay connected with them when the children no longer understand the family language? Can parents maintain their roles as authority figures, teachers, and moral guides if they are not listened to? We discern in Rodriguez's poignant description a family that has lost its intimacy — the closeness between parents and children. Children learn what it means to be parents by observing their own parents. In this family, the children saw shadows only and not true pictures of who their parents were and what they were like as persons. Rodriguez reveals how greatly the loss of language and intimacy in the family changed the very structure of the family as well. The loss of language in this family severed the spiritual bond between parents and children:

> The silence at home, however, was finally more than a literal silence.
> Fewer words passed between parent and child, but more profound was
> the silence that resulted from my inattention to sounds. (p. 25)

That is the dilemma. That is what is lost. One might argue that despite all of this, Rodriguez has been a success. He is a talented writer; he is thoughtful and sensitive; and he has accomplished a great deal in his life. But what his writings reveal to this reader is a deeply conflicted and lonely man who is trying to figure out who he is, where he belongs, and what his culture means. Does it matter that children lose their family language as they learn English as long as it does not interfere with their educational development and success in school? I think it does.

For immigrant children, learning English as a second language and dealing with school successfully are just one set of problems to be faced. Hanging on to their first language as they learn English is an equally great problem. Hanging on to their sense of worth, their cultural identities, and their family connections as they become assimilated into the school and society is a tremendous problem for all immigrant children. What is at stake in becoming assimilated into the society is not only their educational development but their psychological and emotional well-being as individuals as well (Cummins, 1996).

The questions we educators need to consider are these: How and why do children give up and lose their primary languages as they learn English? What is involved, and what role are the schools playing in the process?

How Is a Language Lost?

Language loss is not a necessary or inevitable outcome when children acquire second languages. Otherwise the world would have no bilinguals. In many places around the world, bilingualism and even multilingualism are commonplace. In the United States, however, and in other societies like it, powerful social and political forces operate against the retention of minority languages. To many and perhaps most Americans, English is more than a societal language; it is an ideology. The ideological stance is this: to be American, one must speak English.

30   English gives access to participation in the life of the society, but it is also proof of an individual's acceptance of and loyalty to the American ideal. Conversely, the inability to speak English is a sign that a person has not accepted the conditions of being American. These sentiments are powerful forces in how people see and deal with one another, especially in places like California, which have heavy concentrations of recent immigrants.[3] How do these forces affect the children discussed in this article?

---

[3] According to the Immigration and Naturalization Service, one of every four immigrants to the United States eventually resettles in California. When I was recently called for jury duty, I overheard three separate remarks from individuals complaining about

The inability to speak English in school is a handicapping condition in many communities, particularly in places that have no programs designed to help children who are limited in English proficiency. Children in such situations, irrespective of background or age, are quick to see that language is a social barrier, and the only way to gain access to the social world of the school is to learn English. The problem is that they also come to believe that the language they already know, the one spoken at home by their families, is the cause of the barrier to participation, inclusion, and social acceptance. They quickly discover that in the social world of the school, English is the only language that is acceptable. The message they get is this: "The home language is nothing; it has no value at all." If they want to be fully accepted, children come to believe that they must disavow the low status language spoken at home.

Children often start using English almost exclusively outside of the home just as soon as they have learned barely enough to get by. Before long, they are speaking English at home as well, even with parents who do not understand the language. If the parents do not realize that this shift in language behavior signals a change in the children's language loyalty, English will supplant the family language completely in the children's speech.

Language loss is the result of both internal and external forces operating on children. The internal factors have to do with the desire for social inclusion, conformity, and the need to communicate with others. The external forces are the sociopolitical ones operating in the society against outsiders, against differences, against diversity. They are the forces behind the passage of various public referendums in California against "immigrants" and "outside influences": Proposition 63 in 1986, banning the use of languages other than English in public life; Proposition 187 in 1994, denying undocumented immigrants health, welfare,

---

"foreigners" who could not speak English well. The young woman who was calling names of prospective jurors on the public address system did so with evidence of Spanish in her pronunciation of English. Her English was nonetheless completely grammatical and intelligible. In the San Francisco Bay area, with its very diverse population, there were many unfamiliar surnames to be called, and she occasionally stumbled over the names she was reading, as anyone might. A woman who was sitting beside me in the jury assembly room complained to those seated around her: "They should not hire people who can't speak English! People who don't speak English properly shouldn't be allowed to deal with the public." That was just one of three such remarks I overheard that day.

and educational services provided by public funds;[4] Proposition 209 in 1996, ending affirmative action programs in jobs and education; and finally Proposition 227 in 1998, eliminating bilingual education as the preferred instructional program for LEP students.

Children may not understand what these public actions mean, but they are aware of the underlying sentiment. They interpret it as saying to them: to be different is to be unacceptable. Thus children do what they believe they must to rid themselves of what makes them unacceptable. Language is an obvious difference, so it is the first to go. Names, dress, haircuts — whatever is obviously different is changed: Chu-mei becomes Sondra, Kai-fong becomes Ken, and Allison is Allison from the start. Baggy legged jeans and oversized T-shirts replace unfashionable homemade garments, and the children are transformed. They are still different from their schoolmates, but not quite as different as before. They are no longer outsiders: they are Americans, not foreigners like their parents.

35   The processes of language loss and social adaptation may differ across individuals in detail from the picture sketched here, but the broad outline of these processes is general enough so that many immigrants will be able to map their own experiences onto it. They know what happens in families when children abandon the family language, and parents are no longer able to communicate easily with them. They know about the gradual erosion of trust and understanding among family members and about the loss of parental control.

Why do people allow this to happen? Few of those who are involved in the process of language loss realize the consequences it can have on their family or children until it is too late. It is difficult for people to believe that children can actually lose a language. They recognize that

---

[4] Proposition 187 was declared to be unconstitutional in 1997 in a legal challenge brought before the federal court in Los Angeles. Invoking the "Personal Responsibility and Work Opportunity Reconciliation Act of 1996," the welfare reform legislation enacted by Congress, Judge M. R. Pfaelzer found in *League of United Latin American Citizens v. Wilson*, that 187 was an effort by the state to regulate immigration by restricting access to welfare and educational services. The regulation of immigration is exclusively a federal responsibility, and the state does not have the power to override federal legislation with its "own legislative scheme to regulate access to public benefits," the judge declared. Former Governor Pete Wilson appealed the decision in the Ninth Circuit Court of Appeals, but he was out of office before the case was heard. It was left to the present governor, Gray Davis, to settle the matter. In 1999, Davis asked the court to submit the case for mediation. The state and the opponents of 187 recently came to terms of agreement, ending any future challenges to the ruling.

their children are changing, becoming "Americanized," as it were, or more independent. But few parents doubt that their children, if required to do so, could switch back to their primary language. And indeed, it might be somewhat true for some children. The loss of a primary language is rarely total. But in most cases, when children are not actively using their primary language in everyday interactions, they do not develop it further, as was the case with Chu-mei, or Sondra. She is still able to speak Cantonese, but not at an appropriate level for a child her age.

Suggestions for Educators

What can educators do to make the process of learning the school language and adapting to life in American culture easier on immigrant children and their families? What can they do to make English learning less subtractive than it is now? Ideally children would attend schools where the primary language is used along with English, and they would be given opportunities to develop both languages fully. But that may not be possible under current sociopolitical conditions. Whether or not it is, parents and teachers should be working together to find other ways to support children's development and retention of their primary languages, and to make their adjustment to school an easier one for everyone involved.

Such collaborative efforts between educators and parents, although needed, are not easy. The parents who need the most help are unlikely to speak or understand much English. If teachers can speak their language, they can work directly with them. Otherwise teachers must work through interpreters, and that is never easy. The parents must be convinced that they need to be involved and to find time to work with the school for efforts like this to work.

Many immigrant parents have long workdays and may find it difficult to participate in school activities after work. Others may lack the confidence to work with teachers with whom they are not able to communicate easily. Still others may not understand the need for joint action on the part of the home and school. Undertakings such as the ones I am suggesting require a strong developmental effort on the part of the school. The suggestions that follow are meant to help educators become aware of the need to work with parents to make the situation in their school and community easier on immigrant students.

First, teachers can help parents understand that they must provide children opportunities to attain a mature command of their first 40 language in the home, whether or not it is supported in school. This is done by using more and more mature forms of the language at home in talking with the children as they grow older and expecting more mature speech from them. Parents should be encouraged to find time to talk with their children, read to them (if this is a practice in the culture of the home), and teach them things that interest educated members of their group. Families that come from cultures with a rich oral tradition will have many stories and histories to share with the children. Teachers should encourage them to use these materials and to regard them as equal to written materials that other families might use with their children at home.

Second, teachers and parents should be aware of the traumatic experiences children may be undergoing as they try to fit themselves into the social world of the school. They need to be alert to signs of emotional problems and to treat such problems gently and supportively rather than cause children to withdraw further from family and teachers.

Third, teachers and parents need to work together to neutralize some of the negative forces that operate on children in our society. When children become alienated from parents in the process of becoming Americans, the parents do not always know what is going on in their children's lives. Teachers sometimes see what is happening with children that the parents do not (Olsen, 1997).

Finally, teachers should help parents understand that the only way ethnic languages and cultures can survive in societies like the United States is through community action. Immigrant communities have historically been involved in supporting heritage language and cultural programs. This requires community action, and such action can be taken only by members of the immigrant community. Community action is necessary if the family's language and culture are to survive the process of becoming Americans.

REFERENCES

Benjamin, R. (1993). *The maintenance of Spanish by Mexicano children and its function in their school lives.* Unpublished doctoral dissertation, The University of California at Berkeley.

Cummins, J. (1996). *Negotiating identities: Education for empowerment in a diverse society.* Ontario, CA: California Association for Bilingual Education.

Fillmore, L. W. (1991a). Language and cultural issues in early education. In S. L. Kagan (Ed.), *The care and education of America's young children: Obstacles and opportunities* (The 90th yearbook of the National Society for the Study of Education) (pp. 30–49). Chicago, IL: University of Chicago Press.

Fillmore, L. W. (1991b). When learning a second language means losing the first. *Early Childhood Research Quarterly, 6,* 323–346.

Fishman, J. A. (1996). What do you lose when you lose your language? In G. Cantoni (Ed.), *Stabilizing indigenous languages* (Monograph series, special issue) (pp. 80–91). Flagstaff: Center for Excellence in Education, Northern Arizona University.

Fishman, J. A., & Hofman, J. E. (1966). Mother tongue and nativity in the American population. In J. A. Fishman (Ed.), *Language loyalty in the United States* (pp. 34–50). The Hague, Netherlands: Mouton & Co.

Hinton, L. (1999, December). Involuntary language loss among immigrants: Asian-American linguistic autobiographies. *ERIC Digest,* p. 3. Retrieved July 29, 2000 from the World Wide Web: http://www.cal.org/ericcll/digest/involuntary.html

Kouritzin, S. G. (1999). *Face(t)s of first language loss.* Mahwah, NJ: Erlbaum.

Lambert, W. E. (1977). The effects of bilingualism on the individual: Cognitive and socio-cultural consequences. In P. Hornby (Ed.), *Bilingualism: Psychological, social and educational implications.* New York: Academic Press.

Lau v. Nichols, 414 U.S. 563, 566–69, 94 S.Ct. 786, 788–90, 39 L.Ed.2d 1 (1974).

López, D. E. (1982). *Language maintenance and shift in the United States today.* Los Alamitos, CA: National Center for Bilingual Research.

Macias, R. F. (1998). *Summary report of the survey of the states' limited English proficient students and available educational programs and services, 1996–97.* Washington, DC: National Clearinghouse for Bilingual Education.

Olsen, L. (1997). *Made in America: Immigrant students in our public schools.* New York: New Press.

Portes, A., & Hao, L. (1998). *E pluribus unum: Bilingualism and language loss in the second generation.* (Economics Working Paper Archive at Washington University, St. Louis). Retrieved July 29, 2000 from the World Wide Web: http://ideas.uqam.ca/ideas/data /Papers/wpawuwpma9805006.html

Portes, A., & Rumbault, R. G. (1990). *Immigrant America: A portrait.* Berkeley: The University of California Press.

Rodriguez, R. (1982). *Hunger of memory: The education of Richard Rodriguez.* Toronto and New York: Bantam Books.

Glossary of Grammatical Terms

Many of the terms listed in this glossary are introduced in Chapter 2, "The Sentence's Working Parts." Terms in boldface within a definition have their own glossary entries.

Absolute phrase   A **modifier** that is headed by a **noun** and modifies the whole sentence to which it is attached. The noun in an absolute phrase works like a **subject**, beginning an assertion, but there is no complete **verb**; the verb either appears as a **verbal** or is absent altogether.

> She spent most of her time at the church, her ivory-and-silver rosary draped over her right fist, her left hand wearing the beads smoother, smaller.

> It was the middle of September on the reservation, the mornings chill, the afternoons warm, the leaves still green and thick in their final sweetness.

Active voice   In an active voice construction, the **subject** performs the action described by the **verb**. (*Compare to* **passive voice**.) In the sentences below, the subjects and verbs have been underlined.

ACTIVE VOICE	Corwin shut the door.
PASSIVE VOICE	The door was shut by Corwin.
ACTIVE VOICE	Traditionally, Americans have regarded marriage as a relationship exclusively between a man and a woman.
PASSIVE VOICE	Traditionally, marriage has been regarded as a relationship exclusively between a man and a woman.

Adjectival   A word, **phrase**, or **clause** that modifies a **noun**. (*See also* **adjective**, **adjective clause**, and **adjective phrase**.)

Adjective   A word that modifies a **noun**, typically by naming a quality or characteristic.

Anyone could see that he had been <u>handsome</u>, and he still cut a <u>graceful</u> figure, <u>slim</u> and of <u>medium</u> height.

In our loss, we were cut off from the <u>true</u>, <u>bright</u>, <u>normal</u> routines of living.

Adjective clause   A **dependent clause** that modifies a **noun**. Most adjective clauses are introduced by the words *who, whom, whose, which, that, when,* or *where.*

Grandmother had chronic headaches, <u>which often immobilized her</u>.

Americans <u>who believe in the words of the Declaration of Independence</u> cannot sit by while this wrong continues.

Adjective phrase   A **phrase** that is headed by an **adjective** and that stands outside the **noun phrase** it modifies.

Anyone could see that he had been handsome, and he still cut a graceful figure, <u>slim and of medium height</u>.

Another argument, <u>vaguer and even less persuasive</u>, is that gay marriage somehow does harm to heterosexual marriage.

Adverb   A word that modifies a **verb**, an **adjective**, or another adverb. When modifying verbs, adverbs describe when, where, why, how, or under what conditions an action takes place. When modifying adjectives or other adverbs, they typically specify degree or extent, as in *very* cold or *somewhat cold.*

Kai-fong was <u>severely</u> reprimanded by Father, Mother, and Grandmother, and he <u>gradually</u> began to withdraw.

From a <u>strictly</u> pragmatic perspective, what happened to this immigrant family appears unfortunate but <u>hardly</u> tragic.

Adverb clause   A **dependent clause** that does the work of an adverb, telling where, when, why, how, or under what conditions an action takes place. An adverb clause is introduced by a **subordinating conjunction** and contains a **subject-verb pair.**

If someone with absolute pitch is asked to name tones or intervals, MRIs will show focal activation in certain associative areas of the frontal cortex.

He sometimes experiences a certain difficulty in hearing intervals or harmonies because he is so conscious of the notes that compose them.

Appositive   A **noun phrase** that appears in a sentence next to another noun phrase with the same **referent**.

I'd like you to meet Jerry Allen, my brother-in-law from Texas.

I saw no unity of purpose, no consensus on matters of philosophy or history or law.

Auxiliary   A word that combines with a main **verb** to establish the time, duration, or certainty of its action. Auxiliaries include forms of *be, have,* and *do* as well as modals such as *can, will, shall, should, could, would, may, might,* and *must.*

Most of this I've told before, or at least hinted at, but what I have never told is the full truth.

I did leave the Valley, that very fall, packing my bags for New Haven.

Clause   A group of words containing a **subject** and a **predicate**. (*See also specific types of clauses:* **adjective clause, adverb clause, dependent clause, independent clause,** and **noun clause.**)

Complement   In a clause with a **linking verb,** the complement is an **adjective phrase** or **noun phrase** that follows the **verb.**

Amy Tan's work is popular among book-club members.

Her first novel became a bestseller.

Conjunction   A word such as *and, or, but,* or *so* used to join words or larger grammatical units. (*See also* **coordinating conjunction, correlative conjunction,** and **subordinating conjunction.**)

My father always struck me as the sort of man who, under the right circumstances, might have invented the microwave oven or the transistor radio. You wouldn't seek him out for advice on a personal problem, but he'd be the first one you'd call when the dishwasher broke or someone flushed a hairpiece down your toilet.

Coordinating conjunction A word used to join similar syntactic units within a sentence. The seven coordinating conjunctions are *and, or, nor, but, for, yet, so.*

Correlative conjunction A two-part conjunction used to join similar syntactic units within a sentence. The correlative conjunctions are *both/and, either/or, neither/nor, not/but,* and *not only/but* (*also*).

Cumulative sentence A sentence that begins with the **independent clause**, then continues with a series of **modifiers**. In the sentences below, the modifiers have been underlined.

Sitting at the control board was my dad the engineer, <u>years younger,</u> <u>examining a printout no larger than a grocery receipt.</u>

The men drank from quart bottles of Mountain Dew <u>as they paused from</u> <u>their work to regard my father,</u> <u>who stood at the water's edge,</u> <u>staring at</u> <u>the</u> shoreline with a stick in hand.

Dangling modifier A **modifier** that is not attached carefully to a **clause**, leading to ambiguity about what is being modified.

DANGLING MODIFIER	<u>After reading Gates's essay,</u> our understanding of ethnic identity changed.
REVISED	After reading Gates's essay, we had a new understanding of ethnic identity.
DANGLING MODIFIER	Once, <u>while rifling through the toolshed,</u> an old poster caught my eye.
REVISED	Once, while rifling through the toolshed, I noticed an old poster.

Dependent clause A **clause** (a group of words with a **subject** and **predicate**) that cannot stand on its own as a sentence. (*See also* **adjective clause, adverb clause,** and **noun clause.**) Dependent clauses are sometimes referred to as **subordinate clauses.**

Another difficulty was mentioned to me by the neurologist and musician Steven Frucht, <u>who himself has absolute pitch.</u> He sometimes experiences a certain difficulty in hearing intervals or harmonies <u>because he is so</u> <u>conscious of the notes</u> <u>that compose them.</u>

Early modifier A **modifier** that appears early in the sentence; initial modifiers open their sentences and medial modifiers are embedded within the **independent clause.**

As children, we placed a great deal of faith in his ability but learned to steer clear while he was working.

The experience of watching was ruined, time and time again, by an interminable explanation of how things were put together.

End modifier A **modifier** that appears at the end of a sentence, following the **independent clause.**

Sitting at the control board was my dad the engineer, years younger, examining a printout no larger than a grocery receipt.

The men drank from quart bottles of Mountain Dew as they paused from their work to regard my father, who stood at the water's edge, staring at the shoreline with a stick in hand.

Fragment A grammatical unit punctuated as a sentence but lacking an **independent clause.**

Because that was the cheapest way to eat.

Some thought he had no redeeming value whatsoever. A sociopath. A clever manipulator, who drugged himself dangerous each weekend.

Headword The key word in any phrase — the **noun** in a **noun phrase**, the **verb** in a **verb phrase**, the **adjective** in an **adjective phrase.**

NOUN PHRASE	a man of great compassion
VERB PHRASE	introduced herself to the neighbors
ADJECTIVE PHRASE	always ready to help a friend

Human subject A **noun phrase** in the subject position that refers to a person or people rather than to objects or abstract ideas.

My mother was in the room.

And it was perhaps the first time she had heard me give a lengthy speech using the kind of English I have never used with her.

Independent clause A clause (a group of words with a **subject** and **predicate**) that can stand on its own as a complete sentence.

Of the four children in the Chen family, <u>three are doing well in school</u>. <u>Only one has gotten lost</u>, but <u>that can happen in any family</u>.

<u>The curriculum of the home is taught by word and example</u>, by the way adults relate to the children of the family, beginning at birth and not ending until the children are mature and on their own.

Intransitive verb A **verb** that does not take an **object.**

The Chen family <u>settled</u> in Daly City.

Ethnic languages and cultures <u>can survive</u> in a society like the United States only if parents and educators <u>work</u> collaboratively.

Linking verb A verb that links the **subject** to a word or **phrase** that appears after the **verb,** called the **complement.** The most common linking verb is *be.*

In many ways, the Chen family <u>is</u> typical of Chinese immigrants to the Bay Area.

The rapprochement of Civil War military history with social and cultural concerns <u>is</u> far from complete; audiences <u>remain</u> largely separate and segmented.

Main clause Another term for **independent clause.**

Modifier A word, **phrase,** or **clause** that elaborates upon some other element in the sentence, describing it, limiting it, or providing extra information about it.

My father kissed her, spoke <u>gently</u> <u>into her ear</u>, combed her hair <u>into a shawl</u> <u>around her shoulders</u>.

Nonrestrictive adjective clause An adjective clause that provides extra information about a noun; also called a "non-defining" adjective clause. (*Compare to* **restrictive adjective clause.**)

In the morning, after gassing up, I headed straight west along the Rainy River, <u>which separates Minnesota from Canada</u>.

Diana Deutsch, <u>who has absolute pitch</u>, compares it to color, suggesting that recognizing the pitch of a sound is similar to recognizing the color of an object.

Noun   A word that names a person, place, thing, or idea.

My father kissed her, spoke gently into her ear, combed her hair into a shawl around her shoulders.

At its best, marriage is a stable bond between two individuals who work to create a loving household and a social and economic partnership.

Noun clause   **A dependent clause** that performs the function of a **noun**, serving as a **subject, object,** or **complement.**

What I remember more than anything is the man's willful, almost ferocious silence.

Unlike a horse or a Seeing Eye dog, the whole glory of being a bird is that nobody would ever put you to work.

Noun phrase   A **noun** and its **modifiers.** A noun phrase can serve as a **subject, object, complement,** or a **modifier.** (*See also* **appositive** and **absolute phrase.**)

Although his arm was so twisted and disfigured that his shirts had to be carefully altered and pinned to accommodate the gnarled shape, he had agility in that arm, even strength.

My father kissed her, spoke gently into her ear, combed her hair into a shawl around her shoulders.

Object   In a clause with a **transitive verb,** the object is a **noun phrase** that follows the **verb,** naming the person or thing that receives the action.

Corwin shut the door.

He had taken the old man's fiddle because he needed money.

Parallel structure   When items in a pair or series are the same kind of grammatical unit and fit into the same "slot" in the sentence, they are said to be parallel in structure.

My speech was about Vietnam, abortion, and civil rights, about the sense of community our class shared, since so many of us had been together for twelve years, about the individual's rights and responsibilities in his or her community, and about the necessity to defy norms out of love.

I pretended to sleep, not because I wanted to keep up the appearance of being sick but because I could not bear to return to the way things had been.

Passive voice   In a passive voice construction, the **subject** names the person or thing that receives the action of the **verb.** (*Compare to* **active voice.**) In the sentences below, the subjects and verbs have been underlined.

ACTIVE VOICE	From that rock, I could see all that happened on the water.
PASSIVE VOICE	From that rock, all that happened on the water could be seen (by me).
ACTIVE VOICE	In the Ojibwa language that we speak on our reservation, . . .
PASSIVE VOICE	In the Ojibwa language that is spoken on our reservation, . . .

Periodic sentence   A sentence in which the **modifiers** come at the beginning, building toward the **independent clause.** In the sentences below, the modifiers have been underlined.

Throughout the first year of this campaign, against all predictions to the contrary, we saw how hungry the American people were for this message of unity.

If all citizens have a constitutional right to marry, if state laws that withdraw legal protections of gays and lesbians as a class are unconstitutional, and if private, intimate sexual conduct between persons of the same sex is protected by the Constitution, there is very little left on which opponents of same-sex marriage can rely.

Phrase   A group of words that serves a grammatical function. Unlike **clauses,** phrases do not contain a **subject-verb pair.** (*See also* **absolute phrase, adjective phrase, appositive, noun phrase, prepositional phrase,** and **verbal phrase.**)

Predicate   The **verb** in a clause and any elements (**modifiers, objects, complements**) that accompany it. Typically, the predicate states what the **subject** is or does.

If we walk away now, if we simply retreat into our respective corners, we will never be able to come together and solve challenges like health care or education or the need to find good jobs for every American.

Preposition   A word that indicates the relationship between a **noun phrase** and the rest of the sentence. English has a large but finite set of prepositions; examples are *about, above, across, after, against,* *as, at, before, behind, below, beside, between, by, down, during, for, from, in, into, like, of, off, on, out, over, past, since, through, toward, under, until, up, upon, with, without.* Some prepositions are more complex: *according to, apart from, because of, by means of, except for, instead of, such as.*

There, lashed <u>to</u> a crosspiece <u>in</u> the bow, was a black case <u>of</u> womanly shape that fastened <u>on</u> the side <u>with</u> two brass locks.

Prepositional phrase   A phrase made up of a **preposition** and its object, a **noun phrase.**

There, lashed <u>to a crosspiece</u> <u>in the bow</u>, was a black case <u>of womanly shape</u> that fastened <u>on the side</u> <u>with two brass locks</u>.

Pronoun   A function word that takes the place of a noun. (*See also* **relative pronoun.**)

As children, <u>we</u> placed a great deal of faith in <u>his</u> ability but learned to steer clear while <u>he</u> was working.

Ask <u>my</u> mother how the radio worked and <u>her</u> answer was simple: "Turn <u>it</u> on and pull out the goddamn antenna."

Referent   Something referred to, something named by a word or phrase. The word *rain* refers; those drops of water falling from the sky are the referent.

Relative clause   Another term for **adjective clause.**

Relative pronoun   A word used to introduce an **adjective clause.** The relative pronouns are *who, whom, whose, which,* and *that.*

I undertook a survey of Civil War books reviewed since 1976 in the *Journal of Southern History,* <u>which</u>, despite its title, considers studies on both Northern and Southern aspects of the conflict.

The American public loved *The Civil War* because it was about individual human beings <u>whose</u> faces we could see, <u>whose</u> words we could hear, as they confronted war's challenges.

Restrictive adjective clause   An adjective clause that provides information essential to identifying the **referent** of the noun being modified; also called a "defining" adjective clause. (*Compare to* **nonrestrictive adjective clause.**)

In the morning, after gassing up, I headed straight west along the river <u>that separates Minnesota from Canada</u>.

People <u>who have absolute pitch</u> often compare it to color — they "hear" G-sharpness as instantly and automatically as we "see" blue.

Subject A **noun phrase** that appears before the **verb**, typically naming the actor or topic of the clause.

<u>My own scientific curiosity</u> eventually blossomed, but <u>I</u> knew enough to keep my freakish experiments to myself.

When <u>my father</u> discovered my colony of frozen slugs in the basement freezer, <u>I</u> chose not to explain my complex theories of suspended animation.

Subject-verb pair The core of a **clause**: the **headword** of the **noun phrase** that serves as **subject**, and the **verb** itself (with **auxiliaries**) within the **predicate**. Stripping away **modifiers** to isolate the subject-verb pair highlights the key elements of the clause.

My own scientific <u>curiosity</u> eventually <u>blossomed</u>, but <u>I</u> <u>knew</u> enough to keep my freakish experiments to myself.

When my <u>father</u> <u>discovered</u> my colony of frozen slugs in the basement freezer, <u>I</u> <u>chose</u> not to explain my complex theories of suspended animation.

Subordinate clause Another term for **dependent clause**.

Subordinating conjunction A word used to introduce an **adverb clause**. English has a large but finite set of subordinating conjunctions; examples are *although, as, as if, as soon as, because, before, if, since, though, unless, until, when, where, whereas, while.*

I chose to run for president at this moment in history <u>because</u> I believe deeply that we cannot solve the challenges of our time <u>unless</u> we solve them together.

Subordinator Another term for **subordinating conjunction**.

Transitive verb A **verb** that takes an **object**.

The Chen family <u>rented</u> a house in Daly City.

Ken Burns's *The Civil War* <u>broke</u> television records in the fall of 1990 when it <u>attracted</u> an audience of 14 million. By the end of the decade more than 40 million Americans <u>had watched</u> one or more episodes.

Verb A word that identifies an action or state of being.

My father always <u>struck</u> me as the sort of man who, under the right circumstances, <u>might have invented</u> the microwave oven or the transistor radio.

We dragged Fisher to the car, ducking the bottles and cans as we sped away.

Verbal   A word derived from a **verb** but performing some other function; instead of being paired with a **subject**, a verbal behaves like a **noun**, an **adjective**, or an **adverb**. Verbals appear in three forms: the present participle (*-ing*), past participle (*-ed* or irregular form), and infinitive (*to*).

Bobbing there on the Rainy River, looking back at the Minnesota shore, I felt a sudden swell of helplessness come over me.

I saw a sixteen-year-old kid decked out for his first prom, looking spiffy in a white tux and a black bow tie.

Verbal phrase   A group of words headed by a **verbal**.

Bobbing there on the Rainy River, looking back at the Minnesota shore, I felt a sudden swell of helplessness come over me.

I saw a sixteen-year-old kid decked out for his first prom, looking spiffy in a white tux and a black bow tie.

Verb phrase   A group of words headed by a **verb**.

My father was an engineer.

We dragged Fisher to the car, ducking the bottles and cans as we sped away.

Index